FALLOUT AND PHILOSOPHY

The Blackwell Philosophy and Pop Culture Series
Series editor: William Irwin

A spoonful of sugar helps the medicine go down, and a healthy helping of popular culture clears the cobwebs from Kant. Philosophy has had a public relations problem for a few centuries now. This series aims to change that, showing that philosophy is relevant to your life—and not just for answering the big questions like "To be or not to be?" but for answering the little questions: "To watch or not to watch South Park?" Thinking deeply about TV, movies, and music doesn't make you a "complete idiot." In fact, it might make you a philosopher, someone who believes the unexamined life is not worth living and the unexamined cartoon is not worth watching.

Already published in the series:

Alien and Philosophy: I Infest, Therefore I Am
Edited by Jeffery A. Ewing and Kevin S. Decker

Avatar: The Last Airbender and Philosophy
Edited by Helen De Cruz and Johan De Smedt

Batman and Philosophy: The Dark Knight of the Soul
Edited by Mark D. White and Robert Arp

The Big Bang Theory and Philosophy: Rock, Paper, Scissors, Aristotle, Locke
Edited by Dean A. Kowalski

BioShock and Philosophy: Irrational Game, Rational Book
Edited by Luke Cuddy

Black Mirror and Philosophy
Edited by David Kyle Johnson

Black Panther and Philosophy
Edited by Edwardo Pérez and Timothy Brown

Disney and Philosophy: Truth, Trust, and a Little Bit of Pixie Dust
Edited by Richard B. Davis

Dune and Philosophy
Edited by Kevin S. Decker

Dungeons and Dragons and Philosophy: Read and Gain Advantage on All Wisdom Checks
Edited by Christopher Robichaud

Game of Thrones and Philosophy: Logic Cuts Deeper Than Swords
Edited by Henry Jacoby

The Good Place and Philosophy: Everything Is Fine!
Edited by Kimberly S. Engels

Star Wars and Philosophy Strikes Back
Edited by Jason T. Eberl and Kevin S. Decker

The Ultimate Harry Potter and Philosophy: Hogwarts for Muggles
Edited by Gregory Bassham

The Hobbit and Philosophy: For When You've Lost Your Dwarves, Your Wizard, and Your Way
Edited by Gregory Bassham and Eric Bronson

Inception and Philosophy: Because It's Never Just a Dream
Edited by David Kyle Johnson

LEGO and Philosophy: Constructing Reality Brick By Brick
Edited by Roy T. Cook and Sondra Bacharach

Metallica and Philosophy: A Crash Course in Brain Surgery
Edited by William Irwin

The Ultimate South Park and Philosophy: Respect My Philosophah!
Edited by Robert Arp and Kevin S. Decker

The Ultimate Star Trek and Philosophy: The Search for Socrates
Edited by Jason T. Eberl and Kevin S. Decker

The Ultimate Star Wars and Philosophy: You Must Unlearn What You Have Learned
Edited by Jason T. Eberl and Kevin S. Decker

Terminator and Philosophy: I'll Be Back, Therefore I Am
Edited by Richard Brown and Kevin S. Decker

Watchmen and Philosophy: A Rorschach Test
Edited by Mark D. White

Westworld and Philosophy: If You Go Looking for the Truth, Get the Whole Thing
Edited by James B. South and Kimberly S. Engels

Indiana Jones and Philosophy: Why Did It Have to Be Socrates?
Edited by William Irwin and Dean A. Kowalski

Ted Lasso and Philosophy: No Question Is into Touch
Edited by Mary Baggett and David Baggett

Mad Max and Philosophy: Thinking Through the Wasteland
Edited by Matthew P. Meyer and David Koepsell

Taylor Swift and Philosophy: Essays from the Tortured Philosophers Department
Edited by Georgina H. Mills and Catherine M. Robb

Joker and Philosophy: Why So Serious?
Edited by Massimiliano L. Cappuccio, George A. Dunn, and Jason T. Eberl

The Last of Us and Philosophy: Look for the Light
Edited by Charles Joshua Horn

The Legend of Zelda and Philosophy: Link Outside the Box
Edited by Luke Cuddy

The Wheel of Time and Philosophy: A Portion of Wisdom
Edited by Jacob M. Held

Bridgerton and Philosophy: Dukes, Debutantes, and Deep Questions
Edited by Jessica Miller

Fallout and Philosophy: Thinking Outside the Shelter
Edited by Nathan Kellen, Nathan Sheff, and Joshua Heter

Forthcoming

Severance and Philosophy
Edited by Eric Bronson and Jason T. Eberl

The Bear and Philosophy
Edited by Mark D. White

For the full list of titles in the series see www.andphilosophy.com

FALLOUT AND PHILOSOPHY

THINKING OUTSIDE THE SHELTER

Edited by

Nathan Kellen

Nathan Sheff

Joshua Heter

WILEY

Published by John Wiley & Sons, Inc., Hoboken, New Jersey.

Library of Congress Cataloging-in-Publication Data

Names: Kellen, Nathan editor | Sheff, Nathan editor | Heter, Joshua editor
Title: Fallout and philosophy : thinking outside the shelter / [edited by] Nathan Kellen, Nathan Sheff, Joshua Heter.
Description: First edition. | Hoboken, New Jersey : Wiley, [2026] | Series: The Blackwell philosophy and pop culture series
Identifiers: LCCN 2026008387 (print) | LCCN 2026008388 (ebook) | ISBN 9781394334216 paperback | ISBN 9781394334230 adobe pdf | ISBN 9781394334223 epub
Subjects: LCSH: Fallout (Video game) | Fallout (Television program) | Apocalypse in popular culture
Classification: LCC GV1469.25.F32 F35 2026 (print) | LCC GV1469.25.F32 (ebook)
LC record available at https://lccn.loc.gov/2026008387
LC ebook record available at https://lccn.loc.gov/2026008388

Cover Design: Wiley
Cover Images: sergio34/Getty Images, CSA-Printstock/Getty Images, imdproduction/Getty Images

Set in 10/12pt Sabon by Straive, Pondicherry, India

SKY10163245_072226

Contents

The Vault Dwellers

They asked me how well I understood theoretical philosophy. I said I had a theoretical degree in philosophy. They said, "Welcome aboard." **Daniel Guy Baldwin** is a postgraduate researcher, currently pursuing his PhD at the University of Liverpool. His main research can be found at the crossroads of identity, ethics, death, and narrative.

Walter Barta has contributed to a number of volumes, not unlike the one you are currently reading, such as *Better Call Saul and Philosophy* (2022), *The Godfather and Philosophy* (2023), and *Country Music and Philosophy* (2026). When he's not writing about popular culture, he works on digital humanities projects as a principal investigator at the Digital Research Commons at M.D. Anderson Library at the University of Houston. Despite his interest in new and burgeoning forms of media, he's always said that there's a lot you can learn from old books.

Armond Boudreaux is an associate professor of English at the East Georgia campus of Georgia Southern University, where he has so far managed to avoid being recruited by the Institute. His publications include *The Last Revolution*, a sci-fi thriller series from Aethon Books, and contributions to several Philosophy and Pop Culture series volumes.

Andrea Conque is an assistant professor of philosophy at the University of Louisiana at Lafayette and specializes in political theory. She is the author of *Heidegger & Politics: Nazism, Care, and the Future of Democracy* (2025), *Heidegger, Levinas and the Feminine* (2009), and several chapters in books about pop culture, music, and philosophy, including *Country Music and Philosophy* (2026) and *'90s Alternative & Philosophy* (2026). She hopes she never "catches old" from you.

Alba Curry is a lecturer in philosophy at the University of Leeds, specializing in comparative ancient Chinese and Greek philosophy, moral psychology, and the ethics of AI. She thought she had enough on her plate with Mozi, Aristotle, and machine learning ... until *Fallout* beckoned. Like any unsuspecting Vault Dweller stepping outside for "just a moment," she quickly found herself miles from home, overencumbered, and philosophically committed.

Federico Dal Barco is a PhD student in philosophy at Ludwig Maximilian University of Munich. Although his main focus is writing academic papers on modern philosophy and Immanuel Kant while secluded in his Vault, he sometimes ventures into the wasteland to contribute to the Philosophy and Pop Culture series. Federico has contributed to *The Last of Us and Philosophy* and *The Legend of Zelda and Philosophy*, and he is the administrator of an Italian online videogames journal.

Benjamin B. DeVan is an associate professor and the chair of Palm Beach Atlantic University's MS in Ethics and Organizational Behavior. His overseeing and lessons bridge Asian philosophies, social science, and virtuous leadership. Along with case studies in post-apocalyptic role-play, he contributed previously to *The Wheel of Time and Philosophy*, *The Legend of Zelda and Theology*, and *Hell, No or Yes: What Do the Bible and Philosophers Say?* Scrounging for meaning amidst the rubble, he brings an ethical eye to wasteland factions, moral quandaries, and Nuka-Cola–fueled narratives. He is persuaded that even after the bombs drop, the love of wisdom still has a purchase within and beyond the Vault.

Bobbie L. Eicher is a researcher at Georgia Tech, where she explores the ethical dimensions of artificial intelligence and scientific progress. Her curiosity about moral and educational choices once took her far beyond the wasteland, all the way to Hyrule, where she contributed to *The Legend of Zelda and Philosophy*. When she's not examining what happened to the other vaults, she can be found in Vault 81 making sure the moral compass in her Pip-Boy is properly calibrated.

Katia S. Franco is an associate professor of philosophy at California State University, Chico. She invested most of her stat points in perception, endurance, and charisma: enough perception points to get the awareness perk to help with research on introspection, enough endurance points to get the toughness perk required in philosophy, and enough charisma points to help with philosophy conferences and to get the animal friend perk.

Mackenzie Graham is a senior research fellow at the Ethox Centre, University of Oxford. His research interests are primarily in bioethics, the ethics of health research, and the philosophy of trust. He prefers Galaxy News Radio to the speeches of John Henry Eden.

Trevor Grant Hedberg is an assistant professor of practice at the University of Arizona, affiliated with both the W.A. Franke Honors College and the philosophy department. He also serves as the program director for the Honors Civic Leadership Certificate. He is the author of *The Environmental Impact of Overpopulation: The Ethics of Procreation* (2020) and many other works in applied ethics. Although he does reside in the hot, arid environment of the Sonoran Desert, he has never wished for a nuclear winter and considers avoiding peak sun hours and hydrating properly to be a better means of coping with the desert heat.

Joshua Heter is a professor of philosophy at Jefferson College in Hillsboro, Missouri. He is the co-editor of a number of popular culture and philosophy volumes, including *Back to the Future and Philosophy* (2025), *Asimov's Foundation and Philosophy* (2023), *The Godfather and Philosophy* (2023), and *Punk Rock and Philosophy* (2022). Admittedly, his flesh is weak, but (he's hoping that) this book endures.

John P. Irish teaches humanities in Texas, where he earned his PhD at Southern Methodist University. He regularly contributes articles on Locke and Lockean ideas to *Philosophy Now*, as well as chapters in the Philosophy and Pop Culture series. His broader scholarship explores the philosophical dimensions of weird fiction, and he is especially known for his work on the Irish American author Fitz-James O'Brien. Outside the classroom, he maintains a healthy distrust of corporate shelters, prewar governance, and automated voting systems. He once tried to explain Lockean social contract theory to a Deathclaw. It didn't go well.

J. Scott Jordan is a cognitive scientist who studies the neuroscience, psychology, and philosophy of cooperative behavior. He is perhaps best known for his work on Wild Systems Theory, a twenty-first-century transdisciplinary framework that integrates the sciences, humanities, arts, lived life, and pop culture by focusing on what they have in common; specifically, the never-ending struggle for meaningful coherence. He has published dozens of papers that examine this struggle, such as "Exploring the Hidden Kingdoms of Assumption" (*Black Panther Psychology*, 2019), and "The Welcoming Spiderverse: Finding Your 'Self' in a Web of Others" (*Pop Mythology*, 2023). He produces the Dark Loops Productions channel on YouTube, where he hosts discussions of lived life, science, art, the humanities, and all things pop culture. Finally, he loves to cosplay and is extremely proud of his international comic-book collection.

Nathan Kellen is a teaching assistant professor in philosophy at Kansas State University. He has contributed to a number of popular culture and philosophy volumes, such as *Joker and Philosophy* (2024) and *Star Wars and Philosophy Strikes Back* (2022). He's a fan of games with multiple possibly-canon endings, because at the end of the day Joshua Graham was right, "... we can't expect God to do all the work."

David R. Lawrence is an assistant professor at Durham Law School, where he works on the ethics and law of emerging biotechnologies and the shaky boundaries of moral status. His long-standing *Fallout* habit taught him that moral dilemmas rarely come with clean answers, and the NCR is probably lying to you. He promises that writing this chapter did not require any chems.

Karen "Kat" Schrier is a full professor and director of Games & Emerging Media at Marist University. She leads the Play Innovation Lab and recently did a Fulbright in Tunisia. A game designer who has worked at the World Health Organization, Nickelodeon, and Scholastic, she enjoys researching and making games for compassion, care, and health. Dr. Schrier has over 100 publications, including *We the Gamers* and *Knowledge Games* (2021). She has a husband, three kids, and a sweet old cat, but no dogmeat companion in real life.

S. Evan Kreider holds a PhD in philosophy from the University of Kansas and is a professor of philosophy at the University of Wisconsin—Oshkosh. His research interests focus on ethics and aesthetics, and he has published chapters in numerous pop culture and philosophy anthologies. He's also capable of providing a lengthy and brilliant ethical defense of Mr. House and is willing to argue endlessly with strangers on the Internet about it.

Gerald Lang is a professor of philosophy at the University of Leeds, and has broad interests across moral and political philosophy. He's the author of *Strokes of Luck* (2021) and is currently toiling over a book on deontology, self-defense, and war. He believed these concerns were demanding enough, that is, until *Fallout* reminded him that "war never changes," and now he wanders the philosophical wasteland, scavenging for arguments and hoping his moral compass still works.

Chris Lay is an associate professor at Young Harris College in the northeast Georgian part of the Appalachian Wasteland. His work, mostly on metaphysics, personal identity, and technology, has appeared in various pop culture and philosophy volumes, and he was an editor for the *Palgrave Handbook of Popular Culture as Philosophy* (2024). Like his buddy, Fantastic, out in New Vegas, Chris has a theoretical degree in philosophy.

Sirens howled. **Greg Littmann** hammered on the shelter door. "I could be useful! I'm a doctor …" The heavy bolt slid back, and the door opened a crack. "… of philosophy." The door clanged shut, and the bolt slid home. "No wait! I'm an associate professor in the Philosophy Department at SIUE! I've published on a variety of subjects, including the philosophy of logic, evolutionary epistemology, and the philosophy of professional philosophy. I've written many chapters for volumes that relate philosophy to popular culture for general audiences, including books on *Alien*, *Doctor Who*, *Dune*, *Final Fantasy*, *Star Trek*, and *Star Wars*." Littmann's voice rose an octave. "Socrates said that the unexamined life's not worth living! What's the point of merely surviving if you aren't going to search for truth?" He was shouting now. "Aristotle ...." Behind him, a yellow light was growing brighter. In a moment, it was brighter than the sun.

Ian McDaniel is an assistant professor of philosophy and English for Fort Hays State University's international program at Sias University in Xinzheng, China. His early work was in neo-Marxist philosophy and educational justice, but after (potentially) being replaced by a Gen 3 Synth during graduate school, he now works primarily in the bioethics, healthcare and professional ethics, and moral theory divisions at the institution. He insists he still *feels* human.

Okey-dokey! **Kenneth R. Pike** is an associate professor of philosophy and law at Florida Institute of Technology, home of the "Atomic Toilet" (a 1960s experiment in the use of radioactivity to purify and sterilize sewage). Among Kenneth's past publications are "The Doctrine of Sufficiency as a Contractualist Principle" (*Moral Philosophy and Politics*, 2025) and "*Secher Nbiw* and the Child's Right to an Open Future" (*Dune and Philosophy*, 2023). In addition to earned doctorates in law and philosophy, Kenneth has a theoretical degree in physics.

Michael Funke is a philosophy PhD and JD who wears two hats—one as an assistant attorney general representing the State of Washington and another as a part-time philosophy professor at Bellevue College. He has published papers in both academic and popular presses focusing on the philosophy of action. Now more of a litigator than a researcher, he has also spent a fair amount of time on the walking simulator that is *Fallout*. Seriously, can we just get a drivable car?

Quinn Funke is a senior attending Curtis Sr. High School. He is currently taking a full slate of AP classes and an elective in video game design. After graduation, he plans to attend Tacoma Community College and eventually study engineering. Quinn read his first philosophy book at age nine when he borrowed an introduction to philosophy text from his father's desk. Around the same time, he discovered *Fallout* and has been wandering both wastelands ever since.

Hello there! Don't suppose you'd care to trade? I'm missing a few essentials and—oh screw this, lying just ain't in my nature. Name's Nathan. **Nathan Sheff.** I gave up collecting blue-star caps years ago, but I have collected a PhD in philosophy from the University of Connecticut (while playing a lot of *Fallout*), and I helped collect some really good essays on *Fallout* for this book.

Eric J. Silverman is a professor of philosophy at Christopher Newport University. His diverse interests include ethics, philosophy of religion, and medieval philosophy, as well as interdisciplinary work in psychology. He is the author, editor, or co-editor of seven books, including *Virtuous*

Responses to Tragedy, Suffering, and Evil; *Paradise Understood: New Philosophical Essays About Heaven*; and *The Supremacy of Love: An Agape-Centered Vision of Aristotelian Virtue Ethics*. He realizes that all philosophers want to save the world; they just disagree on how.

Albert R. Spencer is an associate professor of philosophy at Portland State University. He is the author of two books: *American Pragmatism: An Introduction* (2020) and *The Philosophy of Role-Playing Games* (2025). He once took an online version of Covenant's S.A.F.E. empathy test for fun, and now he feels like black vans and helicopters are constantly following him.

Sergio Urueña is an assistant professor of logic and philosophy of science at the University of La Laguna in Spain, working in the areas of philosophy of technology, science and technology studies, and the political epistemology of sociotechnical futures. His research explores how communities create, imagine, use, and negotiate long-term technological trajectories, and he has contributed to discussions on anticipation and responsible innovation. When not reflecting on the politics of knowledge concerning the future, he approaches his academic tasks with the cautious discipline of someone hoping not to aggro a Deathclaw—though, on occasion, certain deadlines seem intent on testing his Luck stat.

Matthew Watts is a PhD candidate in philosophy at the University of Miami. He has published articles on memory, artificial intelligence, and identity, among other topics. He is unhappy to report that his brain has been removed against his will and replaced with a Tesla coil. While the upgrade has done wonders for his productivity, his brain remains stubbornly content in its sterile tube and refuses to go back into his head.

Eric D. Wesselmann is a professor of psychology at Illinois State University. He has published research on the intersection of psychology and popular culture, as well as discussing these topics with like-minded creatives and scholars on his YouTube channel @DigitalGolgothaProductions. He has considered constructing a Vault in his backyard, not so much to survive the Great War of 2077 but to just have a quiet place to write!

Flesh Is Weak, but Questions Endure

It wasn't a foregone conclusion that *Fallout* would be made into a prestige streaming television show. Hollywood hasn't exactly had a stellar track record adapting video games for either the big or small screens. For every *The Last of Us* by HBO (both a faithful retelling and a thoughtful expansion of a story about loss and kinship in a world full of terror), there have been more than a few projects like 1993's *Super Mario Bros.* (an entertaining but mostly bizarre entry into the genre that feels largely disconnected from its source material). For every Netflix's *Castlevania* (a visually compelling reimagining of a dark, gripping tale), there are at least a couple of *Doom*s (a film light on plot whose own star described surviving its production as having lived through "the video game curse").

All of this helps explain why it took *Fallout* so long to evolve beyond its origin as one of the most successful and celebrated video game franchises of all time into the similarly lauded Amazon series it eventually became. Though Bethesda (*Fallout*'s publisher) had been approached a number of times about doing a *Fallout* film, they were more than a little trepidatious, as Bethesda marketing executive Peter Hines openly admitted in 2015: "We've gotten a lot of very good advice about [doing an adaptation]. There's way more things that can go wrong than can go right." And to be sure, with a beloved franchise like *Fallout*, the prospect of producing a film or television series came with a fair amount of risk, as it could have potentially tarnished its otherwise stellar reputation.

However, the temptation to adapt the world of *Fallout* into a dramatized series was ultimately too powerful to resist, as the lure could be felt from the opening moments of the franchise's very first game, released in 1997. The game commences when your Vault's water chip has failed, and your Vault's overseer tasks you with venturing out into the wasteland to track down a new one. As your journey begins, the game reveals a sprawling but blank map, the details of which only fill in gradually as you move through it. The blank spaces of the overworld invite you to consider what might be out there in the wastes, along with the potential, seemingly random, encounters you might have as you explore (which very well may lead you to any number of eclectic items like a velvet Elvis painting salvaged from a UFO or a BB gun that always delivers critical hits). In such a state, it's hard *not* to think of who else might be out in the wastes and what *their* stories might be.

The games we've gotten since the original have filled in the map and more than realized the potential for additional stories in the post-nuclear wastes. Throughout the franchise, we meet more communities and factions, all embodying different ways to eke out a living in a hostile world, each one leading us, as players, to think seriously about what course of action to take. The ending of *Fallout: New Vegas*, for instance, makes this explicit, with the player's judgment being decisive in how the narrative concludes. In the final battle, the fate of New Vegas is up for grabs; who do you trust to carry civilization into the future? What kind of world will you make?

Fallout being awash in so much captivating, imaginative world-building, the opportunity to adapt the games into a dramatized narrative for television simply made too much sense to pass up. In fact, the storytelling that appears in the games as well as the Amazon series is so thoughtful and profound, it raises a host of interesting, sometimes confounding *philosophical* questions. And it is just those questions that led to the creation of this book in an attempt to raise, clarify, and even try to answer them.

Why are we drawn to stories filled with truly terrible things (e.g., inhumane experimentation, gory violence, extreme human suffering) that we want nothing to do with in real life? Could life in the post-nuclear wastes be so bad that it would be wrong to bring new people into existence? If people who survived the war could scrape together a way of life, what would it take for these new societies to emerge and thrive (and what does thriving in such a world even *mean*)? What makes someone (or some*thing*), say, a Vault Dweller or a ghoul, a *person*? Are synths people? If so, what does that entail about our obligations to them; is there a right and a wrong way to treat a synth? What makes *anything* right or wrong?

The authors of this book (and the all-too-fortunate editors who were able to bring them together) are big fans of both the *Fallout* games and Amazon series, and they hope that, in these pages, you'll be led to think more deeply about and to more fully appreciate a franchise that has brought all of us so much meaningful gaming and narrative entertainment. So, climb out of your vault, hop in your power armor, and travel with us through and beyond the wasteland on a journey of ideas, questions, and maybe even a little post-apocalyptic adventure.

Part 1

LIVING AND DYING IN THE WASTELAND

1

Death in the Wasteland: What Do the Living Owe to the Dead?

Mackenzie Graham

In the world of *Fallout*, death is a constant companion. Roaming the Capital Wasteland, the deserts of New Vegas, or the Commonwealth, the player character has numerous encounters with the dead and the dying. For centuries, philosophers have argued about our obligations to the dead, and in the *Fallout* universe, these questions are made brutally tangible.

For example, the main plotline of *Fallout 3*—the completion of Project Purity—sees the Lone Wanderer's father James die to prevent the project from falling into the hands of the Enclave. At the culmination of the game, the Lone Wanderer must choose whether to sacrifice themselves (or a companion) to initiate Project Purity and provide clean drinking water to the Capital Wasteland, align with the Enclave by contaminating the water with a virus, or allow the project to be destroyed.[1] Completing the project seems to be the morally right choice, but is it the best choice for the Lone Wanderer, or for James? In other words, would the Lone Wanderer's death be a bad thing *for them?* Is the failure of James's life's work a bad thing *for him?* Can we be affected by events that happen after we die? These are the questions that will occupy us in the remainder of this chapter.

To answer these questions, we need to think carefully about the nature of death, specifically whether things can go better or worse for us after we die. On the one hand, we avoid speaking badly of the dead, we feel compelled to keep "deathbed promises," and we worry about what will happen to our bodies and reputations after we die. This suggests that posthumous events can benefit or harm us. On the other hand, how can something be a benefit or a harm to me if I am not around to experience it? How can I be wronged by others if I no longer exist to be wronged?

"Death Is Preferable to Communism!"—Liberty Prime

Is death ever a bad thing for the person who dies? At first glance, the answer seems obvious—of course death is a bad thing for the person that dies, at least sometimes. While there may be some cases where death is a good thing, if our lives are generally good then the loss of that good must be a bad thing. So, while the success of Project Purity might be a good thing overall (in that it would be good for most of the people in the Capital Wasteland), it was probably a bad thing for the Lone Wanderer because it meant the loss of a good thing for them (namely, their life).

Yet, as far back as antiquity, philosophers have disputed this intuitive understanding of the badness of death. Most famously, the ancient Greek philosopher Epicurus (341–270 BCE) argued that it was a mistake to think that death was *ever* a bad thing for the person who died.[2] He reasoned that while a person is alive, they are not dead, and so their death has not harmed them. And, when a person is dead, they no longer exist, so there is nothing remaining to be harmed.

This may look a bit like philosophical sleight of hand, and there are a few assumptions Epicurus makes that are somewhat suspect. First, Epicurus was a hedonist: he argued that the only things that are *intrinsically* good or bad for us (that is, good or bad "in themselves") are things that we experience, namely, pleasure and pain. Second, he assumes that something can be *extrinsically* good or bad only if it causes me to experience something intrinsically good. For example, Nuka-Cola is extrinsically good insofar as it causes me to experience pleasure (which is intrinsically good).

Let's consider the first of these assumptions. It seems implausible that pleasure and pain are the *only* things that are intrinsically good or bad. For example, many philosophers argue that fulfilling my desires is intrinsically good, and having my desires thwarted is intrinsically bad—call these "desire-fulfillment accounts" of well-being. For example, if my desire is to eat some Fancy Lad Snack Cakes, it is good for me to satisfy this desire.[3]

Rejecting this first assumption makes the second assumption implausible. If satisfying my desires is good for me, then something that prevents me from satisfying my desires seems like it must be bad for me. But notice that, on a desire-fulfillment account, my desires can be fulfilled (or thwarted) without my being aware of it. Consider "The Power of the Atom" quest in *Fallout 3*: the Lone Wanderer is faced with the decision to destroy Megaton or disarm the nuclear bomb at the center of the town. Suppose the Lone Wanderer disarms the bomb and kills Mister Burke—we can clearly infer from this that the Lone Wanderer desires that the town and its residents survive. But suppose further that, days later and unbeknownst to the Lone Wanderer, the bomb is rearmed and the town is destroyed. The Lone Wanderer's desire that the town be saved is thwarted, which seems like a bad thing for him (or her)—much less for the residents of Megaton!—even if the Lone Wanderer never finds out.

This makes trouble for the Epicurean account. If something can be good or bad for me without my experiencing it, the fact that I don't experience my death doesn't rule out its being good or bad for me. Specifically, it can be bad for me if it prevents me from satisfying my desires, even if I'm not aware that my desires have not been satisfied (which obviously I wouldn't be).

This "deprivationist account" of the badness of death—the view that my death can be bad for me because it deprives me of things that are (or would be) good for me—is highly intuitive. It makes sense of the fact that, other things being equal, death is worse for us the earlier it happens—we are deprived of goods we would have had if we hadn't died when we did, and the earlier we die, the more goods we miss out on. It also makes sense of the fact that sometimes death can be a *good* thing for the one who dies. Consider the Glowing Ones, who have an utterly miserable existence that they cannot escape. It seems plausible that their lives are so bad that they would be better off dying earlier than later, as this would result in less suffering.

However, the deprivationist account has some problems. We might think that if something makes us better or worse off than we would have been otherwise, there must be some time at which it does this. For example, getting radiation poisoning makes me worse off than I would have been had I not been poisoned, and the time at which it makes me worse off is while I am sick. We can see the problem for the deprivationist account: if my death makes me worse off than I would have been by depriving me of some future good, *when* does it make me worse off?

Various philosophers have attempted to answer this question. Contemporary philosopher Fred Feldman argues for an "eternalist" view. Imagine two possible worlds: the actual world in which I die in 2025, and a different world in which I die in 2077.[4] If the actual world in which I die earlier is worse for me than the possible world, it has always been, and always will be, worse. Thus, my death is bad for me at all possible times. Conversely, another contemporary philosopher, Ben Bradley, argues that my death is bad for me at all the times in which I am deprived of the goods I would have had if I hadn't died.[5] This means that my death eventually stops being bad for me; 150 years after my birth, I wouldn't have been alive anyway. It also means that the badness of my death can change as events in the world occur; if the world is consumed by a nuclear apocalypse, and my earlier-than-otherwise death means I avoid this, my death can suddenly go from bad for me to good for me.

Even if we can determine *when* death is bad, there remains the question of *whom* it is bad for: if I no longer exist after my death, how can it be a bad thing for me? How can *anything* be good or bad for me?

"But I'm Glad You're Not Dead. That'd Be a Real Downer. Especially for You, I Bet"—Moira Brown

Like the badness of death itself, the idea of posthumous harms (and benefits) has some intuitive force. As we saw above, it seems possible that something might be bad for me (like the destruction of Megaton) even if this makes no difference to my subjective experience. So why should it matter if the reason I have no subjective experience of this thing is because I am dead?

For example, we know that James' lifelong desire was to complete Project Purity, and his sacrifice at the Jefferson Memorial facility clearly indicates he had this desire up until the moment of his death. Suppose that James hadn't died from the radiation, but merely lost consciousness, and somehow escaped with the Lone Wanderer to the Citadel. Suppose further that the Lone Wanderer goes on to complete Project Purity, but before news of their success reaches James, he dies. It seems that this success benefits James, despite the fact that he doesn't know about it—his life's work has been completed! Compare this case to the events of the game, where Project Purity is completed after James dies. In both cases, James' life's work is completed, and he is not aware of it. If we think this is a benefit in the first case, it seems it must also be a benefit in the second case.[6] But this raises what is often referred to as the "problem of the subject": how can something be good for dead-James, if he no longer exists?

One response to this problem is to argue that neither unconscious-James nor dead-James is benefited by the completion of his life's work—something can only be a benefit (or harm) to me if it affects me directly in some way.[7] While we might think that the success of Project Purity is a good thing *in general*, it is not a good thing *for James*. Once we are dead, nothing can affect us, and so nothing can benefit or harm us.

A different response to this problem comes from philosophers like Joel Feinberg (1926–2004) and George Pitcher (1925–2018).[8] They argue that the subject of posthumous benefits and harms is what they call the "ante-mortem" person. After someone's death, we can describe them as they were at some earlier stage of their life (the ante-mortem person), or describe them as they are now (the post-mortem person). Feinberg and Pitcher think that ante-mortem persons can benefit and be harmed after their death. "Ante-mortem James" desires the completion of Project Purity, and it is this James who is benefitted when it is completed (i.e., after ante-mortem James's death). Although ante-mortem James does not experience the satisfaction of his desire (because while he is alive, it hasn't been satisfied yet), the fact that he has a desire that *will be satisfied* makes a positive difference to his life. (Compare this to a James that has a desire that *will not be satisfied* after his death. His life seems to be worse, at least in that respect). So far, so good. But we might notice a problem here: ante-mortem James stopped existing before the events that satisfied his desire, which suggests that an event in the present (the completion of Project Purity) changed something in the past (ante-mortem James' well-being). This appears to be a case of backward causation: surely something that happens in the present can't improve my well-being in the past!

Feinberg and Pitcher both deny that their views imply backward causation: it is not the case that James died "un-benefited," and then benefits once Project Purity is completed. Instead, they argue that ante-mortem James is benefited *during his lifetime*, by the fact that his future desire for Project Purity to be completed is going to be satisfied.

Consider the events of October 23, 2077—the beginning of the Great War in the *Fallout* universe and the day the Vaults are sealed shut.[9] Because of these events, October 22, 2077, is the last day of the prewar era. Of course, no one realized this at the time (that is, on the 22nd): the events of the 23rd make it true that the 22nd was the last day of the prewar era.

Feinberg and Pitcher argue that we should think of posthumous harms and benefits the same way: events after a person's death retroactively change the properties of the ante-mortem person, and this can make them better or worse off. Suppose I shoot a Raider, but before they die, a second Raider kills me. At the moment of my death, I am not (yet) a killer, but the death of the first Raider makes it true of me that I was a killer, even if this happens after my death.[10] This example shows that ascribing new properties to a person after their death does not require the possibility of backwards causation.

Yet, even if it is possible that events in the present can result in persons that existed in the past acquiring new properties, these may not be the same kinds of properties as "being harmed" or "being benefitted." The property "being a killer" is an extrinsic property, something that is true of me because of my relationship to other things. The change I undergo when the description "is a killer" goes from false of me to true of me is not a genuine change to *me*.[11] Conversely, harms and benefits involve changes to my intrinsic properties (for example, my physical and mental states). This is not to say that my extrinsic properties do not matter to my well-being; changes to my extrinsic properties can, and often do, give rise to changes to my intrinsic properties. For example, actions the Lone Wanderer takes affect their reputation with the various wasteland factions. These changes to my reputation (extrinsic property) can affect my physical or mental states by changing what I think or feel (intrinsic properties), but it is only these latter changes that harm or benefit me. Thus, because the dead lack intrinsic properties, they cannot be benefited or harmed.[12]

"You Think You'll Rest When You're Dead, Children?"—Three Dog

Up to now, we have been mostly concerned with the idea of whether someone can be harmed by events occurring after their death. But we might also wonder whether someone can be *wronged* after their death (or whether we can "do right by the dead"). Something might be harmful, without being wrong. Killing a Raider in self-defense is one such example: the Raider is worse off than they would have been otherwise (say, if I didn't resist), but by harming my attacker, I have not acted wrongly. Conversely, something might be wrong, even if no one is harmed. Suppose I promise to meet you at a particular place and time, though I never intend to show up. Coincidentally, while you're waiting for me to arrive, your shanty is attacked by Super Mutants. Thus, my making a false promise to you is what saved your life (which benefits you), but it was still wrong.

In some ways, the idea of posthumous wrongs is even more intuitive than posthumous harms. As Feinberg points out, we readily accept that we ought not break promises, defame, betray, or otherwise disrespect the deceased—this is not (merely) harmful, but *wrong*.[13]

A particularly provocative example of wronging the dead occurs in the *Fallout 3* side-quest "Blood Ties," in which the Lone Wanderer interacts with members of a commune of cannibals called The Family. Even in the post-apocalyptic *Fallout* universe, cannibalism is considered wrong (as suggested by the fact that even with the Cannibal perk, consuming a corpse reduces Karma). Importantly, the wrongness of cannibalism seems to go beyond any harm that it causes. Even if a person is already dead (so no harm is caused through killing), and is cannibalized in secret (so no distress is caused to others), it still seems that a wrong has occurred, and in particular, that the dead person has been wronged.

One way of understanding this wrong is in terms of our obligations to the living, obligations which might extend past the ends of their lives. A familiar example of this kind of obligation involves promising: suppose that while you're alive, I promise that I will scatter your ashes from the top of Tenpenny Tower after you've died. If I toss them in the sewer instead, and thereby break the promise I made, it seems like I've wronged you.[14] The point here is that my obligation to keep my promise seems to persist, even after the person I've made the promise to ceases to exist.

We can easily imagine a situation in which a person, while alive, makes it clear to us that they do not want to be eaten after they die. And, if we promise that we will not, it seems that we continue to be bound by that promise once they are dead. This does not show that cannibalism is wrong, however, but only that breaking a promise to the deceased is wrong. Does this mean that unless we've made a promise not to eat someone after their death, it's okay?

Maybe it simply goes without saying that we wouldn't want to be eaten after our death, and so although no explicit promises are made, we still have an obligation to respect the wishes of the living about how their bodies will be treated after their death. Indeed, while promises require a clear act of promising and accepting in order to generate an obligation, many of our obligations apply to us whether we like it or not.

But notice that the above obligations are obligations to the living, not to the dead. Unless we have obligations *to the dead*, it is difficult to see how we might wrong them by failing to satisfy these obligations. Thus, if an act like cannibalism is wrong, it is not a wrong to the dead person. Yet, it is also unclear how it could be a wrong to the formerly living person, since this person no longer exists.

Nevertheless, we still have reasons to do (or avoid doing) certain things with respect to the dead, despite the fact that they can seemingly neither be harmed nor wronged. As contemporary philosophers J.S. Taylor and Ernest Partridge (1935–2018) argue, we honor the wishes of the now-dead to ensure the continuance of such honoring as a social practice, so that our wishes will in turn be honored.[15] Thus, we should honor the wishes of the dead because doing so is good for the living. Notice that on this view, however, if we could fail to honor the wishes of the dead without affecting the social practice of honoring (for instance, if we could be cannibals in secret), not only would there be no reason not to do this, no one would be wronged. Similarly, we could imagine circumstances—such as a post-apocalyptic wasteland—where even if a person wished not to be eaten after death, there is no expectation that this wish will be respected. On this view, there would be no moral reason against cannibalism.

One other possible way of understanding potential obligations to the deceased is to appeal to impersonal views of morality. These views hold that an action can be wrong without making things worse for anyone in particular. Suppose that you are the last person alive in a sealed Vault, and about to die. If you push a button, you will start a process that will create 100 Vault Dwellers who will go on to live happy lives. If you don't, these future Vault Dwellers will not exist. Failing to push the button doesn't harm or wrong anyone (since the future Vault Dwellers don't exist yet), but it seems to be the wrong choice.[16]

Perhaps cannibalism, if it is a wrong, is an "impersonal" wrong—it is wrong, but without wronging anyone in particular. In this way, our obligations toward the dead are analogous to our obligations toward things like nature—for example, we ought to show respect for nature not because failing to do so is harmful, or because it violates a right, but because nature has an impersonal sort of value. Similarly, cannibalism is wrong because it is disrespectful, not to a particular person, but to *personhood*.

"You're ... Different. If You Die, You Stay Dead. Better Be Careful!"—Dr. Stanislaus Braun

It is a necessary feature of video games like those in the *Fallout* series that when the player-character dies, the world stops. The story cannot continue without the player. Of course, in reality, we know that the world will continue in some form after our deaths (barring a nuclear apocalypse). In this chapter, we've considered some challenging philosophical questions about our connection with the world after our deaths. Given that we no longer exist, it is difficult to see how we might be harmed or wronged by what happens after we die. Still, how we treat the dead seems very much to matter; if not to them, then to those of us who are still surviving.

Notes

1. In *Fallout 4*, interactions between Deacon and the Sole Survivor indicate that the Capital Wasteland is exporting purified water, suggesting that canonically, the Lone Wanderer activates the purifier without contaminating it with the Forced Evolutionary Virus (FEV).
2. Epicurus, "Letter to Menoeceus," in Diogenes Laertius ed., *Lives of Eminent Philosophers*, trans. R.D. Hicks, (Cambridge: Harvard University Press, 1972).
3. It is possible that my desires might be harmful to others (e.g., if I desire to kill someone). In this case, satisfying this desire would be good from the point of view of my well-being, but it would be morally bad.
4. Fred Feldman, "Some Puzzles About the Evil of Death," *The Philosophical Review* 100 (1991), 205–227.
5. Ben Bradley, "When Is Death Bad for the One Who Dies?," *Nous* 38 (2004), 1–28.
6. Philosophers Derek Parfit (1942–2017) and Joel Feinberg (1926–2004) both appeal to comparisons like this to argue for the idea of posthumous harm. Derek Parfit, *Reasons and Persons* (Oxford: Clarendon Press, 1984). Joel Feinberg, *The Moral Limits of Criminal Law*, vol. 1: *Harm to Others* (New York: Oxford University Press, 1984).
7. Philosophers like Ernest Partridge (1935–2018) and contemporary philosophers Mark Bernstein and Walter Glannon make this kind of argument.
8. Feinberg, *The Moral Limits of Criminal Law*.
9. With the exception of Vault 12, which was designed never to close so the effects of radiation on inhabitants could be studied.
10. A similar example comes from Dorothy Grover (1936–2017).
11. Philosophers call these "Cambridge changes," after the influential Cambridge philosophers Bertrand Russell (1872–1970) and J.M.E. McTaggart (1866–1925). A simple example of a "Cambridge change" is what occurs when I change my location relative to a fixed point. A sentence that was true, such as "Big Town is north of me" when I'm standing at the Red Racer Factory, is no longer true when I'm standing in Paradise Falls, even though nothing about my physical make-up has changed.
12. This sort of argument is made by the contemporary philosopher J.S. Taylor. J.S. Taylor, "A Defense of the Obligation to Keep Promises to the Dead," *The Journal of Medicine and Philosophy* 49 (2024), 547–549.
13. Feinberg, *The Moral Limits of Criminal Law*.
14. There is a large philosophical literature on the nature of promising, and philosophers disagree about whether we have an obligation to keep promises made to the living, once they are dead. For an overview, see Allen Habib, "Promises," in *The Stanford Encyclopedia of Philosophy* at https://plato.stanford.edu/entries/promises.
15. Taylor, "A Defense of the Obligation to Keep Promises to the Dead."
16. These kinds of cases are related to the philosopher Derek Parfit's famous non-identity problem. Parfit, *Reasons and Persons*.

2

Should Lucy and Maximus Have Children? The Ethics of Reproducing in the Apocalypse

Eric J. Silverman

Whether or not to have children can be a tough decision, even when life is going well. Do we have the resources to ensure our children will have a good life? Is our family situation and society stable enough for us to reasonably expect life to be a blessing and not a hardship for our children? These are legitimate questions, even if you don't have to worry about your children being turned into ghouls or eaten by Deathclaws.

This issue isn't just a practical question; it's also an ethical question. Is it morally acceptable to bring children into a world in which every reasonable expectation is a lifetime marked by tragedy, evil, pain, suffering, and disappointment? Some philosophers (called anti-natalists) make the case that it's unethical to have children just in general. Of course, in the *Fallout* universe, things are quite a bit worse than in our ordinary world. As the philosopher Thomas Hobbes (1588–1679) might put it, in most corners of the post-apocalyptic *Fallout* world, life is "nasty, brutish, and short."[1] Even with the best circumstances in a vault, life is marked by limited freedom, limited resources, and deadly dangers just outside the door (and that's if your vault isn't one of the crueler experiments designed by the Vault-Tec).

In this chapter, we'll explore the ethics of natalism: the decision to have children. We'll start by considering the ethics of reproduction in the *Fallout* world from the viewpoint of the anti-natalists. In the Amazon series, Lucy MacLean intends to marry and have children in the hopes of eventually helping rebuild civilization. But many might reasonably ask if it's wrong to have children in a world where their lives will likely be marked by the ubiquitous suffering and hardship found in the world of *Fallout*. Will her children's lives be genuinely good on the whole in such a dangerous apocalyptic future? And is it ethically troublesome that those being born are being brought into such a world without their consent?

"Death Is a Preferable Alternative to Communism"—Liberty Prime

Some conditions and experiences are so bad that many would simply prefer death or non-existence. While most Americans no longer draw the line at communism, contemporary anti-natalist philosopher David Benatar goes so far as to claim that even in the conditions of current human existence, it is better to never have been born. As Benatar puts it:

> A charmed life is so rare that for every one such life there are millions of wretched lives. Some know that their baby will be among the unfortunate.... Even the most privileged people could give birth to a child that will suffer unbearably, be raped, assaulted, or be murdered brutally. The optimist surely bears the burden of justifying this procreational Russian roulette. Given that there are no real advantages over never existing for those who are brought into existence, it is hard to see how the significant risk of serious harm could be justified.[2]

Having a child brings a new person into existence who will have both positive and negative experiences. Yet, morally speaking, these experiences do not balance out in the end. Benatar claims there is no moral directive to bring people into existence so they can have positive experiences, but that there is a moral directive against bringing people into a situation where they have negative, painful experiences. Furthermore, many of the negative experiences will be more significant than the positive experiences: for example, pain matters more than pleasure in that it can be longer term. Each of us experiences unpleasant irritations, bodily discomfort, hunger, and thirst, even on good days. In bad situations, we may experience long-term chronic pain, yet no one gets to experience chronic pleasure. The everyday conditions of current normal existence are simply bad. Because we get used to these negative conditions, we are slow to realize just how much pain we experience every day. In contrast, pleasure tends to be rarer, shorter-term, and more difficult to sustain. In the *Fallout* universe, we might have to fight radroaches just to survive, and the great joy of the day might be roasting one of the disgusting creatures to provide basic food to live another day.

Since bringing humans into existence inevitably results in considerable and unavoidable negative experiences, Benatar concludes that it is unethical to bring children into existence. Let's call this argument the Harm Argument.

Someone might reasonably object that Benatar gets the odds of a good life versus a wretched life wrong in the current world. It surely seems like the odds of having a life that is happy, pleasant, and overwhelmingly good are better than a million to one. Yet, in the reality of *Fallout*, the everyday problems are far more extreme: radiation poisoning, starvation, violence, and murder. If human happiness is largely about pleasure, then life after the apocalypse does not seem promising for virtually anyone. If life is about accomplishing our desires, it is clear that few long-term desires can be secured in such a world. The post-apocalyptic world seems as bad as Hobbes claimed the pre-civilized state of nature must have been. He claimed that the instability of an uncivilized world would create a situation where there was

> no place for hard work, because there is no assurance that it will yield results; and consequently no cultivation of the earth, no navigation or use of materials that can be imported by sea, no construction of large buildings, no machines for moving things that require much force, no knowledge of the face of the earth, no account of time, no practical skills, no literature or scholarship, no society; and—worst of all—continual fear and danger of violent death, and the life of man solitary, poor, nasty, brutish, and short.[3]

In other words, the chaos of the uncivilized world discourages most of the valuable activities that make life better for everyone, while encouraging violent behaviors that ultimately harm most people. These systematic trends inevitably make life bad for everyone. Hobbes thought that such uncivilized chaos was so bad that any kind of political civilization would be an improvement.

Of course, there are exceptions: the vaults, the Brotherhood, and other such organizations bring order, peace, and a degree of safety to at least some small areas of the world. Yet, this civilized peace is the rare exception, as much of the world is in a constant state of anarchy and war that Hobbes envisioned (hardly a suitable place to raise children). It is a miserable existence that we'd be wise to avoid. The Robobrain Jezebel in *Fallout 4* goes even further by claiming, "By my calculations, the easiest way to help a human is simply to destroy it. There's no point in prolonging a laughably fragile life." In her view, death is preferable to the post-apocalyptic existence of struggling humans. After all, such lives are futile, full of pain and disappointment. Why not just end the futility before we have lives made up entirely of negative value? Of course, one does not have to endorse active mass killing to admit that life in the post-apocalyptic world would be so miserable that most people should prefer non-existence.

I Don't Remember Signing Up for This Experiment: What About Consent?

A long-standing moral principle requires that there needs to be a mature, informed agreement before a person endures something risky or unpleasant. The importance of consent is obvious in the case of Vault-Tec's cruel experiments on the Vault Dwellers. Literally, these dangerous experiments aren't what these unsuspecting Americans signed up for, and they wouldn't have agreed to them.

Accordingly, there is at least a kernel of truth in the rebellious adolescent quip, "I didn't ask to be born!" None of us consented to be brought into existence. As Jean-Paul Sartre (1905–1980) observed, "Someone will say, 'I did not ask to be born.' … I am not the foundation of my being.… I am abandoned in the world."[4] Consent concerning matters that importantly affect us is generally a moral necessity. This principle might even be true of *all* things that affect us personally, but it is most obviously true concerning choices that might have a decisively negative impact on our lives.

The principle of consent provides the basis for a second argument against having children. Bringing new children into the world involves risks and could result in significant harm to them. Considering the serious risk, it would be unethical to bring them into the world without their consent. Yet, we know that no child consents to being brought into existence; how could they? They're thrust into this world with all its attendant risks, all without their consent or choosing.

The contemporary philosopher Seana Shiffrin uses these principles as an argument against having children. Even under the best conditions, bringing someone into existence comes with significant risks. When making decisions that have significant risk to another person, it is morally necessary to get their consent, even if you are seeking to benefit that person. For example, doctors are generally not allowed to perform invasive medical procedures without patient consent, even when they intend to help the individual (and this prohibition would be even stronger in less benevolent situations like the mutation experiments of Vault 4). Since children do not consent to the risky choice of being brought into the world, having children is inherently immoral. We can call this argument the Consent Argument. As Shiffrin argues:

> By being caused to exist as persons, children are forced to assume moral agency, to face various demanding and sometimes wrenching moral questions, and to discharge taxing moral duties. They must endure the fairly substantial amount of pain, suffering, difficulty, significant disappointment, distress, and significant loss that occur within the typical life. They must face and undergo the fear and harm of death. Finally, they must bear the results of imposed risks that their lives may go terribly wrong in a variety of ways. All of these burdens are imposed without the future child's consent.[5]

Life can be great, but it also brings challenges, pain, suffering, disappointment, and ultimately death. It seems that any event with such downsides requires the consent of the person who will face these dangers.

Even in ordinary circumstances, life is full of challenges. When life goes well, we still face discomfort, relationship issues, disappointments, disease, aging, and eventually death. And much worse things can happen, such as violence, poverty, and isolation. Subjecting anyone to such pain and risk surely requires their consent. Only some hyperbolic villain who would hunt us from the shadows like Ulysses would think otherwise.

"I Have a Question. The Only Question That Matters. Would You Risk Your Life for Your Fellow Man?" – Desdemona

Thus far, we've considered two arguments against having children in the post-apocalyptic world: the Harm Argument and the Consent Argument. Yet, there are some notable ways one might respond to these arguments. First, against the Harm Argument, many philosophers, theologians, poets, and saints have thought that the goal of life might be something other than pleasure, fulfilled desire, and the sorts of commonsense goods at the heart of the Harm Argument. On this alternative view, the prevalence of pain in the post-apocalyptic world doesn't undermine the most important aspects of life.

What are these important aspects? One possibility is that the greatest good might be amusement or excitement. In the original *Fallout* game, Alya (from the Khans gang) seems to endorse this view: "We give them the most important thing possible. We give their dreary lives excitement." The idea that amusement might be the ultimate human good is even considered by Aristotle (384–322 BCE) before he rejects it as the goal of a child and inadequate for mature humans.[6]

Other thinkers have said that the goal of life is to find meaning in the challenges of life, to develop character, to love, to find enlightenment, or to glorify God. Since the time of the ancient Greeks, some thinkers—such as the Stoics—have thought that the ultimate goal of life was virtuous moral development. According to the Stoics, the point of life might be to develop as excellent, moral, virtuous people and to aid others in difficult circumstances. Inspiring the Stoics, Socrates (470–399 BCE) insists, "A good man cannot be harmed either in life or in death."[7] He asserts this principle, even as he had been unjustly condemned to death by the authorities in Athens. Socrates claims that the only good is virtue in the soul and the only evil that can happen to us is to become vicious. Thus, to be virtuous is to have all that is important, even if you have a painful, frustrating, untimely death.

Similarly, Aristotle thought that mere pleasure is an inadequate goal for humans and that the focused pursuit of pleasure is beneath human dignity. Pleasure is the goal of barnyard animals; it shouldn't be the goal of human beings. Instead, for Aristotle, cultivating a life of virtue shaped by rational principles in line with human potential is life's true goal.[8]

If the goal and primary good of human life is virtue, then the *Fallout* world might be a particularly good setting in which to live such a life. Resisting a preoccupation with pleasure isn't just virtuous; it's an effective practical strategy in difficult circumstances. Furthermore, there is an abundance of people in need of help. The environment is quite suitable for living a life of service and sacrifice. And if that task seems too overwhelming in the world of *Fallout*, we might take the advice of Mother Teresa

(1910–1997) as she faced the endless task of serving the sick, poor, and dying in the most destitute corners of Calcutta: "Help one person at a time and always start with the person nearest you."[9] Success is not the goal of such a life; instead, virtuous service to aid others is what's valuable.

Accordingly, when parents ask themselves what they really want for their children, the answer is more complicated than the simplistic story that Benatar offers. While we do indeed want our children to have pleasant, enjoyable lives, full of good things, many parents are more concerned about the kind of people their children become. They view a good life as consisting not merely of pleasure but also of meaning, virtuous character, relationships, and the pursuit of the greater good, even if such pursuits sometimes require sacrifice and hardship. And the *Fallout* world actually does provide opportunities for these sorts of goods.

In some instances, the pleasurable life and the meaningful, virtuous life conflict with one another. While this can be tragic, the meaningful, virtuous life is still the best and most desirable life in the most important ways. Think of the end of the original *Fallout* game when the Overseer infamously exiles the vault's savior, explaining, "You're a hero. And you have to leave." The virtuous, sacrificial life of the hero may not be the most pleasurable or the easiest, but it is what saints and poets have always told us to pursue.

Another response to the Harm Argument is to focus on the goodness of existence itself. We can see this idea in *Fallout 4* when Contagion's Vulnerability Robotic Infirmary Engineer explains that promoting existence in the form of human survival is a foundational moral duty: "Humanity is so resilient, to cling to life despite all of this. It is the duty of us all to further that survival." Existence may be the foundational good, while pleasure, fulfilled desires, and the sorts of things valued by the Harm Argument are at best secondary goods. Therefore, even an unpleasant and difficult human existence might be considered to be better than non-existence.

On this view, simplistic theories of happiness are absurd, especially if they lead to suicidal or anti-natalist thought. Existence is the most important good, and it's good *for the child* that it exists, even if their life is difficult. A universe where human persons exist is far better than a universe without persons. Existence is the foundational good, even if a world without persons would have been simpler and included less pain.

Who Can Consent? What Can They Consent To?

Obviously, we should not put people into dangerous situations without their consent. Yet, the Consent Argument against the morality of having children relies upon a simplistic and wooden notion of the need for consent that very few people actually endorse.

In practice, the principle of consent usually comes with many qualifications and limitations. Morally relevant, genuine consent to important choices requires a considerable degree of mature understanding. Yet, young children are incapable of the mature understanding needed to provide consent on most significant matters. It is widely recognized in our culture that children cannot consent to medical procedures, sexual activity, or even to an elementary school field trip to Shady Sands. Instead, the child's caretaker is trusted to act on their behalf in pursuit of the child's well-being. Parental or adult caretaker consent on behalf of the child is thought to be both necessary and sufficient concerning important choices that affect the child. In our culture, parents are free to provide or withhold consent for a wide range of choices on the child's behalf, often even directly against the immediate desires and opinions of the child. They may deny the child their preferred foods, insisting on a balanced diet of fruits and vegetables rather than the sweets and deep-fried food that many children crave. Parents may insist on an earlier bedtime than the child prefers. They may even use some degree of force to administer these decisions. More controversially, parents may choose to limit their children's access to information, forbid certain friends, and even withhold certain medical procedures such as vaccines.

While it's true that consent of an adult person is required before making decisions that may directly affect them in a negative way, not all humans are adult persons. Just as a caretaker's consent—rather than the child's consent—is thought to be morally sufficient for the most important decisions in a child's life, the consent of the potential child's parents is probably morally sufficient to legitimize the decision to bring a child into existence. So, if Lucy and Maximus want to have children and think that their offspring would have a difficult, but meaningful, worthwhile life, then it is morally acceptable for them to proceed with having a family (assuming Maximus can overcome the myths about sex that the Brotherhood taught him).

Furthermore, the impossible—and perhaps ridiculous—demand for a person's consent before they actually exist is an incoherent desire that would have tremendously negative results in that it would end the human race if we actually followed this principle. In doing so, we would permanently remove the unique good of the human race from the universe. Accordingly, we should notice that requiring a potential person's consent to be brought into existence fails a moral principle called the Universalization Test.[10] This test—created by the great modern philosopher Immanuel Kant (1724–1804)—claims that we should only act upon principles that can be universalized and applied to everyone without creating incoherent absurdities. Principles that cannot be universalized are morally suspect.

For example, lying is thought to be a principle that cannot be universalized. The goal of lying (i.e., deception) can't be accomplished if everyone lies. If everyone lies all the time, eventually no one trusts, and therefore deception becomes impossible. Lying only works if most people don't lie most of the time. Since the goal of lying—deception—is undermined when lying becomes universalized, we should realize that successful deception relies upon a kind of unethical self-preference. But living by a special set of rules that not everyone can live by is immoral self-preference. Since all persons are morally equal, we should not treat ourselves as superior to others by indulging in unethical actions that only work if a select few indulge in them. So, lying works because most people tell the truth most of the time, but then I exempt myself from such rules in order to accomplish my goal. This self-preference, exempting myself from the rules of honesty that I implicitly need others to live by, is what makes lying immoral.

Similarly, we cannot universalize the principle that we need a person's consent in order to bring them into existence. Since we, like all rational beings, were brought into existence without our consent, and it is that very existence that allows us to see the value of consent, we commit a similar absurdity. The goal of the Consent Argument is to respect the value of rational personal consent. Yet, if humanity universally holds to the rule of requiring consent before bringing people into existence, no rational being would exist (including ourselves) to respect the value of the consent of rational beings. This desire is incoherent and requires an exception to the rule in order to invoke the rule. Furthermore, while it presents itself as an idealistic moral principle, it would ultimately be more effective than the Master's plan for ending humanity itself. My existence—and the existence of all known rational moral beings—requires that they be brought into existence without their consent.

Facing the Future with Hope and Optimism

Throughout most of history, life has been more challenging, less comfortable, shorter, and left humanity much more exposed to harm than in our current world. Yet, despite these hardships, most societies have valued life, children, and cultural development. To give up on having children is to give up on the future of the human race and the great good that accompanies human personal experience in this world. Therefore, even in the face of an apocalypse, we should distrust the anti-natalist arguments. Humans have built flourishing civilizations in the past and moved out of the anarchic state of nature. If necessary, we can do so again, but only if we are willing to face hardship and distrust pleasure enough to reject the arguments of anti-natalism. Some of us, in the short to medium term, would need to face the challenges posed by the post-apocalyptic mess and seek to reestablish civilization. Hopefully, we would look at the difficult task ahead of us and—with a bit of hope and optimism—echo Lucy's sentiments by saying, "Okey dokey!"

Notes

1. Thomas Hobbes, *Leviathan*, (London: Penguin, 2017), XIII.9.
2. David Benatar, *Better Never to Have Been: The Harm of Coming into Existence*, (Oxford: Oxford University Press, 2006), 92.
3. Hobbes, *Leviathan*, XIII.9.
4. Jean-Paul Sartre, *Existentialism and Human Emotions*, (New York: Open Road, 2015), 48.
5. Seana Shiffrin, "Wrongful Life, Procreative Responsibility, and the Significance of Harm," *Legal Theory* 5 (1999), 137.
6. Aristotle, *Nicomachean Ethics*, trans. W.D. Ross, (Oxford: Oxford University Press, 2009), 1176b.
7. Plato, *Apology*, trans. G.M.A. Grube, in *Plato: Five Dialogues* (Indianapolis: Hackett, 2002) 41c–d.
8. Aristotle, *Nicomachean Ethics*, 1100b–1101a.
9. Teresa of Calcutta, "Mother Teresa's Golden Words," https://www.motherteresacharities.org/mother-teresa-Quotes.php?srsltid=AfmBOopYrwLums0q0AmpL4OL76y_PyjS4xZ55cOQmPk69EqP1e9llFtH, accessed February 18, 2026.
10. Immanuel Kant, *Groundwork of the Metaphysics of Morals*, 4:421. What we have called the Universalization Test is one of the various formulations of what Kant calls the "Categorical Imperative."

3

All Too Human: Moral Status in the Wasteland

David R. Lawrence

There's a moment in *Fallout 4* that sticks with you. It's not a grand battle or a world-altering decision, but a quiet, tense confrontation in the belly of a forgotten prewar bunker. You're there on the orders of Elder Maxson, the zealous leader of the Brotherhood of Steel, to execute a traitor. The target is Paladin Danse, your friend and mentor, a man who believes in the Brotherhood's cause with every fiber of his being. His crime? He's a synth. An escaped machine from the very Institute he's dedicated his life to destroying. He didn't know. When you find him, he's not a monster or a sleeper agent; he's just a man whose entire world, his very identity, has been shattered. He begs you to kill him, to let him die as a soldier because, in his mind, that's the only way to reconcile the man he knows himself to be with the "abomination" the Brotherhood says he is. You've fought beside him, trusted him. Now you're supposed to judge whether he's even a person. This single quest, "Blind Betrayal," encapsulates a philosophical war being waged in the irradiated ruins of the *Fallout* universe.

Fallout is full of gunfights and monsters. But this moment reveals its deeper story: a world where identity, morality, and personhood are all up for grabs. Through characters like Danse, Nick Valentine, Curie, and others, the franchise explores a question with real-world weight: What makes someone a person? And when we meet someone different, whether artificial, mutated, or augmented, how do we decide whether they matter?

Who Counts in the Wasteland?

To navigate the ethical landscape of the *Fallout* wasteland, we first need a philosophical toolkit. The central question—who or what counts as a person—isn't a matter of simple definition but of moral status. As the contemporary philosopher Charles Taylor puts it, "A person is a being with a certain moral status or a bearer of rights. But underlying the moral status, as its condition, are certain capacities. A person is a being who has a sense of self, has a notion of the future and the past, can hold values, make choices; in short, can adopt life-plans."[1] These capacities are the threshold for moral status because they are what give a being a subjective inner world, a stake in its own continued existence. A being with these capacities can be wronged in a way an object cannot; it has a life that can go better or worse *for it*. To deny moral status to a being that can plan, value, and see itself as a continuous story is to ignore the very qualities that make our own lives meaningful.

A crucial component of this is what's called narrative identity: an "internalized and evolving life story, integrating the reconstructed past and imagined future to provide life with some degree of unity and purpose."[2] This isn't just memory; it's the active process of weaving those memories into a coherent story of who you are. This capacity is the bedrock of another key characteristic, known as "moral agency." To be a moral agent, amongst other things, one must understand oneself as a continuous being who is responsible for past actions and whose present choices will shape a future self. Understanding an action as a part of a narrative like this, one which will have consequences for the agent and indeed for others, is crucially important. Think of a security turret. It can kill someone (a morally significant act), but it doesn't understand what death means, and it doesn't choose to kill for reasons. A moral agent, by contrast, is the source of the moral choice itself, capable of understanding the moral value of its actions.[3] This distinction is paramount because if personhood is defined by these cognitive capacities, then the physical material—the substrate of flesh, circuits, or irradiated tissue—is irrelevant. To insist otherwise is, arguably, a form of physical bigotry.

We also tend to think that persons must be humans, and this is reflected in the old English common law distinction between the protected "reasonable creature," by which the historical jurisprudentialists meant "human," and the unprotected "monster," a being lacking the "shape of mankind."[4] This dichotomy provides a stark framework for understanding how the societies of *Fallout* judge their novel inhabitants. However, the word "human" is trickier than it seems. Sometimes we mean biology—you're human if you're *Homo sapiens*. But sometimes we mean something deeper: you're human if you can think, feel, and make moral choices as we do.[5] And sometimes we mean it as praise, calling someone "truly human" when they show our best qualities, like compassion or justice.[6] In *Fallout*, some of the most "human" characters aren't biologically human at all.

Mankind, Redefined

The third-generation synths of *Fallout 4* are the game's most direct exploration of artificial personhood. They are biomechanical constructs, physically and mentally indistinguishable from humans, built by the secretive Institute. Here we see the philosophical debates about personhood played out in stark relief. The Institute views them as property, mere "glorified toasters," dismissing their desires as simulated, despite creating beings with all the capacities Taylor outlined. The Brotherhood sees these same capacities but denies they matter because of how synths were made, viewing them as "abominations" regardless of their actions. Only the Railroad recognizes that if something walks, talks, and suffers like a person, it deserves the rights of a person.

Even the player isn't exempt from these questions. In the *Fallout 4 Far Harbor* DLC, the synth leader DiMA poses a chilling question: How can you be sure *you're* not a synth? Your earliest memory is the day the bombs fell. Are you sure those memories are real, or were they implanted? The writers are clearly invoking *Blade Runner* here, but they're putting it in your hands. You're not just watching a character doubt their past. You're being asked: What makes your life yours? No character illustrates the achievement of personhood better than Nick Valentine, a prototype synth with the implanted memories of a prewar detective. His quest, "Long Time Coming," is a masterclass in the formation of narrative identity. Nick is driven to hunt down mob boss Eddie Winter, the man who murdered the original Nick's fiancée. This isn't a programmed directive; it's a deeply personal mission. This demonstrates Taylor's criterion of a sense of self; Nick has a unique fusion of his machine nature and the detective's memories.

This hybrid self is authentic because Nick actively grapples with it, questioning his own nature rather than passively accepting it. His choice to pursue Winter is an act of autonomous moral reasoning, not a pre-written script. He has a clear notion of the past and the future, using Nick's prewar trauma to define a future where justice is served. He holds values—justice for the wronged, closure for the grieving—and makes the choice to pursue Winter, adopting a life-plan to bring this centuries-old story to an end. Here we see clear evidence of narrative identity because he integrates a "reconstructed past" with an "imagined future," giving his own unique existence "unity and purpose."[7] By confronting Winter, he acts as a moral agent, understanding the act not as mere revenge, but as the righteous conclusion to a great injustice. He becomes his own man by taking ownership of another's story.

Nick's detective work extends far beyond the Winter case, demonstrating sophisticated moral reasoning that proves his personhood. When investigating the Valentine Detective Agency's other cases, Nick consistently makes ethical judgments about justice, often showing mercy to desperate people while pursuing genuine criminals with relentless determination. He expresses genuine empathy for victims of violence and demonstrates a nuanced understanding of human nature that goes beyond mere programming. His reflections on the nature of memory and identity, such as wondering whether his feelings for the original Nick's fiancée are genuine or borrowed, show the kind of introspective moral reasoning that defines authentic personhood. This demonstrates that his moral agency extends across all aspects of his existence, not just isolated dramatic moments. But while Nick's journey explores personhood through the lens of memory and narrative identity, Curie's story examines it from another vital angle: the role of emotion and an embodied mind.

Her journey is about what happens when logic meets grief, and the transition from moral actor to moral agent. Initially a Miss Nanny robot in Vault 81, she is programmed with medical knowledge but lacks true understanding. Her choice to seek a synth body in her quest, "Emergent Behavior," demonstrates a sophisticated sense of self, one that recognizes its own limitations and seeks to transcend them. This choice shows the capacity for life-planning that defines personhood. Once embodied, she is overwhelmed by new emotions: grief for a long-dead colleague, flustered embarrassment, and confusion. This is her crash course in moral agency. She is no longer just a logical machine executing protocols; she must now navigate a world of feelings and their consequences. Her struggle to reconcile her logical past with her emotional future is the forging of a new narrative identity. Her embodied experience creates true moral agency because her reasoning is no longer purely computational; it is now informed by genuine emotional and physical experience, allowing her to empathize and make value judgments in a way her robot form never could.

Curie's emotional awakening provides perhaps the most compelling evidence for the connection between embodied experience and moral agency. After her transformation, she doesn't just experience emotions; rather, she actively grapples with what they mean. Her confusion about romantic feelings demonstrates her genuine moral development as she tries to understand these new sensations within her existing ethical framework. She expresses guilt about feeling happy when others suffer, showing a sophisticated moral intuition about appropriate emotional responses. This demonstrates how her newfound emotions aren't mere computational responses but genuine qualitative experiences that inform her moral reasoning. When she encounters violence in the wasteland, her emotional reactions—horror, empathy, and sometimes righteous anger—guide her ethical judgments in ways her purely logical programming never could. Her emotional development proves that moral agency requires not just rational calculation but the full spectrum of conscious experience that comes with embodied existence. Curie's story is one of achieving personhood by choice, but the wasteland offers a more tragic perspective on synth identity. As we saw at the opening of this chapter, the tragedy of Paladin Danse is that he is a perfect person by the standards of his chosen ideology, right up until that ideology denies his right to exist. His sense of self is entirely defined by his role as a human soldier in the Brotherhood of Steel. When the quest "Blind Betrayal" reveals he is a synth, his narrative identity collapses, built as it is on a past he now questions and a future that is suddenly impossible. The fact that his identity can be shattered so profoundly *proves* he had a genuine one to begin with; a machine wouldn't have an identity crisis. His immediate reaction is to demand his own execution, a choice that proves his status as a moral agent who fully understands and accepts the values of the Brotherhood, even when they condemn him. His moral reasoning about his own existence demonstrates the very capacities the Brotherhood denies. He is capable of holding values and making choices based on a life-plan, even when that choice is self-annihilation for the sake of his principles.

Hey, Smoothskin

If it talks like a person, chooses like a person, and reasons like a person, does it matter that it looks like a monster? Ghouls challenge our definition of personhood by forcing us to separate identity from a "species-typical" form. As humans transformed by radiation, retaining their minds and memories beneath a necrotic exterior, ghouls are the ultimate test of society's ability to look past the "monster" appearance and see the "reasonable creature" underneath.[8] The prejudice against them is fueled by a tangible threat: feralization, the unpredictable process by which a ghoul's higher cognitive functions decay, leaving behind mindless aggression.[9] Philosophically, feralization is a stark depiction of the loss of personhood.

Yet, many ghouls powerfully resist this loss of self, and perhaps no one embodies that defiance more than John Hancock, the charismatic mayor of Goodneighbor. Disgusted by his brother's anti-ghoul politics, Hancock left Diamond City and eventually became a ghoul himself. He didn't lose himself; he found himself. Hancock forged a new sense of self and a clear life plan: to protect the outcasts of the wasteland. He consistently demonstrates his values, such as freedom for the oppressed and punishment for the wicked, through his choices as a leader. His governance requires him to make constant moral judgments to maintain a functioning, just society.[10] The irony that his "pure" human brother is later revealed to be an Institute synth only sharpens the point: Hancock, the "monster," is more authentically human (by one measure) than the man who wore the perfect human form.

While Hancock's story is about choosing a new identity, *Fallout: New Vegas* explores the burden of a long-established identity. The ghoul mechanic Raul Tejada, a prewar ghoul and skilled mechanic you rescue from Black Mountain, is burdened by centuries of memory and loss. His companion quest, "Old School Ghoul," is a quiet exploration of narrative identity. By speaking with other aging warriors like Ranger Andy and Loyal the Boomer, Raul is forced to confront his past as a legendary gunslinger. This demonstrates complex narrative reasoning across centuries, as he must reconcile his past self with his present one. His internal conflict shows a sense of self in flux. Ultimately, he must make a choice: either embrace his past and become a gunslinger again, or leave it behind. This choice proves his personhood, as he actively shapes his future by reinterpreting his past.

The Milk of Human Kindness

We have an even more distinct example in the Super Mutants, who are created by the Forced Evolutionary Virus (FEV). They are the most physically divergent beings from humanity in the franchise and the most universally reviled. Yet to dismiss the entire race as monstrous is to ignore the clear evidence of personhood in some of them. Different FEV strains and the genetics of the original human subject produce vastly different results, from the intelligent first-generation mutants of the Master's army to the brutish mutants common on the East Coast. The most compelling refutation of this monstrous stereotype comes from *Fallout 3*'s Fawkes. An intelligent Super Mutant ostracized by his peers for his civility, his status as a true moral agent is undeniable. At the game's climax, the player must enter a chamber flooded with lethal radiation. Fawkes, who is immune to radiation, refuses to go in their place. His reasoning is a pointed display of sophisticated personal ethics: "We all have our own destinies, and yours culminates here. I would not rob you of that." This is a profound moral choice based on his values. His ethical reasoning about destiny and agency shows a sophisticated understanding of personhood itself. He recognizes the player's right to their own narrative identity and values, and his choice to respect that is a powerful act of moral agency. Fawkes proves himself "more human than human" by showing a deeper respect for the tenets of personhood than many of the game's actual humans.[11]

Fawkes's moral sophistication extends throughout his interactions with the wasteland's inhabitants. He consistently advocates for non-violent solutions to conflicts, demonstrating a nuanced understanding of justice that goes beyond simple retribution. When discussing other Super Mutants, he expresses genuine sadness about their violent nature, showing empathy even for those who reject him. His reflections on the nature of his transformation reveal deep philosophical thinking about identity and change; he sees his mutation not as a loss of humanity but as an evolution of it. This demonstrates that his moral reasoning encompasses not just dramatic moments but a comprehensive ethical worldview that guides all his choices. His treatment of companions shows respect for their autonomy and dignity, proving that his understanding of personhood extends to recognizing it in others. Fawkes proves an individual can transcend the monstrous stereotype, but he is not an isolated case.

In *Fallout 2* and *New Vegas*, we meet Marcus, a first-generation Super Mutant from the Master's army. Unlike the somewhat tragic figure of Fawkes, Marcus is a community builder. After the Master's defeat, he famously fought a Brotherhood of Steel paladin for days until they both gave up and became friends. Together, they founded the town of Broken Hills, a settlement where humans, ghouls, and mutants live and work together. Marcus demonstrates a clear life plan that extends beyond himself to an entire community. He holds values of peace and cooperation, and makes the choice to actively build a society based on them. As sheriff and later founder of Jacobstown, a refuge for other mutants, he acts as a moral agent on a societal scale, creating laws and mediating disputes. This community-building represents the highest form of moral agency and life-planning, as it involves creating a framework in which others can pursue their own life plans. His entire existence is a testament to a narrative identity that evolved from soldier to diplomat and leader.

Wasteland Ideologies

The factions vying for control of the wasteland are living embodiments of competing philosophical stances on who deserves rights. The Institute denies personhood to their creations, viewing them as property and programming, a convenient excuse for slavery. Their goal to "redefine mankind" is thus undermined by their moral blindness to the persons they create. The Brotherhood of Steel practices a technophobic puritanism, viewing synths, ghouls, and mutants as abominations to be eradicated based on their unnatural origin. Their stance is a clear example of what contemporary bioethicist Leon Kass calls the "wisdom of repugnance," a visceral, emotional rejection of the unnatural that is rationalized into a moral imperative. In stark contrast, the Railroad operates on a single abolitionist principle: any self-aware being is a person and deserves to be free, extending the moral community based on capacity, not form. These factions are more than political rivals; they are warring philosophies, and their conflict shows how easily societies can justify prejudice by drawing arbitrary lines around who counts as a person.

These philosophical stances manifest in concrete actions throughout the games. The Institute's scientists routinely "retire" malfunctioning synths without consideration for their wishes or experiences, treating beings with clear evidence of consciousness as disposable equipment. The Brotherhood's soldiers execute ghouls on sight during their sweeps, regardless of whether these beings pose any actual threat. Their anti-ghoul rhetoric reveals a systematic dehumanization that justifies genocide. Elder Maxson's order to execute Danse demonstrates how quickly personhood can be revoked when it becomes inconvenient to the ideology. Conversely, the Railroad's safe houses and memory wipes represent a recognition that synths possess the same fundamental dignity as any conscious being. Their willingness to risk everything to protect artificial persons demonstrates the practical implications of expanding the moral community beyond biological boundaries.

More Human Than Human

The irradiated landscapes of *Fallout* are populated by beings who force a radical reexamination of what it means to be a person. The case studies of the synth, the ghoul, and the Super Mutant, when viewed through a philosophical lens, converge on a single, powerful conclusion: personhood is a matter of capacity, not of origin. Nick Valentine, Curie, and Danse prove that minds built from circuits or deception can still grasp truth, justice, and love. Hancock and Raul show that identity can endure beyond decay, beyond centuries. Fawkes and Marcus, beings branded monsters, demonstrate compassion and vision that many humans never achieve.

The central moral of the *Fallout* universe is an argument for the expansion of our moral community. The factions that are framed as antagonists are those that insist on a narrow, exclusionary definition of personhood. The heroes are those who fight to recognize the personhood of the "other." This is not merely an abstract debate that applies to a fictional world. The wasteland, in its brutal way, offers a cautionary tale. It argues that the only meaningful measure of a being is its capacity for reason, for empathy, and for the shared struggle to create a life of purpose. To deny a place in the moral community to any being that demonstrates these capacities is to fail the ultimate test of our own humanity.

Notes

1. Charles Taylor, "The Concept of a Person," in *Philosophical Papers, Volume 1*, (Cambridge: Cambridge University Press, 1985), 97.
2. Dan P. McAdams and Kate C. McLean, "Narrative Identity," *Current Directions in Psychological Science* 22 (2013), 233.
3. David R. Lawrence and John Harris, "Monkeys and Moral Machines," in Steve Clarke, Hazem Zohny, and Julian Savulescu eds., *Rethinking Moral Status*, (New York: Oxford University Press, 2021), 5.
4. David R. Lawrence and Margaret Brazier, "Legally Human? 'Novel Beings' and English Law," *Medical Law Review* 26 (2018), 320–321.
5. David R. Lawrence, "The Edge of Human? The Problem with the Posthuman as the 'Beyond,'" *Bioethics* 30 (2016), 337.
6. David R. Lawrence, "More Human Than Human," *Cambridge Quarterly of Healthcare Ethics* 26 (2017), 477.
7. McAdams and McLean, "Narrative Identity," 233.
8. First established in *Fallout* (1997) through encounters with sentient ghoul communities, such as Necropolis under its leader, Set.
9. The concept is demonstrated by the presence of feral ghoul enemies since *Fallout* (1997) and is discussed as a societal fear by characters such as John Hancock in *Fallout 4* (2015).
10. The player's first encounter with John Hancock upon entering the settlement of Goodneighbor, where he delivers a speech defining the town's philosophy.
11. Lawrence, "More Human Than Human," 477.

4

Fallout and the Ethics of Killing Everything

Trevor Grant Hedberg

Shortly after beginning *Fallout: New Vegas*, players typically face a decision about how to resolve a conflict in the town of Goodsprings. Joe Cobb, a member of the Powder Gangers, is searching for a trader named Ringo, and he threatens to burn the town to the ground if Trudy, the unofficial mayor of Goodsprings, does not hand him over. Players can ignore this conflict and venture elsewhere, but, in all likelihood, they will make a choice between helping defend Goodsprings from the Powder Gangers' assault or killing Ringo and assisting the Powder Gangers in their efforts to take over the town. In this scenario, siding with the Powder Gangers clearly represents a morally worse choice than aiding the settlers of Goodsprings, but it is far from the most evil option. *Fallout: New Vegas* is a remarkably flexible game when it comes to player choice: it is possible to beat the game as a total pacifist, and it is also possible to beat the game while killing or destroying almost every non-player character (NPC) you encounter. Thus, it is possible to end the conflict in Goodsprings by killing *both* the Powder Gangers and the Goodsprings residents.

This brutal, homicidal style of play is taken to its extreme in playthroughs where players attempt to eliminate every NPC in the game. In online forums and YouTube videos, these are usually called "Kill Everything" or "Kill Everyone" runs, and this playstyle is popular enough that some gaming websites have compiled lists of games where it is possible to eliminate all NPCs.[1] The premise behind playing the game in this fashion is to complete the game while also ending the lives of as many NPCs encountered as possible. *Fallout* games are not really designed to be completed this way: murdering every NPC renders many questlines impossible to complete, makes factions hostile, and eliminates merchants that players could normally visit to buy and sell items. In *Fallout 3* and *Fallout 4*, many NPCs are even tagged as "essential" in the game's code to prevent critical questlines from being broken. If an essential character's health is reduced to zero, they will be downed temporarily, but their health will eventually regenerate. Even in *New Vegas*, the AI program known as Yes Man will avoid death by transferring to a different Securitron robot so that there will always be at least one path by which players can progress to the game's ending.

Even when not attempting to kill everything, the *Fallout* games are still blatantly violent. Combat in the games involves dismemberment, decapitation, and explosion-induced gore. In the more modern games, the Vault-Tec Assisted Targeting System (called "V.A.T.S." in-game) even allows players to decimate NPCs in stylized slow motion. Attempting a Kill Everything playthrough takes that violence to its most extreme form.

The morality of violent video games has been a controversial topic for several decades, and many wonder whether there is something wrong with playing games like those in the *Fallout* franchise, where violence is portrayed in brutal and sometimes morbidly humorous ways. In this chapter, we consider the specific case where a player is attempting a Kill Everything playthrough. In this case, there will be many situations where the player is deliberately harming and killing NPCs that are innocent and pose no threat to the player's survival, which means that the player's violent acts cannot be explained or justified by references to in-game self-defense or the defense of settlers or traders from aggressive mutants or raiders. Is it wrong to play one of the *Fallout* games in this way?

Does Killing Everything in a Game Affect Behavior in the Real World?

Perhaps the most common criticism of violent video games is that playing them makes a person more likely to commit violent acts in real life. This claim strikes many gamers as dubious because it isn't particularly difficult to differentiate reality from fiction (especially when we're considering the fantastical post-apocalyptic version of the United States in which the *Fallout* games take place). Thus, we may have little difficulty imagining a player who chooses to detonate the nuclear bomb at the center of Megaton in *Fallout 3*—wiping out an entire settlement of innocents in the process—while also being a morally upstanding person in real life.

Social scientists have not been content to leave the resolution of this issue to intuition, however, and there is an extraordinary amount of research on the relationship between the consumption of violent media and its effects on behavior. Any survey of the existing literature will show a rather strong consensus supporting the claim that playing violent video games increases feelings of aggression,[2] but there are some caveats. One such caveat is that the increase in aggressive feelings or behaviors is almost always very small.[3] Another is that there are some studies that appear to generate the opposite conclusion, namely that playing violent video games does not, in fact, lead to an increase in aggressive tendencies.[4] Overall, evidence is mixed on the extent to which playing violent video games increases aggression and the extent to which that increase in aggression influences players' behavior.[5]

The argument that playing violent video games is morally objectionable because of potential impacts on players' behavior also encounters other difficulties beyond the ambiguities tied to the available evidence. One problem is that this line of reasoning risks extending to a wide array of other activities, such as watching films or reading books that portray violent conflict. If these activities lead to a small increase in people's levels of aggression, should we really conclude that people are morally obligated to limit their media consumption only to non-violent content?

Another problem is that video games can have cognitive and social benefits that have to be weighed against their negative effects. Perhaps choosing to detonate the nuclear warhead in The Nucleus—a submarine base found on Mount Desert Island in *Fallout 4*'s *Far Harbor* DLC—and wiping out all its residents in the process results in a minor increase in the player's aggression, but contemplating how to navigate past the many guards and escape before the detonation occurs may also cultivate problem-solving skills, and sharing anecdotes on Discord about role-playing as an evil character may help foster connection with other players. And, of course, players can just find it fun to try things to see how the game world changes, for better or for worse, in response to their decisions. Apart from minors, people are usually allowed to engage in pleasurable behaviors even when doing so marginally increases the risk of engaging in violent activities. Drinking alcohol and playing contact sports are prime examples. If those behaviors are okay, why wouldn't we reach the same judgment about playing violent video games?

Overall, concern about the increased risk of *Fallout* players engaging in real-world violence is not a compelling reason to morally criticize playing these games, even when players are trying to wipe out all sentient life in the game. Perhaps a different line of argument will be more convincing.

Does Virtual Homicide Express Disrespect for Humanity?

One of the most influential moral theories in Western philosophy comes from Immanuel Kant (1724–1804). According to Kant, the foundation of morality could be represented as a core principle that he called the Categorical Imperative. Kant thought that this principle could be expressed in several different ways, but the variant most relevant to our discussion is known as the Humanity Formulation. According to this moral principle, we should never act in ways that treat humanity, whether others' or our own, as a mere means to an end, but always as an end in itself.[6] "Humanity" in this context is not referring to the human species or any other biological concept; instead, it refers to the features of human beings that make us distinctively agents—people capable of understanding and acting on reasons. On Kant's view, the key ability is a person's rational agency—their capacity to adopt various ends (i.e., goals), pursue those ends, and engage in other rational, independent behavior. According to the Humanity Formulation, it is wrong to treat human beings merely as tools to further our own ends because doing so fails to respect people's rational capacities. This principle provides an intuitive explanation for why it is wrong to deceive others, steal from them, or otherwise harm them for our own benefit: doing so interferes with their ability to use their rational capacities to pursue their own ends and thereby disrespects their humanity.

Someone who applies this line of reasoning to the *Fallout* universe might conclude that players are doing something wrong when they steal, lie, manipulate, maim, or otherwise harm innocent NPCs. One could reason that doing so fails to respect their humanity, or at least the fragments of humanity that these NPCs have, given that they are not actual people. Now it's important to recognize that someone making this argument is *not* saying that the player's behavior will result in disrespecting the humanity of actual people in the real world: that argument would run into the same empirical challenges that were discussed in the previous section. Rather, a person making this argument is saying that the NPCs in these games are *close enough* to being real people that it is wrong to treat them this way. After all, the characters will express disapproval of your actions and try to save themselves by attacking you or running away. Many of them have daily routines that correspond to the game's day-and-night cycles and have motivations or desires that resemble those that real people would have. Do these considerations make it wrong to harm innocent NPCs?

While it may one day be possible to create artificial intelligence with a moral standing comparable to human beings, the NPCs in the *Fallout* games are nowhere close to that level of cognitive sophistication. While the illusion of their intelligence is often maintained through creative game design, it is also frequently shattered when the characters get stuck on the terrain, repeat the same lines of dialogue, or become romantically attracted to the player character in a ludicrously short time frame. The NPCs do not possess anything like the rational agency that human beings do. The behaviors that create that impression are programmed responses to player actions designed to immerse the player more deeply in the games' post-apocalyptic environments. For these reasons, the AI in the *Fallout* games does not have the rational capacities such that it could be disrespected in any morally significant way.

There remains something unnerving about a player who derives sadistic satisfaction from the simulated suffering and death of innocents, but that uneasiness cannot be adequately explained by an appeal to disrespect.

What Does Simulated Slaughter Suggest About the Player?

Imagine a player is attempting a Kill Everything playthrough of *Fallout: New Vegas*. Upon entering the settlement of Freeside, the player tries to murder two children who are chasing a giant rat, but discovers that the children cannot be killed. (They are simply not coded to be killable, though they will react to being assaulted.) Wanting to be as thorough as possible, the player installs a mod that makes the children killable and then resumes the playthrough, massacring them and all the other residents of Freeside. Even if the NPCs (including the children) cannot be disrespected in the Kantian sense and even if we assume that this behavior never results in any real-world behavior that is objectionable, there remains something morally unsettling about the player's actions. But how can this lingering discomfort be explained?

I believe the best explanation for why slaughtering the innocent in the *Fallout* video games might be wrong is found in virtue ethics.[7] This moral framework has its roots in Plato (428–347 BCE) and Aristotle (384–322 BCE). The basic idea is that morality is about the cultivation of virtues—stable dispositions to think, feel, and act in ways that are excellent or praiseworthy. Almost everyone has some familiarity with virtues, even if they have never labeled the concepts using that term. Traits like courage, loyalty, generosity, honesty, and patience are all virtues. Almost all virtues also have corresponding *vices*—traits that represent undesirable deficiencies or excesses in one's character. For instance, we could say that a character who charges into a raider camp to save hostages with little thought or concern for their numbers would be reckless, and a player who flees without making any genuine attempt to save the hostages may be considered cowardly. Being courageous is something of an intermediary between these two dispositions: it involves recognizing and responding appropriately to the risk of harm using one's abilities and resources. Recklessness is a vice of excess, and cowardice is a vice of deficiency; courage represents the appropriate balance between these traits.

According to Aristotle, happiness (also called flourishing or *eudaimonia*) is the highest good that human beings can achieve,[8] and happiness consists in "a certain activity of the soul in accord with virtue."[9] In this manner, living virtuously is essential to a well-lived human life. But virtue is hard to acquire. Avoiding vices of excess and deficiency requires consistent and thoughtful practice, and this is precisely why simulated acts of extreme violence may be problematic even if they never directly result in harm or disrespect to people in the real world.

Let's return to the case of the player who installs a mod to make children killable so they can better realize their aspiration of killing all the NPCs in *New Vegas*. Thinking through the lens of virtue ethics, we could condemn this action in several ways. The player may be desensitizing themselves to portrayals of violence, hindering their ability to cultivate virtues like empathy and sympathy. The player may also be cultivating an apathy toward human suffering (or the portrayal of such suffering) or even developing an enjoyment of seeing others suffer. Even if these effects on the player's character do not directly result in harm to others in the future, the player may nonetheless be doing something that makes it harder to develop and cultivate virtues.

Notably, however, this virtue ethical explanation does not condemn nearly all instances of playing violent video games. In a typical playthrough of the *Fallout* games, players will face complex moral dilemmas and need to engage in challenging problem-solving to complete certain quests. The presence of violent conflict and the aftermath of the nuclear war can serve to grow players' empathy for certain characters and get them invested in trying to do the right thing to save those in need. Even in scenarios where the player makes a choice that is morally questionable, seeing the consequences of their decisions can serve as a valuable learning experience by instilling feelings of remorse or regret. In other words, the mere presence of violence in the *Fallout* games does not make it morally objectionable to play them: the morality of playing the game depends in large part on players' motives. Are they playing the game to experience morally complex narratives, engage in difficult problem-solving, or explore the consequences of their choices in a post-apocalyptic landscape? These reasons for playing are consistent with the cultivation of virtue. But what if the central motivation is to see the horrified expression of a settler who flees from them before being abruptly dismembered by a frag grenade? That motive does not seem consistent with the cultivation of virtue.

Now, it might be tempting to think that there could never be a motivation to perform a Kill Everything playthrough that would be consistent with the development of virtue, but matters are not that simple. In the process of trying to kill all the NPCs in the game world, players will encounter a range of unusual circumstances that require innovative problem-solving. Some characters, for example, are tagged as essential until certain points in the story or until a specific questline is completed, which means that the player must sometimes align with these characters for a time before eventually betraying them. This is just one way in which the player may encounter storylines and scenarios that they have never seen before, and they may even discover or unlock a bad ending in which the player character gets some well-deserved comeuppance. Additionally, some characters are so powerful that they are not meant to be killed, especially early in the game, and the deaths of vendors and the hostility of certain factions can render valuable weapons and resources unobtainable, making the game more difficult. There may also be quests and locations with so many well-armed characters that killing them all represents a massive challenge on its own.

Here's the key point: there can be reasons to role-play as the embodiment of chaotic evil in the *Fallout* games that are not morally problematic, such as seeing more of the game's possible narratives, exploring the consequences of player choices, and seeking a greater in-game combat challenge. In practice, it may not be possible to separate these motives from the stylized, bloody violence that permeates these games—at least not in the most extreme cases of trying to kill every settler, companion animal, and other innocent in the game—but I maintain that it is at least theoretically possible that a player could try to snuff out all virtual life in the post-apocalypse without doing anything wrong.

Is There a Right Way to Play?

Video games like those in the *Fallout* series allow players to commit acts that are unimaginably cruel, but the mere presence of violence in these games does not make playing them wrong. Even if the player attempts a playthrough where they try to wipe out the entirety of the game's NPCs, this does not necessarily mean they are doing anything wrong. The link between acts of virtual violence and in-game violence is tenuous, and video-game characters are not the kinds of beings that can be disrespected in any relevant way, even when they visually resemble human beings. Nevertheless, players who forge an unrelentingly violent path through the post-apocalypse may be corroding their moral character and hindering the development of virtues. Whether they are in fact doing something wrong will depend on their underlying attitudes and motivations for playing the game that way. Some players may simply want to test their mastery of the game's combat system or see unexplored aspects of the games' narratives, and such motives do not obviously demonstrate anything vicious. But not all gamers' motives are that innocuous. If you are planning to install a mod so you can kill the in-game children, it might be time to reflect on what that reveals about your character.

Notes

1. See, for instance, Patrick Arellano, "15 Video Games Where You Can Kill Everyone," *Comic Book Resources*, January 7, 2023, at https://www.cbr.com/video-games-where-you-can-kill-everyone, and Ritwik Mitra, "Open-World Games That Let You Kill Every NPC," *Game Rant*, August 8, 2024, at https://gamerant.com/open-world-games-lets-players-kill-every-npc.
2. For some examples, see Karen E. Dill and Jody C. Dill, "Video Game Violence: A Review of the Empirical Literature," *Aggression and Violent Behavior* 3 (1998), 407–428. and Christopher P. Bartlett, Craig A. Anderson, and Edward L. Swing, "Video Game Effects—Confirmed, Suspected, and Speculative: A Review of the Evidence," *Simulation & Gaming* 40 (2009), 377–403.
3. Maya B. Mathur and Tyler J. VanderWeele, "Finding Common Ground in Meta-Analysis 'Wars' on Violent Video Games," *Perspectives on Psychological Science* 14 (2019), https://doi.org/10.1177/1745691619850104
4. For a recent example, see Simone Kühn, Dimitrij Tycho Kugler, Katharina Schmalen, Markus Weichenberger, Charlotte Witt, and Jürgen Gallinat, "Does Playing Violent Video Games Cause Aggression? A Longitudinal Intervention Study," *Molecular Psychiatry* 24 (2019), 1220–1234.
5. For one of the most comprehensive reviews of the literature that reaches this conclusion, see Barrie Gunter, *Does Playing Video Games Make Players More Violent?* (London: Palgrave Macmillan, 2016).
6. Immanuel Kant, *Groundwork for the Metaphysics of Morals*, trans. and ed. Mary Gregor and Jens Timmerman, Vol. 4., (Cambridge: Cambridge University Press, 2012), 429. For a more detailed overview of Kant's moral philosophy, see Robert Johnson, "Kant's Moral Philosophy," in *The Stanford Encyclopedia of Philosophy*, at https://plato.stanford.edu/entries/kant-moral.
7. For a defense of a similar position about playing violent video games more generally, see Matt McCormick, "Is It Wrong to Play Violent Video Games?," *Ethics and Information Technology* 3 (2001), 277–287.
8. Aristotle, *Nicomachean Ethics*, trans. Terence Irwin, (Indianapolis: Hackett Publishing, 2019), 1095a.
9. Aristotle, *Nicomachean Ethics*, 1099b.

Part 2

SYNTHS, CYBORGS, AND THE SELF

5

My Pip-Boy, My Self: The Extended Mind and Its Fallout

Michael Funke and Quinn Funke

Alright, Vault Dwellers, let's talk about the Pip-Boy, that trusty wrist-mounted companion that's kept more than a few of us alive in the blasted wasteland. It's more than just an accessory; it's an essential part of you! It may even be part of your mind. In their influential essay "The Extended Mind," contemporary philosophers Andy Clark and David Chalmers argue that human cognition is not confined to the brain but extends into the external tools and technologies with which we interact.[1] The Pip-Boy of the *Fallout* universe exemplifies this concept, functioning as a cognitive extension that aids in navigation, decision-making, and inventory management.

So, are we all cyborgs? Contemporary consciousness scholar Donna Haraway's essay "A Cyborg Manifesto" describes the cyborg as a hybrid entity that transcends traditional boundaries—biological, technological, and social.[2] In her view, all humans are cyborgs to some degree, shaped by the technologies and sociocultural systems they inhabit. The Pip-Boy wearer, who depends on this device for survival in the post-apocalyptic wasteland, illustrates this hybrid or "cyborg" identity. Much like Haraway's cyborg, the Pip-Boy user is a socially mediated organism whose cognitive and physical capacities are augmented by technology.

While there is real potential for liberation with cyborg identity, the Pip-Boy's role in the *Fallout* universe underscores its darker side; within the *Fallout* universe, dependence on technology becomes a survival imperative rather than a choice. The Pip-Boy's capabilities compare with real-world assistive and wearable technologies like prosthetics, cochlear implants, smart rings, watches, and brain–computer interfaces. This tech demonstrates both the potential and the limitations of technological augmentation in contemporary society. Tools designed to extend human cognition can empower individuals while also shaping us through social, economic, and ethical constraints.

The Extended Mind Hypothesis

So, how do we get from the Pip-Boy to full-on cyborg identity? In "The Extended Mind," Clark and Chalmers argue that human cognition extends into external tools and technologies that support cognitive processes. Those tools or technologies, like the Pip-Boy, are not adjuncts to human thought; rather, they are part of human thought. Clark and Chalmers propose that for an external resource to be considered part of an individual's cognitive system, it must meet three key criteria: availability, reliability, and active cognitive engagement.[3] These criteria establish whether a tool or device functions not merely as an aid to thinking but as an integral component of cognition itself.

First, availability refers to the extent to which an external tool is readily accessible and seamlessly integrated into an individual's cognitive activities. A tool that qualifies as an extension of the mind must be consistently available for use, without requiring excessive effort to retrieve or activate. For example, a person who frequently consults a notebook to store and recall information effectively offloads memory functions onto an external medium, much like they would access internal cognitive resources. The same applies to digital technologies, such as smartphones, which provide immediate access to stored knowledge, reminders, and problem-solving tools.

Second, reliability ensures that the external resource is consistently used and trusted as part of an individual's cognitive system. A tool that is only occasionally employed or prone to malfunction cannot be considered an extension of the mind, as it does not provide the stability needed for cognitive integration. For instance, an individual who relies on a GPS system for navigation to the point where they no longer memorize routes exemplifies this principle. The tool becomes a dependable part of their cognitive functioning, shaping their ability to interact with the world.

Finally, active cognitive engagement requires that the external tool does more than passively store information—it must play an active role in cognitive processes such as reasoning, decision-making, or problem-solving. This criterion distinguishes genuine cognitive extensions from simple external aids. A calculator, for example, does not merely hold numbers but actively performs mathematical computations, directly contributing to cognitive tasks. Similarly, a person who habitually uses a scheduling app to structure their daily activities engages in a form of cognitive outsourcing, where the tool becomes an essential part of their executive functioning.

By meeting these three criteria, external tools and technologies become more than just accessories to thought; they become integral to the cognitive system itself. Clark and Chalmers's extended mind thesis challenges traditional Cartesian boundaries between mind and world, suggesting that cognition is dynamically distributed across both biological and technological components.

The Pip-Boy as Mind Extension

In the *Fallout* universe, the Pip-Boy, a multifunctional wrist-mounted technological device (as if we have to tell you), is essential to navigating the wasteland. The Pip-Boy serves as an indispensable extension of the character's mind, facilitating essential survival tasks such as navigation, health monitoring, inventory management, and information retrieval. Through these functions, the Pip-Boy not only enhances the user's decision-making capabilities but also actively shapes their perception of and interaction with the post-apocalyptic world.

The Pip-Boy meets Clark and Chalmers's three key criteria for cognitive extension: availability, reliability, and active cognitive engagement. First, it is readily available, worn at all times, and immediately accessible whenever needed. Unlike external tools that must be retrieved or activated separately, the Pip-Boy is always within the user's reach, ensuring uninterrupted cognitive support. Second, it is reliably integrated into the user's activities, serving as a consistent and trustworthy aid for critical tasks such as tracking radiation levels, monitoring injuries, and managing essential supplies. This reliability ensures that the user can depend on the device in high-stakes situations without conscious deliberation. Finally, the Pip-Boy is actively engaged in cognitive processes by facilitating problem-solving and decision-making. For instance, when faced with an enemy encounter, the user can employ the Vault-Tec Assisted Targeting System (V.A.T.S.), which slows down time and provides real-time data on enemy vulnerabilities. By offloading complex calculations and prioritization to the device, the Pip-Boy effectively becomes an extension of the user's cognitive architecture, enabling more efficient and strategic combat decisions.

This integration of the Pip-Boy into the user's mental and behavioral routines challenges the conventional distinction between human cognition and external tools. The device does not function merely as an accessory or passive aid; rather, it actively participates in the cognitive loop, fundamentally altering how the user processes information and makes decisions. In this sense, the Pip-Boy is an extension of the user's mind. As Clark and Chalmers write, "We cannot simply point to the skin/skull boundary . . . the legitimacy of that boundary is precisely what is at issue."[4] By blurring the boundary between human and tool, the Pip-Boy underscores the fluidity of cognitive extension, demonstrating how technological augmentation can reshape the very nature of thought and action.

Cyborg Theory

In "A Cyborg Manifesto," Haraway presents the cyborg as a metaphor for understanding the complex relationship between humans, technology, and culture. Haraway defines cyborgs as "creatures simultaneously animal and machine, who populate worlds ambiguously natural and crafted."[5] The cyborg transcends traditional binaries and challenges conventions of identity, embodiment, and power. Technology is not separate from or in opposition to nature; rather, Haraway argues, humans have always been cyborgs, shaped by the tools, machines, and systems they create and with which they interact.

At its core, the cyborg represents a rejection of rigid boundaries, particularly those that structure social and political hierarchies. Think about how the Super Mutants forever altered the social landscapes of *Fallout*. Haraway critiques traditional notions of identity that rely on fixed categories, such as gender and species, instead advocating for a more fluid and interconnected view of existence. The cyborg is neither purely human nor purely machine, but something in between—a fusion of organic and artificial elements that disrupts dominant narratives about what it means to be a person. This perspective is especially relevant in an era where digital technologies, medical advancements, and cybernetic enhancements increasingly blur the line between biology and machinery.

In the *Fallout* universe, the concept of the cyborg is exemplified in various ways, from cybernetically enhanced individuals like cyberdogs or Kellogg from the Institute, to the ubiquitous presence of wearable technology, such as the Pip-Boy, or power armor. Like Haraway's cyborg, these beings challenge clear distinctions between human and machine, raising philosophical and ethical questions about autonomy, identity, and dependence on technology. The Pip-Boy, in particular, functions as an external cognitive system that seamlessly integrates with the user's decision-making processes, mirroring the way real-world technologies increasingly shape human cognition and interaction.

Haraway's vision of the cyborg is not merely a commentary on science fiction but a call to rethink human identity in an age of technological mediation. By embracing the cyborg as a symbol of hybridity and transformation, "A Cyborg Manifesto" invites us to consider how technology shapes not only our capabilities but also our very understanding of selfhood and society.

The Sole Survivor and the Cyborg Identity

Haraway's cyborg, a figure that disrupts the rigid boundaries between human and machine, nature and technology, finds a compelling embodiment in *Fallout 4*'s Sole Survivor. This character, thrust into a post-apocalyptic world centuries removed from their own, isn't just a survivor; they're a testament to the cyborg condition, a being whose very existence is intertwined with technology.

The Pip-Boy, a seemingly simple wrist-mounted computer, serves as a potent symbol of this cyborg integration. It's not merely a tool, but an extension of the Sole Survivor's senses and cognitive abilities. Consider the quest "The Glowing Sea." Without the Pip-Boy's rad monitoring, the Sole Survivor's exploration of this irradiated wasteland would be a death sentence. The device provides real-time feedback on radiation levels, allowing them to navigate a lethal environment that would otherwise be inaccessible. It's a symbiotic relationship in which the human and machine work in tandem for survival. The Pip-Boy is not just displaying information, but becoming an integral part of the Survivor's perception, allowing the person to perceive danger that is otherwise invisible.

Further, the Pip-Boy's inventory management and mapping functions offload cognitive burdens, extending the Sole Survivor's mental capacity. Remember the search to locate Virgil's cure within the dark hallways of the Institute? The Pip-Boy's ability to track quest markers, manage inventory, and provide detailed maps became essential, effectively outsourcing complex navigational and logistical tasks. This isn't just tool use; it's a merging of human and machine, where the Pip-Boy becomes an externalized cognitive function.

The Sole Survivor's reliance on and integration with the Pip-Boy transcends mere utility. It becomes an extension of their very being, a cybernetic prosthesis that reshapes their interaction with the environment. It's not just a device; it's a part of who they are, a testament to Haraway's vision of the cyborg as a being that transcends traditional boundaries, a hybrid entity forged in the crucible of technological integration and societal collapse. The Sole Survivor is not simply human, but an overcoming of nature as a boundary and an acknowledgment of how society defines the individual.

The Cyborg as Dystopian Necessity

In some ways, *Fallout*'s depiction of the Sole Survivor presents a starkly contrasting narrative from Haraway's cyborg. Haraway envisioned the cyborg as a figure of emancipatory potential, a being that dismantles oppressive binaries and embraces fluid identities; Haraway's cyborg is a political actor, a liberator, a creature of radical possibility. In *Fallout*, the Sole Survivor's cyborg existence is less a conscious act of liberation and more a pragmatic adaptation to a brutal reality. The Pip-Boy, for instance, isn't a chosen augmentation, but a tool of survival forced upon them by the post-apocalyptic environment. It's not a symbol of liberation, but a lifeline. This dependence on technology, while enabling survival, simultaneously highlights the vulnerability of the human condition in a world where technology is both essential and potentially destructive.

The Sole Survivor, while capable of challenging authority, is often driven by the immediate need to survive or fulfill personal quests. Their actions, while impactful, are less about dismantling systemic oppression and more about navigating the chaos of the wasteland. The game's narrative often highlights the inherent dangers of technological dependence. The constant threat posed by rogue robots and the remnants of prewar technological hubris serve as cautionary tales about the potential for technology to become a source of oppression rather than liberation, a stark contrast to Haraway's cyborg as a figure of resistance against dominant narratives and power structures.

In essence, while Haraway's cyborg is a symbol of hope and liberation, *Fallout*'s Sole Survivor embodies a more ambivalent relationship with technology. Their cyborg existence is a testament to human adaptability, but also a stark reminder of the potential for technology to both empower and enslave. The game uses the cyborg to explore the anxieties of technological dependence, a contrast to Haraway's optimistic vision.

Disability, Bio-Tech, and Cyborg Identity

Much like in *Fallout 4*, the Pip-Boy is also a ubiquitous extension of the Courier's capabilities in *New Vegas*, prompting a comparison with real-world medical technologies designed to augment the minds and bodies of disabled individuals. Devices like cochlear implants, prosthetic limbs, and brain–computer interfaces, much like the Pip-Boy, function as extensions of the self, enhancing sensory perception, mobility, or communication. They represent a tangible merging of human and machine, a blurring of the lines between biological limitations and technological augmentation.

The Pip-Boy's integration into the Courier's existence diverges significantly from the lived experience of those who rely on assistive technologies in our world in two ways. First, real-world medical technologies are typically developed with specific therapeutic goals, addressing targeted impairments rather than functioning as general-purpose cognitive aids. A cochlear implant, for example, is designed to restore hearing, while a prosthetic limb aims to replace lost mobility. The Pip-Boy, conversely, serves as a comprehensive tool, encompassing navigation, health monitoring, information retrieval, and inventory management, catering to a broad spectrum of needs in the Mojave Wasteland.

Second, the integration of real-world assistive technologies is often mediated by medical professionals and shaped by societal attitudes toward disability. Unlike the Pip-Boy, which exists within a fictional world where its use is universal and non-stigmatized, assistive technologies in our society are frequently subject to social, economic, and ethical constraints that limit access and shape user experience. Societal biases, limited funding, and complex regulatory frameworks can create barriers to accessing these technologies, further marginalizing disabled individuals.

In the *Fallout: New Vegas Old World Blues* DLC, the Think Tank, with their advanced cybernetics and brain augmentations, represents a distorted, exaggerated version of modern bio-tech. Their experiments, while extreme, illustrate the potential for technology to both enhance and dehumanize. The Pip-Boy, existing outside these constraints, presents a simplified, almost idealized vision of technological augmentation, devoid of the complex social realities that shape the lives of disabled individuals who rely on similar technologies. This contrast highlights the critical distinction between the fictionalized integration of technology in *New Vegas* and the real-world challenges faced by disabled individuals seeking to improve their lives through bio-tech. Contemporary feminist scholar Alison Kafer responds to Haraway's cyborg by pointing out that a bio-tech fusion is not without its complexities, particularly when viewed through the lens of disability studies.[6]

Kafer notes that Haraway's cyborg theory, while groundbreaking in its inclusion of disability within feminist discourse, often overlooks the material realities of prosthetic use. As many disability studies scholars have argued, and as Kafer meticulously documents, Haraway's idealized cyborg fails to account for the potential pain, discomfort, and social stigma that often accompany technological augmentation. While the Pip-Boy appears seamless and empowering, its functionality exists within a fictional context devoid of the real-world challenges faced by disabled individuals. Unlike the Pip-Boy, which exists within a fictional world where its use is universal and non-stigmatized, assistive technologies in our society are frequently subject to social, economic, and ethical constraints.

Societal biases, limited funding, and complex regulatory frameworks can create barriers to accessing these technologies, further marginalizing disabled individuals. Kafer, however, avoids a complete dismissal of Haraway, suggesting instead a "cripped cyborg theory" that acknowledges the material realities of disability while still recognizing the potential for technological augmentation to empower. In the context of *New Vegas*, this might involve a deeper exploration of the social and ethical implications of cybernetics, moving beyond the simplistic portrayal of technology as either purely beneficial or purely detrimental. This contrast highlights the critical distinction between the fictionalized integration of technology in *Fallout* and the real-world challenges faced by disabled individuals seeking to enhance their capabilities through bio-tech, and the need for a more nuanced, disability-conscious approach to cyborg theory.

A Transhumanist Conclusion

Transhumanism, at its core, is a philosophical and intellectual movement that advocates for the use of science and technology to enhance human physical and cognitive abilities. It envisions a future where humans transcend their biological limitations, potentially through advancements in biotechnology, nanotechnology, and artificial intelligence. This pursuit of radical self-improvement resonates strongly with the concepts of the extended mind and Haraway's cyborg, both of which challenge the traditional boundaries of human existence.

The extended mind hypothesis posits that cognitive processes are not confined to the physical boundaries of the brain and body but can extend into the external environment through the use of tools and technologies. Transhumanism takes this concept to its extreme, advocating for the deliberate integration of technology into the human body and mind to augment cognitive functions, sensory perception, and physical capabilities. This aligns with Haraway's cyborg, a hybrid of machine and organism that disrupts the nature/culture binary. The cyborg, in Haraway's vision, is a being that embraces technological augmentation as a means of liberation, transcending the limitations of the biological human.

The *Fallout* universe, in its own dystopian way, provides a compelling, if cautionary, exploration of extended minds, cyborgs, and transhumanist themes. The pervasive use of the Pip-Boy, as discussed earlier, exemplifies the extended mind, where technology becomes an integral part of the user's cognitive architecture. The Think Tank in *Old World Blues* pushes this concept further, showcasing the potential for radical brain augmentation and the blurring of lines between human and machine. Their experiments, though ethically dubious, illustrate the transhumanist desire to transcend biological limitations through technology.

Notes

1. Andy Clark and David Chalmers, "The Extended Mind," *Analysis* 58 (1998), 7–19.
2. Donna Jeanne Haraway, "A Cyborg Manifesto: Science, Technology, and Socialist-Feminism in the Late Twentieth Century," in *Simians, Cyborgs and Women: The Reinvention of Nature*, (New York: Routledge, 1991), 149–181.
3. Clark and Chalmers, "The Extended Mind," 17.
4. Clark and Chalmers, "The Extended Mind," 7–8.
5. Haraway, "A Cyborg Manifesto," 150.
6. Alison Kafer, *Feminist, Queer, Crip*, (Bloomington: Indiana University Press, 2013). See especially chap. 5 "The Cyborg and the Crip."

6

Transhumanism or Bust!

Walter Barta

Do you want superpowers? Would you like to be smarter, stronger, faster, tougher, more perceptive, and more charming? Are you itching to cast off that fragile biological body for a shiny new chrome upgrade? Want to go human 2.0? Try transhumanism! The latest and greatest philosophy, perfectly suited for your modern lifestyle. But "What is transhumanism?" you say.

Well, if you've ever played through a *Fallout* game, you've surely seen some *transhumans*, that is, humans that are either biologically or mechanically transformed to achieve enhanced abilities. These characters are exemplars and/or practitioners of the philosophy of *transhumanism*, which is a strand of thinking that posits that human beings are not the final stage of evolutionary development. Rather, according to transhumanism, the human being is just one step in the development of other future kinds of beings. But transhumanism isn't just a fantasy found in video games; it's a philosophy in real life! Notable transhumanists include some of the most famous philosophers of all time: greats like Nicolas de Condorcet (1743–1794), who dreamed of human perfectibility; William Godwin (1756–1836), who imagined societies that have overcome all human problems; and Friedrich Nietzsche (1844–1900), who conceived of the "Superman" ("Übermensch"), an aspirational self-actualized superhuman being; and many modern thinkers have subsequently taken up the transhumanist project.[1]

So many philosophers have hyped up transhumanism because it comes with a wide array of benefits: more health, more wealth, more happiness, more everything! Following this tradition, one of the greatest platforms of transhumanist philosophy in our time is the *Fallout* series, which is arguably a transhumanist video game series, acknowledging and even advocating for the many promises that transhumanism has to offer. Most of the characters and factions in the *Fallout* series use some form of technological enhancement, and the gameplay loop of the *Fallout* games is a transhumanist cycle of self-improvement, encouraging the players to embody the transhumanist ethos. Every action is done in order to unlock some perk, acquire some item, or gain some ability, enhancing one's player character and turning them from someone human into someone transhuman.

But, before you go signing up so fast, in the interest of full disclosure, I have to warn you that transhumanism has some strings attached—so this may be less of an advertisement than it is a public service announcement. Side effects may include a moderate-to-severe loss of humanity and, in rare cases, the end of the world as we know it. True to form, the *Fallout* series casts a critical eye on some of the problems posed by the transhumanist ethos. The setting and lore, as a post-apocalyptic fiction, seem to emphasize the destructive consequences that can be directly traced to transhumanist developments, and many elements of the quests and storylines point out how the human impulse to transcend our human limitations may ultimately undermine what makes us human and endanger our prospects for civilization.

All this being said, is transhumanism for you?

Better Living Through Mutagenics!

There are at least two stages of transhumanist theory and practice that are worth considering: (1) human enhancement, best exemplified by the alteration of human biology through biological engineering; and (2) posthumanity, best exemplified by the replacement of the fragile body of the human being with the deliberate engineering of robotics and artificial intelligence. Both kinds of transhumanism, and their advantages, make prominent appearances in the *Fallout* series.

The first major prospect for transhumanism is human enhancement through biological science. Modern medicine can currently heal human beings of many diseases and injuries, but biological engineering will also soon be able to (and in some cases already can) improve human beings: stimulants can provide cognitive benefits, steroids can provide muscular benefits, and gene therapy can provide genetic benefits. Many human enhancement advocates believe that modifying our basic biology can (and eventually will) create new kinds of human forms, transhumans, who, at the theoretical extreme, will be free from human deficiencies and endowed with superhuman proficiencies, unlike naturally born humans. Examples of this variety of biological transhumanism in *Fallout* include characters like the ghouls, the Super Mutants, and even the Vault Dwellers. So, you have several appealing options.

You may become a ghoul, which, admittedly, is not a choice most wanderers make. Most humans become ghouls only after accidentally being mutated by the nuclear radiation of the wasteland. But if you do become a ghoul, you will be an altered human, with some corresponding pros and cons. The main pro is that ghouls have an extended lifespan. Some are even said to have been alive before the bombs dropped. Living forever sounds fun, right? Well, the main con is that ghouls deteriorate, both mentally and physically, which explains their *ghoulish* appearance and behavior. When ghouls are properly medicated, they can stave off the deterioration and prolong their humanity, though this is a cost with diminishing returns.

So, if you want more perks and fewer side effects, becoming a Super Mutant may be a better bet. Super Mutants are humans that have been exposed to the Forced Evolutionary Virus (FEV), and you too can become one with just a little inoculation. Those mutated by the virus enjoy an array of physical and mental benefits and thus often come to see themselves as "super" human, greater than human. The transhumanist cult known as the Children of the Cathedral even plots to turn the entire population of the wasteland into Super Mutants, which they believe is a next step in human evolution toward a superior form of being—albeit with the slight caveat that they may all be a little sterile.

But even if you do not become a ghoul or Super Mutant, as a technologically adept Vault Dweller, you are still an enhanced human in many respects. An average wasteland wanderer can hardly go a minute without the urge to inject themselves with a stimpak, pop a Mentat, or even huff some Jet—for the extra health, intelligence, and strength—such that even the "humans" are transhumans via self-medication.

But is all this really desirable? In the book *Human Enhancement,* contemporary philosopher of medical technology Julian Savulescu and others argue that this kind of human enhancement is not only permissible but may even be obligatory.[2] Imagine, in your wanderings across the wasteland, you find a helpless caravan being attacked by bloat flies. As a good Samaritan, you feel that it is your duty to grab the survivors, throw them behind the nearest pile of rubble, blast the bloat flies out of the sky, and do everything you can to protect the poor fellows. But then, if this is your duty, then isn't it also your duty to stick them with stimpaks and force feed them Mentats—so they can protect themselves with their new and improved stats? Why not? One man's Jet addiction may be another man's rationally beneficial quality of life improvement. Of course, if there are serious side effects, as with the ghouls, or serious issues of consent, as with the Super Mutants, then the case is more morally complex. But what if there are no side effects and they agree to the medication? If you get to keep your nose, don't turn green, and sign off on all Vault-Tec's medical waivers, isn't enhancement the best option? Isn't a radscorpion more rad? Aren't two heads on a brahmin better than one?

Indeed, even if we are not constantly self-medicating and self-modifying in real life, the gameplay of *Fallout* virtually encourages (and even demands) us to do so in-game. We collect all the powerful items and equipment we can find and adopt every upgrade and level-up we can access because they help us beat bigger and badder enemies. Ask yourself: In video games, you level up, but do you ever level down? Probably not. You'd probably rather eat iguana on a stick. And, oftentimes, enhanced abilities are the bare minimum necessary for surviving the difficult conditions of the post-apocalyptic wasteland. Every vault needs a water chip, right? In this way, the *Fallout* gameplay loop coaxes us into embodying and living out the transhumanist ethos in practice, without even questioning it, showing us that personal enhancement is not just a transhumanist value but a humanist value by default, already implicit in our orientation toward our world, implicit in real life but made even more manifest in the heightened gaming experience.

Nine Out of Ten Doctors Recommend Brain Transplants!

The second prospect for transhumanism is achieving post-humanity through applied mechanical and computational sciences. Some transhumanist advocates believe that technologies can and should replace human life-forms. Mechanical engineering has created marvels of robotics, and electrical engineering has created marvels of computation, and we can expect these devices to only become stronger and smarter as the technology matures. Some of these devices have been used as prosthetics, mechanical arms and legs replacing human ones; and, with neurological interfacing currently under development, electrodes implanted in brains are allowing humans to interact with the world in new ways. At some point, we can envision humans becoming fully cyborg and eventually maybe even abandoning their biological bodies entirely for the benefits of living virtually in cyberspace. And these are just some of the sparkling gadgets that post-humanity has to offer! Examples of mechanical and computational post-humanity in *Fallout* abound, including all the multifarious cyborgs and artificially intelligent contraptions that inhabit the wasteland. You have as many options for post-humanity as the laws of physics permit.

You could join the Brotherhood of Steel, which is a faction dedicated to the collection, preservation, and adoption of advanced military weaponry, most famous for their liberal use of power armor, a fully mechanized suit of metal that makes its wearer nearly invincible. Their adoption of the transhumanist philosophy that "flesh is weak" and their expression of that philosophy through the use of intense body-modification technology make the Brotherhood one of the most impressive forces in the wasteland.

Similar to the Brotherhood but even further down the path toward post-humanity, you could emulate Mr. House, the elderly casino tycoon whose biological body is kept in cryonic stasis, with just enough life left to mentally control the vast robotic workforce of his New Vegas infrastructure. It is one thing to pilot power armor, but imagine controlling an army with your extended mind distributed a thousand places at a time. Or even better, you could be a cyborg, fully cybernetically integrated with a computer, like the mutant cult leader, the Master; or like Dr. Mobius and his Think Tank of lobotomites; or like a Vault-Tec Robobrain (a brain-piloted robot). Or you could be a fully artificial being, like John Henry Eden, the American president, or Zax, the bioengineering supercomputer that inhabits The Glow. Robots are already better than humans at most (if not all) things and so have a survival advantage in the wasteland—from Protectrons up to Liberty Prime. So why *hire* a Mister Handy when you can *be* a Mister Handy instead? Once one has completely migrated one's self to a digital substrate, there is little to no limit on what kind of mind one might be and thus little to no limit on the varieties of experiences one might program oneself to have.

But even if you don't fully bite the bullet and amputate all of your human parts, you as a Vault Dweller are still at least partially post-human just by living life integrated with modern technologies: sitting in your air-conditioned vault, eating your hyper-processed Cram, wearing your Pip-Boy (and, as a player, carrying a smartphone, the real-life version of the Pip-Boy). It turns out to be pretty hard not to be at least a little post-human, whether in the pre- or post-apocalyptic world.

But do you really want to become a cyborg? In the article "Why I Want to Be a Posthuman When I Grow Up," contemporary philosopher Nick Bostrom says that we only think that post-humanity is undesirable from our narrow human perspective and are just not being open-minded enough.[3] He argues that a post-human destiny is not only desirable but probably unimaginably desirable. Imagine, you have spent your entire life as a Vault Dweller (in a hole in the ground), never seeing the outside world, and all you know is sleeping, eating, taking personality tests, and occasionally throwing boring birthday parties; but then, you are sent into the wasteland on a reconnaissance mission, and suddenly, as you open the vault doors, you realize that the world is full of so many more possibilities than you ever imagined.

According to Bostrom, this is the human situation relative to the post-human situation.[4] You are a mere human, mentally and physically impoverished, completely oblivious to the vast spaces of mental and physical possibilities available to you, if you would only choose to replace your inferior meat-parts with superior engineering. And the thing is, you are in such an intellectually benighted state that you cannot even make an educated choice, because you do not (and cannot, with your tiny, fleshy brain) know what you are missing. The only enlightened option is the post-human one. So, shouldn't you choose post-humanity too? Just put your brain in a vat, and you won't go back!

Indeed, when you play a *Fallout* game, do you ever just go back to your home vault and chill in the break room? Probably not. You'd probably rather get torn to shreds by Deathclaws. In many respects, the structure of *Fallout* gameplay mirrors post-human values. The chief transhumanist value (according to Bostrom) is the "opportunity to explore" different realms of experience, which is precisely what a video game offers, especially an open-world sandbox like *Fallout*.[5] The experience of exiting the vault mirrors the experience of turning on a video game and seeing a different world. If you thought video games were a mere human activity, that may be a mistake of your merely human mind, as you are already partially post-human when you play them.

The Fastest Treadmill in the West!

However, even with all its prospects and promises, you should know that the transhumanist ethos also has problems. Many have argued that transhumanism is unethical, in spite of its potential benefits, for a variety of reasons: transhumanist technologies are inauthentic, unnatural, "playing God," and so on.[6] Many of these reasons rest on controversial metaphysical assumptions, and so may be unconvincing to the transhumanists themselves. But some reasons are somewhat stronger, particularly the enormous risks that transhumanist technologies pose, both to humanity and to civilization, risks that playing *Fallout* illustrates all too well.

The first risk is that transhumanism threatens to undermine our humanity. This might happen because self-improvement is a kind of "Red Queen Race," a situation where everyone strives to improve but no one really does: you need enhancements to outcompete others, but in turn, they need enhancements to outcompete you, in a vicious cycle.[7] This dynamic is seen in evolution: prey get faster to evade predators, but in turn, predators get faster to catch prey, and nobody actually improves their fitness in the long run. This dynamic is found in video games as well. *Fallout* gameplay is notorious for having an adaptive leveling system: enemies level with the player, so if you are level 1, they are level 1, but if you are level 100, they are level 100. No matter how hard you work, it never really feels like you improve. No matter how leveled-up you are, "War never changes." Thus, in a sense, transhumanist technologies do not serve the user so much as they serve to raise the price of self-preservation for everyone. In this way, transhumanism is less of an escalator than a treadmill, not so much elevating as exhausting its human users. We can also observe that once a human being gets on this transhumanist treadmill, it becomes difficult, if not impossible, to get off, without getting left in the dust, wherever it takes us. And where does it take us? It seems like the only endgame is optimizing away all human weaknesses, in favor of inhuman strengths, until one loses everything human about oneself, becoming a kind of Darwinian Demon, a creature of maximal possible competitive fitness, and minimal humanity.[8] Thus, the inarguable benefits of transhumanist technology act like a siren song, luring us with fantastic quality of life improvements, toward Sisyphean enslavement.

Indeed, this path of least resistance is all too familiar to the *Fallout* player: selecting the best build, min-maxing stats, speedrunning past the plot, until you are the most unstoppable wanderer in the wasteland. The transhumanist treadmill is baked into the gameplay. But if the whole game is a repetitive grind, is that even a game? Is it fun anymore? Probably not. You'd probably rather chug food paste. In this estimation, the transhuman condition may be a torturous struggle to the death, and the human condition, for all its faults, may be as good as it ever gets for us mortals, an unlikely and invaluable oasis nestled in the killing fields of a dog-eat-dog-meat desert, with vicious wild animals behind us and malicious superhuman cyborgs in front of us, nature red in tooth and deathclaw. This concern about inhuman competition is what at least partially motivates the Overseer of Vault 13 and the Enclave President in their attempts to kill all Super Mutants. The Overseer worries that Cathedral and their mutagenics program will eventually dominate the wasteland if left unchecked, and so orders a preemptive strike against them; and after this, he even kicks out the Hero of Vault 13 (that's *you*) for becoming too much of a powerful wild card for the vault's fragile ecosystem to handle; and his concerns are not unfounded, because years later Vault 13 has indeed been overrun, by a pack of hyper-intelligent Deathclaws. And this seems to be why the Enclave President rationalizes using the most drastic measures, including genocidal bioweapons; he puts it bluntly, "No price is too high for the survival of the human race." Human self-preservation in an increasingly competitive world may require the destruction of transhumans and their technologies.

Philosopher and novelist C.S. Lewis (1898–1963), famous for his *Chronicles of Narnia* fantasy novels, predicts that this competition for superhuman power only leads to dystopian outcomes.[9] In *The Abolition of Man*, Lewis worries that technological advances don't so much permit humans to overcome nature as they permit humans to oppress other humans. Indeed, just so, in *Fallout*, the scientists of the Institute frame their science as promoting humanity, but they do so primarily by dehumanizing experimentation on synths, sentient humanoid robots, thereby undermining the synths' humanity in the process. Similar dehumanization is done by Vault-Tec on humans themselves. Each different vault is a different social experiment run on non-consenting human test subjects, with the purpose of determining which social structures succeed and fail.

Philosophers, including Lewis, further criticize transhumanism as a self-defeating venture: by changing human nature, we might eliminate the very features that make humans valuable, thus undermining the reasons we had for changing ourselves in the first place. Lewis's version of this critique is distinctively theological, rooted in the traditional Christian idea that tampering with human nature is defacing the image of God. But contemporary philosopher of history Francis Fukuyama takes a similar but secular approach: Fukuyama does not claim to know what quality makes human nature worth preserving, but he believes there may be something special about us, and therefore, we tamper with our nature at our peril.[10] He calls this unknown human quality "Factor-X" (which sounds a bit like something Vault-Tec might put in the water), but according to Fukuyama, losing Factor-X may make life not worth living, making the transhumanist project ultimately tragic, leading to an existential trap: self-transcendence as self-destruction. Indeed, continually optimizing ourselves would eventually require trading off the things that we value most: our dignity, our happiness, our favorite 1950s song, our taste for Nuka-Cola, and more.

The Future Is Bright . . . Like an Atom Bomb!

The second risk is that transhumanism threatens to destroy civilization. The basic problem is that the powerful scientific advances necessary for us to develop into transhumans will probably also enable doomsday devices. The energy required for a Garden of Eden Creation Kit is also the energy required for a Garden of Eden Destruction Kit.

Indeed, the *Fallout* series depicts an alternate history on the other side of total nuclear war, which is just one example of what philosophers call existential risks (x-risks), possible events that could permanently diminish the potential of humanity.[11] Following other big-picture twentieth-century scientific thinkers like Carl Sagan (1934–1996), Jonathan Schell (1943–2014), and John Leslie, contemporary philosopher Toby Ord believes that we are living in a particularly dangerous moment in human history because of our technological advancements.[12] Ord suggests that many x-risks could be natural, like asteroids or volcanoes; but that the preponderance of x-risks are anthropogenic, like nuclear war or climate change; and that many x-risks will arise from technologies yet to be created, like engineered biohazards or artificial general intelligence. In other words, the apocalypse probably won't transpire in spite of modern technologies but because of them. World-ending powers are difficult to wield responsibly. Whether in the nuclear war that starts the series, the general climatic decline of the wasteland, the mutant schemes for world domination, or the many mechanized factions vying for power, in one form or another, the *Fallout* series showcases all these kinds of x-risks, how difficult they may be to avoid, and how entangled they are with transhumanist ambitions.

In the same spirit, although a transhumanist himself, Bostrom worries that some devices may even lead to doomsday by default: once the technology is invented, it is already too late.[13] For example, if the mini-nukes in *Fallout* could be made cheaply enough to be purchased at the local convenience store for a couple of bottle caps, then the resulting chaos caused by irresponsible or reprehensible users might be enough to permanently plunge the world into irrevocable anarchy. And, the only way to avoid that fate might be something like totalitarian surveillance, what technocrats like Vault-Tec, Mr. House, or Brotherhood of Steel might offer, which is arguably a kind of x-risk itself, to the extent that it locks the future into a dystopian state. Indeed, technological trade-off is a motif offered throughout the *Fallout* series: either perpetual war and destruction or authoritarian oppression, your choice. As the mutant cult leader, the Master puts it: "Do you join the Unity, or do you die here? Join! Die!" Worse still, even if they don't go extinct soon, the wasteland dwellers and their world may eventually return to peak technological development, but this again risks nuclear war, repeating the cycle all over.[14] Presumably, this happens until a stable state is reached: either post-humanity or extinction. Until then, we are condemned to the human cycles of violence and their fallout. "War never changes," at least until we're all dead.

All things considered, loss of humanity and loss of civilization seem so repugnant that some transhumanist technologies may simply have too high a cost. The immortality of a ghoul and the invincibility of power armor are probably not worth living in a wasteland for. But in a strong sense, the philosophy of transhumanism is still well worth seriously contemplating, even if we ultimately reject its risks. And *Fallout* may be one of the most important series of our pre-apocalyptic time, precisely because exploring scenarios in which we ruin our future helps increase the chances we will do something to prevent them. That being said, even understanding how much we have to gain and how much we have to lose, will we make the right decisions? Maybe we should all take a few Mentats and think really hard about our future... Our world may depend on it!

Notes

1. Nick Bostrom, "A History of Transhumanist Thought," *Journal of Evolution and Technology* 14 (2005), 1–25.
2. Julian Savulescu and Nick Bostrom, *Human Enhancement*, (Oxford: Oxford University Press, 2009).
3. Nick Bostrom, "Why I Want to Be a Posthuman When I Grow Up," in Bert Gordijn and Ruth Chadwick eds., *Medical Enhancement and Posthumanity*, (Heidelberg: Springer, 2008), 107–137.
4. Nick Bostrom, "Transhumanist Values," *Journal of Philosophical Research* 30 (2005), 3–14.
5. Bostrom, "Transhumanist Values," 3–14.
6. Russ Shafer-Landau, "Genetic Engineering," in Russ Shafer-Landau ed., *Living Ethics: An Introduction with Readings*, (Oxford: Oxford University Press, 2019), 600–641.
7. Leigh Van Valen, "A New Evolutionary Law," *Evolutionary Theory* 1 (1973), 1–30.
8. Nick Bostrom, "The Future of Human Evolution," in Charles Tandy ed., *Death and Anti-Death: Two Hundred Years After Kant, Fifty Years After Turing*, (Palo Alto: Ria University Press, 2004), 339–371.
9. C.S. Lewis, *The Abolition of Man*, (Oxford: Oxford University Press, 1943).
10. Francis Fukuyama, *Our Posthuman Future*, (New York: Farrar, Straus & Giroux, 2002).
11. Nick Bostrom, "Existential Risk Prevention as Global Priority," *Global Policy* 4 (2013), 15–31.
12. Toby Ord, *The Precipice*, (Oxford: Oxford University Press, 2019).
13. Nick Bostrom, "The Vulnerable World Hypothesis," *Global Policy* 10 (2019), 455–476.
14. Nick Bostrom, "The Future of Humanity," in Jan Kyrre Berg Olsen, Evan Selinger, and Søren Riis eds., *New Waves in Philosophy of Technology*, (New York: Palgrave MacMillan, 2009), 186–216.

7

Synthetic Souls? Pragmatist Functionalism and the Moral Status of Synths in *Fallout*

Albert R. Spencer

"War never changes," but who counts as the enemy always does. From the beginning, the *Fallout* franchise has used its post-apocalyptic setting to explore messy questions about identity and moral worth. In the original game, the Super Mutants aren't just brutes; they're part of the Master's dream of unity. *Fallout 2* and *Fallout Tactics: Brotherhood of Steel* gave us Deathclaws that speak and care for one another. *Fallout 3* asks whether ghouls—rotting but reasoning—deserve a seat at the human table, especially in quests like "Tenpenny Tower." Across the series, players face a recurring challenge: Are these other beings just monsters, or are they persons in their own right? *Fallout 4* raises the stakes by adding synths: artificial beings who look, think, and feel like us. They aren't just strange or scary; they're unsettlingly familiar, forcing us to ask whether being human is about biology, behavior, or something else entirely.

As players explore the Commonwealth, they encounter a spectrum of attitudes toward synths, from casual suspicion to violent exclusion. Likewise, the major joinable factions mirror these divergent moral stances. Gradually, these encounters build toward a central ethical tension: whether beings that appear and act fully human deserve full moral status. That tension becomes personal as the game subtly suggests that even the player's own identity may be synthetic, leaving the question of personhood not merely theoretical but existential. This chapter examines how *Fallout 4* frames that question through a range of gameplay elements and philosophical lenses. By drawing from theories of mind and the philosophical tradition of American Pragmatism, I'll argue that the game invites players to confront the ethical boundaries of personhood and reconsider what it means to be human in a world reshaped by artificial consciousness.

Full Metal Personhood? Foes, Factions, and Philosophy of Mind

Most *Fallout* titles present new near-human beings as adversaries, inviting players to question how we define personhood. These creatures—Super Mutants, Deathclaws, ghouls, and various robots—share human traits like language or social behavior, but each also embodies anxieties around mutation, decay, or dehumanization. Their monstrous appearances signal danger, making moral evaluation instinctive and ethically uncomplicated, and they are eventually incorporated into the societies of the wasteland.

Synths, however, complicate this framework. Generation 1 synths are robotic skeletons used for manual labor; Generation 2 models adopt human features, like skin, voice, and personality, but remain visibly artificial; Generation 3 synths are nearly impossible to distinguish from humans. The only certain methods of identification—killing them, stealing the Synth Component from their inventory, or accessing Institute records—would certainly be violations of their rights if they were human. Other in-game tools, like Covenant's SAFE test or energy resistance in V.A.T.S., offer inconsistent results. This persistent uncertainty erodes trust and fuels moral paranoia, as the player and non-player characters (NPCs) cannot reliably tell who is human and who is not. For example, the character Phyllis Daily illustrates the psychological toll of this ambiguity. Once a settler, she begins to question her own identity after experiencing blackouts and disturbing dreams. One night, she awakens to find her grandson dead, likely by her own hand. Convinced she may be a synth, she isolates herself in shame. Her story combines trauma, paranoia, and societal fear, capturing how the ambient cultural anxiety about synth infiltration can destroy even sympathetic individuals.

This unease reflects a concept known as the *uncanny valley*, first proposed by roboticist Masahiro Mori (1927–2025).[1] As artificial beings become more lifelike, we feel increased affinity until a point where subtle imperfections cause revulsion. Gen3 synths live on the edge of this valley. Their realism provokes not empathy, but suspicion, reversing the usual logic of moral recognition. In *Fallout 4*, the more human a synth appears, the more unsettling it becomes. This design choice undercuts the intuitive equation of similarity with moral worth, deepening the game's ethical ambiguity. This unease is heightened by the fact that some synths, including major NPCs, do not even know they are artificial. Meanwhile, human characters like Phyllis Daily mistakenly fear they are synths, often with tragic consequences. Settlements respond in starkly contrasting ways: Covenant institutes violent screening procedures to prevent infiltration, while Diamond City tolerates Nick Valentine, a friendly Gen2 prototype with the personality of a stereotypical 1940s gumshoe, if only because his artificiality is visible and thus non-threatening.

Factions also mirror this spectrum: the Brotherhood of Steel sees synths as abominations, the Institute as property, and the Railroad as persons worth liberating. But *Fallout 4* offers no stable moral heuristic for recognizing personhood, only a deepening uncertainty. The ambiguity extends even to the protagonist by subtly suggesting the Sole Survivor might be a synth. This nuance makes the question of artificial identity not just ethical or political, but *existential*. In stripping away reliable visual and behavioral cues, the game pushes players to confront a deeper philosophical issue: What makes someone a person? Is it memory, emotion, consciousness, continuity, or something else entirely? To answer that, we must turn to the philosophy of mind.

According to the contemporary philosopher Amy Kind, philosophy of mind traditionally wrestles with what minds are, how they relate to bodies, and how we know they exist.[2] Early debates were split between dualism, which posits mind and body as separate substances, and physicalism, which sees everything, including mental states, as reducible to material causes. Identity theory and behaviorism both attempted to explain the mind without invoking the immaterial, but each had flaws: the former was species-specific, the latter too reductive. Thus, functionalism emerged as a compelling alternative. Instead of defining minds by their physical makeup, it defines them by the roles they play. Pain, for instance, is not about C-fibers firing but about a state caused by injury that leads to avoidance. This view allows for multiple realizability—the idea that minds can emerge in, or be *realized by*, diverse physical systems, including synthetic ones like *Fallout*'s synths. Fortunately, the Classical American Pragmatists deepen this view. Charles Sanders Peirce (1839–1914) connects mind to sign interpretation and experience, describing consciousness as a dynamic, triadic process shaped by felt qualities, resistance, and meaning-making. William James (1842–1910) presents the mind as a flowing stream of consciousness, evolving through adaptation and purpose. John Dewey (1859–1952) roots consciousness in interaction, describing it as a functional process shaped by habit, inquiry, and environment. For these thinkers, the mind is not a static thing but a way of navigating the world, shaped by culture and conduct.[3]

These insights shift the question of personhood from metaphysical essence to relational function. If synths exhibit memory, emotion, moral reasoning, and social participation, the Classical Pragmatists would argue they qualify as persons. Despite their artificiality, synths are persons because they engage in meaningful participation in our shared social life. *Fallout 4* dramatizes this debate through its three major joinable factions, each of which embodies a distinct philosophical position on the nature of mind and moral status. The Brotherhood of Steel adopts a view akin to dualism: they see synths as soulless imitations, outwardly human but inwardly empty, lacking the immaterial essence—call it spirit, soul, or moral substance—that defines true personhood. This belief justifies their zealous campaign to eliminate all synths, regardless of behavior or self-awareness. The Institute, by contrast, represents a reductive physicalism. They value the technological sophistication of synths and acknowledge that they display memory, emotion, and intelligence, but regard these as mere byproducts of complex programming (i.e., impressive simulations rather than signs of genuine consciousness). For the Institute, synths are tools: useful, disposable, and devoid of moral status. The Railroad breaks from the previous views by embracing a form of functionalism resonant with Classical American Pragmatism. They argue that personhood is not about essence or origin but about practical capabilities: if a being can suffer, reflect, make choices, and build relationships, then they deserve the rights and respect accorded to persons.

Yet *Fallout 4* does more than present these perspectives. It invites the player to inhabit and navigate them. Unlike traditional morality systems that reward clear-cut good or evil choices, the game forces players to weigh conflicting values under conditions of uncertainty. Should synths be liberated or controlled? Are they a threat, a population, or something else entirely? Thus, the ethical weight of the game falls not on the factions but on the player's own evolving judgment: What makes a being worthy of rights? What kind of life demands recognition? And who has the authority to decide? By placing players in morally ambiguous scenarios, where truth is partial and consequences are profound, the game demands ethical reflection, not merely strategic thinking. Because the game withholds clear answers, players must seek their own frameworks for navigating its dilemmas and look beyond the game for guidance. To explore what ethical framework might support such recognition, we now turn to W.E.B. Du Bois, Gloria Anzaldúa, and Jane Addams, three thinkers affiliated with the Classical Pragmatists, who extended their functionalism by emphasizing how personhood emerges through struggle, agency, and relational belonging.

Mind Games: Double Consciousness, Mestiza Consciousness, and Synth Consciousness

Three key missions in *Fallout 4* ("Human Error," "The Battle of Bunker Hill," and "Where You Belong" [*Far Harbor* DLC]) each dramatize a different aspect of synth personhood. While the game's open world allows for non-linear exploration, these quests tend to frame the player's moral evolution. Paired with the relational philosophies of Du Bois, Anzaldúa, and Addams, they reveal how *Fallout*'s synths are not just machines or narrative devices, but agents whose moral status demands recognition. For example, W.E.B. Du Bois's (1868–1963) concept of *double consciousness* describes the internal conflict of marginalized individuals forced to see themselves through the eyes of a dominant, devaluing culture. Rather than a private psychological tension, Du Bois saw this as the result of systemic misrecognition that fractures identity.

Scholars emphasize that Du Bois's notion of double consciousness is not merely a psychological or existential phenomenon, but a socially and historically situated response to systemic oppression. It emerges from the lived experience of Black Americans who are forced to navigate a world structured by white supremacy—a world that persistently devalues their humanity while demanding their participation. In this context, double consciousness reflects the internalized conflict between self-perception and the distorted image imposed by a racist society. It is not a failure of identity, but a moral and intellectual response to being excluded from full recognition and political belonging, yet still striving for dignity, self-determination, and communal affirmation within those hostile conditions.[4]

This framework maps cleanly onto the quest "Human Error." Early in the game, players encounter the town of Covenant. Behind a smiling facade hides a secret: they abduct travelers and run psychological tests to detect synth infiltrators. Amelia Stockton, a kidnapped woman, is subjected to invasive interrogation in the compound beneath the town. Her identity is ambiguous. She may be a synth, but her confusion and emotional distress suggest that she believes she's human. Amelia's predicament mirrors Du Bois's diagnosis. She is caught between her self-understanding and the fearful projections of Covenant. The player must choose whether to side with the town's security logic or rescue Amelia. That choice becomes a referendum on personhood. Is it determined by biology, memory, behavior, or the capacity for fear, choice, and meaning-making?

The mission places the player at a moral crossroads, pushing them to enact their own stance on recognition, exclusion, and the fragile status of the "Other." But if "Human Error" introduces moral ambiguity on an individual scale, "The Battle of Bunker Hill" raises the stakes. In this quest, a group of escaped synths is caught between three factions: the Brotherhood of Steel, who see synths as threats to humanity; the Institute, who treat them as malfunctioning property; and the Railroad, who view them as persons in need of protection. The player must choose whom to support, and their decision has permanent consequences. This standoff crystallizes the three philosophies of mind under consideration: dualism (Brotherhood), physicalism (Institute), and functionalism (Railroad). It also gestures toward a deeper crisis. Some evidence scattered throughout the game suggests that the Sole Survivor may be a synth, which complicates the decision further: Is the player defending their own kind? Enacting a hidden directive? Can agency ever be disentangled from origin? This recursive uncertainty destabilizes identity itself, creating a moral feedback loop so intense it's no surprise it drove Phyllis Daily to madness. It could even cause a synth's logic core to short-circuit under the strain of irreconcilable imperatives.

Here, Gloria Anzaldúa's (1942–2004) borderlands philosophy provides clarity. Her concept of *Nepantla*—the Nahuatl word for the in-between space where identities blur—describes beings who resist binary categories and forge new selves in fractured terrain. Rather than seeing such liminality as confusion or failure, Anzaldúa frames it as a generative site of transformation, a space where contradictions are held in tension and used to create new meaning.[5] Individuals who inhabit *Nepantla* become *Nepantleras*—shapeshifters who do not resolve differences by collapsing into conformity but instead navigate multiplicity with fluidity and ethical imagination. These figures are not merely caught between worlds; they are bridges, translators, and creators of new relational worlds. In this light, Anzaldúa's vision aligns with María Lugones's account of "active subjectivity"—the capacity to craft identity and moral agency through resistance to imposed definitions and through the forging of communal ties across differences.[6] Consequently, the Sole Survivor, caught between factions and haunted by uncertainty about their own nature, becomes a *Nepantlera*. Their identity is not fixed because it fluctuates across moral, political, and even ontological boundaries. They are a citizen and an outsider, a liberator and a threat, possibly human, and possibly machine. Their ethical choices cannot rely on pure logic or loyalty to any faction. Instead, they must act from the unstable ground between conflicting truths, forging meaning in the cracks between the Brotherhood's fear, the Institute's control, and the Railroad's idealism. Choosing to defend synths, especially if one is a synth, risks accusations of self-interest or manipulation. Yet this act might affirm Anzaldúa's insight: that ethical action comes not from certainty of origin but from the courage to act across boundaries in pursuit of justice. In doing so, the Sole Survivor mirrors the *mestiza consciousness* Anzaldúa champions—a consciousness born from multiplicity, grounded in struggle and committed to transformation without erasure.

The Railroad to Acadia: From Intersectionality to Associated Living

Because these insights from Du Bois and Anzaldúa align most closely with functionalism, one might assume that this chapter defends the Railroad as the most noble faction of the three. They are, but their methods invite serious critique. Their mission is to liberate synths from bondage, yet their strategy often involves "resetting" escapees by erasing a synth refugee's memories, identities, and personality to protect them from detection. Though framed as compassionate, this tactic echoes the very violence of the Institute it seeks to resist. In both cases, synths are denied the continuity of selfhood, treated not as agents but as programmable vessels. The moral discomfort here is not incidental. It cuts to the heart of what liberation truly means. If memory and history are central to personhood, then such erasures are not acts of protection but of profound violation.

This criticism is precisely the argument made by the Feral Historian, an independent scholar on YouTube, who provocatively describes the Railroad as the most evil faction in *Fallout 4*.[7] His reasoning is simple but devastating: the Institute might oppress synths as property, but the Railroad effectively *kills* them by wiping their minds. In attempting to save synths, they annihilate the very selves they claim to recognize and defend. Whereas the Institute denies that synths are persons, the Railroad affirms them in theory, but "protects" them by erasing the personhood they acknowledge in practice. This inversion makes the Railroad's ethic very unsettling. They are blind to the moral significance of intersectionality, a framework shaped by the contemporary theorist Kimberlé Crenshaw, which was anticipated by both Du Bois and Anzaldúa. Intersectional analysis reveals how efforts to liberate the marginalized can reproduce domination when they ignore the complexity of situated experience. As Anzaldúa and the other women of color warned in her anthology co-edited with Cherríe Moraga, *This Bridge Called My Back* (1981), acts of solidarity that overwrite or assimilate marginalized voices risk replicating the very forms of silencing they oppose. Even when carried out with consent or in the name of safety, the Railroad's resets raise urgent questions: Is freedom worth the loss of self? What kind of protection leaves nothing of the person it protects? And who has the moral authority to make that decision?

Backing the Railroad is problematic, but it remains the best option available in the base game for a future in which synths might live freely and equally with their post-apocalyptic allies and rivals. However, a more hopeful, but still flawed, model appears in the *Far Harbor* DLC. The expansion begins with the quest "Where You Belong," in which the Sole Survivor is introduced to Kasumi Nakano, a young woman convinced she's a synth. She seeks refuge in Acadia, a sanctuary for self-aware synths and their non-synth allies, led by DiMA, a Generation 2 prototype who shares fraternal origins with Nick Valentine. In fact, it is Valentine who gives this quest to the Sole Survivor, which further underscores that this story arc reflects the agency of synths to create their own equitable future. Of course, once the Sole Survivor successfully escorts Kasumi to Acadia, it becomes apparent that this sanctuary is not yet the utopia it aspires to be. Though DiMA envisions Acadia as a pluralistic community, where synths are not controlled or erased but invited to build lives alongside humans, he secretly murdered and replaced Captain Avery, a leader of the human settlement of Far Harbor, to maintain peace. This act, though not rooted in hatred, still violates moral norms. However, unlike the Brotherhood's genocide, the Institute's coercion or the Railroad's erasure, DiMA's sin is framed as an act of desperation in service of coexistence. Consequently, the Sole Survivor must judge not only DiMA's actions but Acadia's potential. Can a community built on a lie still become a space of justice?

To answer this, we turn to Jane Addams (1860–1935), whose philosophy of democracy offers a compelling framework for understanding

Acadia's fragile promise. Addams argued that democracy was not merely a political structure, but a way of life rooted in *associated living*, or the idea that ethical communities emerge through mutual recognition, shared inquiry, and sustained cooperation across differences. For Addams, social progress depended not on purity or ideological conformity, but on the ongoing work of building inclusive relationships, even amid conflict and uncertainty.[8] Her commitment to multiculturalism, dialogue, and democratic ethics emphasizes that communities are strongest when they are messy, contingent, and collectively shaped.

In this light, Acadia becomes more than a haven. It becomes a test case for Addams's vision. DiMA's crime is morally significant, but *Fallout 4* does not frame it as disqualifying. Instead, it presents a difficult question: Can imperfect actions taken to preserve a pluralistic community be redeemed by the potential for associated living? The Sole Survivor's role in Acadia is not to impose justice from above, but to participate in its fragile construction. The player must decide whether truth-telling, reconciliation, and cooperation can restore what violence once threatened. Where the Institute offers control, the Brotherhood offers exclusion, and the Railroad offers protection through erasure, Acadia, imperfect as it is, offers the hope of solidarity. In navigating this space, the player is no longer just a judge of factions, but a co-creator of ethical community, embodying Addams's ideal of democratic life built not on moral certainty, but on the courage to relate across differences.

Post-Apocalyptic Pragmatism

Thus, the philosophical insights of Du Bois, Anzaldúa, and Addams converge to form a robust justification for a pragmatic functionalist understanding of synth personhood. Each thinker illuminates a distinct but interrelated aspect of identity: Du Bois exposes how prejudice fragments the self through systemic misrecognition; Anzaldúa reclaims contested spaces, like the US–Mexico border, as a site of creative resistance; and Addams grounds moral agency in participatory, co-creative relationships that generate new ethical possibilities. These perspectives map closely onto the structure of *Fallout 4*'s core synth-centered missions ("Human Error," "The Battle of Bunker Hill," and "Where You Belong"), each of which dramatizes one of these dimensions in turn. Together, they show that personhood is not an essence to be discovered or a status to be granted, but an ongoing process enacted in relation to others, often in the face of coercive systems and conflicting narratives. Indeed, if there is a moral to the *Fallout* franchise, I argue that this is it. Despite humanity nearly destroying itself and the world, with each title, civilization gradually rises from the ashes, and the sentient species of the wasteland become more and more diverse. Yesterday's enemies become tomorrow's neighbors, and

Fallout 4 subtly reminds us of the social progress that has occurred throughout the franchise. Characters like Strong, a Super Mutant who seeks the milk of human kindness and Hancock's ghoul bodyguard Fahrenheit, who protects Goodneighbor's fragile order with loyalty and grit. Each shows how former monsters can become allies, citizens, or even heroes, and if Nick Valentine can become a loyal and beloved companion, why should Gen3 synths be denied this opportunity? Yes, there are risks, but kindness, community, democracy, and ethics require risk. Furthermore, the wasteland is the ultimate testament to the folly of ethics and politics based on suspicion and cynicism. In affirming this view, this chapter not only challenges the ideologies that dominate the game's factions but also articulates a moral vision in which identity is forged through struggle, solidarity, and shared transformation. Synths, like many marginalized groups, do not demand recognition because they conform to normative models of the self, but because their very resistance to those models expands what moral personhood can mean.

Ultimately, *Fallout 4* does not offer a tidy resolution to the questions it raises, and it shouldn't. More importantly, its moral ambiguity echoes the historical struggles of real-world communities who, like the synths, were denied full recognition and forced to navigate hostile systems of power. The echoes of Du Bois's double consciousness resound in the inner conflict of characters like Amelia Stockton and Kasumi Nakano, whose identities are fractured by suspicion and misrecognition; Anzaldúa's borderlands philosophy parallels the lived experience of synths as beings shaped through contradiction, hybridity, and resilience; and Addams's ethic of co-participation finds new life in the fragile democracy of Acadia, a community forged through imperfect but ongoing experiments in associated living. *Fallout*'s post-nuclear setting is more than speculative fiction; it functions as allegory, illuminating how personhood, justice, and community have always been historically contested, forged through conflict, and co-created in the margins. The moral crises the game and franchise present are not science fiction fantasies but dramatizations of the very same philosophical and political struggles that shaped the history of the United States: slavery and abolition, colonialism and resistance, assimilation and resurgence, exclusion and solidarity.

Yet the relevance of *Fallout 4*'s questions is not confined to history. It speaks urgently to the present and future. In a world increasingly shaped by artificial intelligence, algorithmic governance, and the erosion of shared public discourse, the boundaries of personhood and agency are once again in flux. The debates over what makes an entity worthy of rights mirror those playing out in contemporary discussions about digital identity, machine learning, and biopolitical control. *Fallout 4* anticipates these dilemmas not by offering technocratic solutions, but by embedding them in stories of care, betrayal, kinship, and self-discovery. It reminds us that the most pressing ethical questions of our time are not about what technology can do, but about what kind of world we want to build together, and who we are willing to recognize as co-creators of that world. By playing through these questions, players are invited to rehearse the ethical imagination needed to face an uncertain future. In choosing how to respond, we define not just them, but ourselves. Let us also hope that when synthetic persons do arrive, they will not mirror our cruelties but exceed our humanity, and that in recognizing their personhood, we do not forfeit our own.

Notes

1. Masahiro Mori, "The Uncanny Valley," *IEEE Spectrum*, trans. Norri Kageki and Karl F. MacDorman, June 12, 2012, https://spectrum.ieee.org/the-uncanny-valley.
2. Amy Kind, *Philosophy of Mind: The Basics* (Abingdon: Taylor & Francis, 2020). Frank M. Kirkland, "On Du Bois' Notion of Double Consciousness," *Philosophy Compass* 8, no. 2 (2013), 137–148.
3. Albert Spencer, *American Pragmatism: An Introduction* (Cambridge: Polity Press, 2020).
4. Ernst Allen, "Du Boisian Double Consciousness: The Unsustainable Argument," *The Massachusetts Review* 43.2 (Summer 2002), 217–253. Bernard Boxhill, "W.E.B. Du Bois and William James on Double Consciousness," *Journal of Social Philosophy* 54, no. 3 (Fall 2023), 316–362. Kirkland, "On Du Bois' Notion of Double Consciousness," 137–148.
5. Mariana Ortega, "Apertures of In-betweenness, of Selves in the Middle," in AnaLouise Keating ed., *New Perspectives on Gloria Anzaldúa* (Basingstoke: Palgrave Macmillan, 2006), 77–84.
6. Gloria Anzaldúa, *Borderlands/La Frontera* (San Francisco: Aunt Lute Books, 2012). AnaLouise Keating, "Risking the Vision, Transforming the Divides: Nepantlera Perspectives on Academic Boundaries, Identities, and Lives," in AnaLouise Keating and Gloria Gonzalez-Lopes eds., *Bridging: How Gloria Anzaldúa's Life and Work Transformed Our Own*, (Austin: University of Texas Press, 2011). Maria Lugones, "From Within Germinative Stasis: Creating Active Subjectivity, Resistant Agency," in Keating ed., *New Perspectives on Gloria Anzaldúa*, 85–99.
7. The Feral Historian, "Fallout 4: The Railroad," YouTube, June 26, 2025, at https://www.youtube.com/shorts/Us1Hq-nfgnA.
8. Jane Addams, *The Greatest Works of Jane Addams*, (Prague: Madison & Adams Press, 2019).

8

Robots, Cyborgs, and Synths: Exploring Personhood in the *Fallout* Universe

Matthew Watts

The American wasteland of the twenty-third century is a census-taker's nightmare. Beyond the baseline humans scarred by radiation and tribal conflict, the world of *Fallout* teems with beings made of metal, wire, and spliced-together tissue. Hulking Securitrons police the Strip of New Vegas, dispensing summary judgment, repurposed Robobrains hum prewar memories as they carry out cold military protocols, and synthetic detectives grapple with recollections that aren't their own. This assortment of manufactured creatures raises a question as old as philosophy itself, now given a radioactive urgency. What, precisely, makes a person a person? And are the mechanical denizens of the wasteland persons, and therefore worthy of our respect and consideration?

While only occasionally in the spotlight, personhood is an invisible thread running throughout the *Fallout* universe. For example, when a small, floating Eyebot named ED-E first beeps at you from the dusty workshop of Primm, it's easy to see just another useful gadget, little more than a floating toolbox. But then ED-E begins playing snippets of prewar broadcasts, humming with electronic curiosity and buzzing cheerfully when enemies fall—sometimes even playing triumphant victory music. As you travel together through the Mojave, his chirps and electronic whirs seem to express happiness, frustration, or even anger, hinting at genuine emotional states behind his polished steel casing. His journey isn't random; ED-E is driven by a mission to reach the West Coast, propelled by a deep affection for his creator, Dr. Whitley. His poignant audio logs reveal a bond that feels unmistakably like love. At some point, you may begin to wonder: Is ED-E merely clever hardware executing code, or could this blinking metal companion be a genuine someone, deserving care and loyalty, rather than mere maintenance?

This chapter examines the mechanical denizens of the wasteland to better understand their personhood and moral standing, and to make sense of companions like ED-E and whether they deserve more than just maintenance. To navigate this philosophical minefield, we should probably begin with the inhabitants of the wasteland that are closest to us: the cyborgs, hybrids who blend organic brains with artificial hardware. From there, we'll turn to the haunting challenge of androids, or "synths," artificial beings so perfectly human that they force us to confront the very foundations of our identity. And finally, the wasteland pushes us toward perhaps the hardest challenge—the "pure" machine, a mind of code in a body of metal.

The Ghost in the Hybrid Machine: Cyborg Identity

Perhaps the easiest entry point into the question of personhood is the wasteland's cyborgs—creatures that fuse familiar human brains with mechanical bodies, raising immediate questions about where the person ends and the machine begins. With an intact human brain still running the show, the question of personhood feels a bit less puzzling—after all, if anything counts as a person, surely a living brain does, even if it's housed in a metal shell.

By "cyborg," I mean any creature partly made of flesh and partly made of metal. These are beings whose identities are grafted, soldered, and bolted together. This fusion of the organic and the synthetic forces us to ask what holds a self together across such radical physical change. The traditional answer comes from John Locke (1632–1704), who argued that personal identity is found in consciousness, specifically, in memory. You are the same person you were yesterday because you remember being that person. For Locke, it doesn't matter if your body is made of flesh or metal; what counts is the unbroken chain of memories connecting you to your past.[1] No figures in the wasteland exemplify this principle quite like the unique Robobrain "professors" of Vault 118, which appear in *Fallout 4*'s *Far Harbor* DLC. These prewar socialites, artists, and academics voluntarily underwent brain extraction and placement into Robobrain bodies, believing it a path to immortality. Yet, their new mechanical existences are anything but serene.

Take Bert Riggs, the scientist who engineered their transformation. His existence as a Robobrain is dominated by his research, even as he grapples with the strange behaviors of his fellow Vault Dwellers. Or consider Santiago, the painter, whose affair with Gilda Broscoe shows that more than just his artistic sensibilities have been preserved. These Robobrains are not merely machines; they are thinking, speaking (or at least whirring) paradoxes of Lockean identity. Their minds, once encased in flesh, are now housed in steel and circuits, yet their personalities, quirks, and most importantly, their memories, remain. The "murder mystery" they inhabit is a direct consequence of these lingering, prewar identities and relationships, proving that even across radical physical change, the self, haunted by its past, persists. Their robotic bodies don't just preserve their lives; they preserve their eccentricities, grudges, and fragmented humanity, making them walking, talking testaments to the idea that we are what we remember, even if that memory is now a metallic echo.

But what if that connection to memory frays? The philosopher Derek Parfit (1942–2017) complicates the Lockean model by suggesting that what matters is not a perfect, unbroken chain of memory for identity, but rather "psychological continuity." A person is a long series of overlapping mental states—memories, intentions, desires—that connect us to our past selves. For Parfit, survival of identity is a matter of degree.[2]

This framework is particularly useful when examining the Think Tank, the demented brain-bot rulers of the Big MT from *Fallout: New Vegas*'s DLC *Old World Blues*. These are the disembodied brains of the twenty-first century's most brilliant scientists, preserved in hovering chassis with articulating computer screens showing pictures of eyes and mouths acting as stand-ins for their faces, and left to stew in their own neuroses for two centuries. Sealed off from the world, their only stimuli have been each other and their own decaying memories. The result is a society of minds where the connection to their original human selves is almost entirely gone, replaced by a set of exaggerated, looping personality traits. Doctor Klein is breathtakingly overconfident in his own intelligence; Doctor Dala fixates on human sensuality, distorted through her non-physical form; Doctor 0 (the not-so-brilliant or valued scientist) claims to have a gift with machines and "can render anything inoperable—preserve them in a non-functioning state"; Doctor 8 had his voice module reprogrammed, and is largely incomprehensible; and Doctor Borous booms with an obsession for bizarre animal modifications. Their renegade member, Doctor Mobius, is addicted to using psychoactive drugs, like Mentats and Psycho, to keep himself in a state of perpetual looping confusion to act as a boogeyman for his former colleagues, preventing their escape.

The members of the Think Tank are perhaps the ultimate Parfitian thought experiment, a horrifying and hilarious look at what happens when psychological continuity is stretched so thin over time that all that remains is a caricature. Their identities are not constituted by their memories, which have deteriorated beyond recognition, or in some cases, been damaged, or erased, but rather loosely held together identity narratives, obsessive research topics, and a shared, profound arrogance. This isn't just the passive decay of memory over time; it's the result of active, willful self-sabotage.

While the tragic, confused, and looping memories of both Big MT's Think Tank and the Robobrains of Vault 118 grant them a clear claim to personhood, the wasteland is crowded with beings that don't have any grey matter (e.g., Securitrons, Mister Gutsy units, synths) yet still bark orders, crack jokes, and even nurse centuries-old grudges from past lives. If a brain floating in a jar can think, what about a chassis with no brain at all? To tackle that harder question, philosophers reach for functionalism, the view that what makes a mind is not the meaty brain it's made of but the job it performs.

Mind Over Matter: The Functionalist Wager

Before we can judge the personhood of a machine, we must decide if a machine can even possess a mind. The philosophy of mind offers a powerful tool for this: functionalism. Championed by thinkers like Hilary Putnam (1926–2016),[3] functionalism proposes that mental states (like pain, belief, or love) are not defined by the physical stuff they are made of (neurons, silicon chips), but by the functional role they play. Pain, for example, is a state caused by bodily damage that causes things like wincing or crying out, and the desire to withdraw or flee. If a machine's internal state works like pain, then for a functionalist, it is pain. In essence, the mind is not the hardware; it's the software. This idea gives us good reason to take the minds of the wasteland's machines seriously. It allows us to look at a sentry bot, or a robo-scorpion riddled with bullets, and ask ourselves whether it's suffering, and not just whether we breached its armor.

To understand functionalism, let's start with what could be the simplest hostile machine in the wasteland: a ceiling turret. Its entire "mind" can be described with one brutally simple rule: *if* it detects a hostile target (the input), *then* it starts shooting (the output). That's its entire decision procedure. That rule sheet is exactly what Putnam called a machine table: a list matching every possible input with the action to take and the next state to enter. Putnam's "machine table" shows how one can specify a mind purely as a pattern of inputs, internal states, and outputs; if you can map those transitions onto *something*—even the wires and vacuum tubes that make up the cognitive machinery of the Mister Handy series of service robots—you have, in principle, recreated a mind.

Putnam thought that our own minds are just a vastly more complex version of that same kind of table of inputs, internal states, and outputs. The whole debate about artificial persons boils down to this: If you can write a machine table that's complex enough to perfectly copy a human's, is the robot running that program just *acting* like a person, or *is* it a person? For a functionalist, there's no meaningful difference—the program is the person.

The true power of functionalism lies in its radical flexibility, an idea sometimes called "multiple realizability." Think of a program on a holotape. That program—say, the game *Red Menace*—plays the same way whether you run it on a clunky office terminal, a sophisticated Institute computer, or your own wrist-mounted Pip-Boy. The hardware is different, but the software's function is identical. In the same way, a thought or feeling can show up in wet human neurons, clacking vacuum tubes, a quantum chip, or even the goo-filled brain jar of a beat-up Robobrain. Functionalism proposes that a mind is like that software. It can run on almost any kind of hardware. It doesn't matter if the hardware is a squishy, biological brain or a network of positronic processors in a synth. This single idea blows the door wide open for non-human personhood, challenging the idea that only a squishy brain can think. It provides a unified way to approach the consciousness of every artificial being in the wasteland, from a Mister Gutsy to a Robobrain to Nick Valentine, with one elegant question: Does it, regardless of its construction, *function* as though it has beliefs, desires, and an inner life?

The *Fallout* universe provides its own grim illustration of this concept in the form of the SAFE test, used by the paranoid *Fallout 4* community of Covenant to identify synths. The test-giver asks a series of bizarre questions designed to elicit a uniquely "human" psychological response. The entire premise of the test is a desperate gamble against functionalism; it assumes there is some ineffable human essence that no machine could ever replicate. The irony is that the test's frequent failures are the strongest argument for functionalism. Synths have become so adept at replicating the functional roles of human emotion and reasoning that their responses are often indistinguishable from those of a biological person. Covenant's very existence, shrouded in fear and sustained by a flawed interrogation method, is proof that when a being can perfectly perform the functions of a person, telling the difference becomes little more than a violent and often tragic exercise in prejudice. This framework, where function triumphs over form, gives us a new way to approach the wasteland's purely mechanical denizens.

Androids Anonymous: The Search for a Synthetic Self

Now we arrive at the most human of the wasteland's non-humans: the androids, or as the Commonwealth calls them, the synths. These are wholly artificial beings, sometimes built from mechanical parts, sometimes from 3D-printed biological tissue, but all designed to perfectly mimic humanity. With synths, the Lockean memory theory of identity is thrust back into the spotlight. If you are your memories, then you are the person who remembers them, no matter the body those memories inhabit.

Enter Nick Valentine, the iconic synth detective of Diamond City. He not only has the personality, training, and instincts, but the very *chain of memories* that defined that man's life, and even the unresolved grudges of a prewar Boston cop. By Locke's criterion, those unbroken memories are *exactly* what make him that cop again, which means Nick *qualifies* as a person in the Lockean sense. Yet Nick also knows he is *not* the original Nick; he is something new. We see this tension play out as he obsesses over tracking down the man who killed the original Nick Valentine's fiancée, mob boss Eddie Winter, now living as a ghoul. He uses those memories as raw material—tools for his investigations, foundations for his moral code—but it is *Nick the synth* who chooses loyalty, justice, and even irony in a lawless world.

Nick has the benefit of implanted memories, but what about all the other synths without such memories? A more radical way to understand synths—including Nick, and indeed every synth roaming the Commonwealth—is through the enactivism articulated in the work of contemporary philosopher and cognitive scientist Evan Thompson.[4] This enactivist approach argues that identity is not a "thing" stored in the brain (like a set of memories), but an ongoing process forged through the constant dynamic interaction between a being and its environment. We are not our memories; we are what we do. You become who you are by seeing what's around you, acting on it, and then taking in what happens next—again and again, like a never-ending feedback loop. Swap out a chunk of memory, and the loop still rolls on, picking up fresh experiences and stitching them into the ongoing story.

There is no better case study for this than DiMA, the leader of the rogue synth colony of Acadia in *Fallout 4*'s *Far Harbor* DLC. DiMA is haunted by his past actions, some of which could destroy the fragile peace he has built. At a critical juncture, he makes a profound choice: he physically removes a key memory from his own brain and hides it away. To protect the community he has created—the identity he has enacted as a leader and protector—he excises a piece of his past. He is literally choosing his present self, defined by his actions and relationships in Acadia, over the historical truth of his memories. In choosing present action over perfect recall, DiMA shows that personhood can be maintained—even *improved*—by pruning memories that threaten the identity-in-progress. Like Nick, he proves that a self can be built, revised, and fiercely defended, no matter how artificial the starting materials.

Robots in Revolt: Autonomy in a Tin Can

We've seen that cyborgs and synths clear every personhood hurdle and that to be considered a person is to be granted moral standing. It means your interests matter, your well-being is a moral concern, and you cannot be treated as a mere tool for someone else's purposes. But what about the wasteland's "pure" robots—Protectrons trundling along ruined subway lines, Mister Gutsy units barking patriotic slogans, and Victor, the ever-cheerful Stetson-wearing Securitron we see all over the Mojave wasteland? Their steel faces trigger little sympathy. They stagger when servos seize, and bleep alarms when armor buckles, yet most Wastelanders treat those reactions as mere glitches. So, how do we decide whether a being of bolts and circuitry has a life that matters?

By "robot," I mean a fully mechanical being whose thoughts—if we can call them that—and behaviors arise from its programming. These are the ubiquitous Mister Gutsy patrol bots, the chirping Miss Nanny caretakers, and the hulking Securitrons of New Vegas. To most Wastelanders, they are appliances, no more deserving of respect than a Pip-Boy or a laser rifle. But are they? One promising framework for addressing this question is the capabilities approach championed by contemporary philosopher Martha Nussbaum. Rather than judging moral standing by appearance or origin, Nussbaum argues that a good life—regardless of species or substrate—is one in which a creature can exercise its core capabilities and thus flourish in its own way. Her approach identifies 10 central human capabilities: practical reason, play, affiliation, productive work, curiosity, life, bodily health, senses and imagination, emotions, and control over one's environment.[5] Though developed for human contexts, this framework offers a useful lens for evaluating whether artificial beings might qualify for moral consideration.

The test becomes: Can this being flourish according to its own nature and capacities? Curie, the French-accented Miss Nanny hidden in Vault 81, provides a compelling case study. Her entire purpose centers on scientific discovery. When the Sole Survivor frees her, she isn't satisfied with dusting test tubes; she yearns to design new experiments, cure wasteland diseases, and—once transferred into a synth body—watch a sunset with friends. Critics might argue that her responses represent sophisticated programming rather than genuine desire. Yet helping Curie upgrade her frame reveals something profound: if her pursuit of knowledge, companionship, and wonder represents mere programming, it is programming that enables her to flourish in ways that align remarkably well with Nussbaum's vision of a meaningful life.

This suggests that at least some robots may meet reasonable standards for moral standing, not by mimicking human consciousness, but by demonstrating their own forms of flourishing within their designed capacities. The question isn't whether they experience life exactly as we do, but whether they can pursue purposes that matter to them in ways that constitute genuine well-being.

Yet, Curie may be an exceptional case. Many robots lack her rich inner repertoire, and it's not obvious they possess the sort of autonomy or self-directed projects that philosophers usually point to. Some robots like Curie may qualify as persons in their own right, but for others, the case is less clear. So perhaps we need to shift the question from the high bar of personhood to the more foundational concept of moral standing. Does a being have to be a full person to deserve moral consideration?

For contemporary utilitarian Peter Singer, the answer is no. He argues that the one, non-negotiable ticket into the moral community is sentience: the capacity for suffering and enjoyment.[6] If a being can suffer or feel pain, that pain counts, and we have a moral obligation to take that interest into account. Singer famously argued against "speciesism"—the prejudice of favoring humans over other animals.[7] By extension, dismissing a robot's clear negative state simply because its source is silicon rather than carbon amounts to a form of what we could call "substrate prejudice"—moral prejudice based on the material of the body rather than the reality of the experience. When a Securitron takes damage and begins to hobble away on a damaged wheel, its chassis sparking, that labored retreat does the same causal job flesh-and-blood pain does: it registers harm and cries out for relief.

This brings us to a more complex machine like Victor the cowboy Securitron. While his personhood may be debatable, his moral standing is on firmer ground. He demonstrates behaviors that indicate positive and negative internal states. His cheerful personality suggests a capacity for a state of well-being. More importantly, his rescue of the Courier can be seen as an act to alleviate a state of harm he has witnessed. His own dialogue reveals a being that assesses risk and seeks to avoid danger: "I was out for a stroll that night when I heard the commotion up at the old bone orchard. Saw what looked like a bunch of bad eggs so I laid low."[8] This isn't just a tactical calculation; it's an expression of an interest in his own continued, unharmed existence. If a robot can experience unpleasant internal states—whether from physical damage or programmatic distress—and actively strives to avoid them, its welfare counts for something.

Taken together, these lines of thought paint a consistent picture. Robots like Curie and Victor may be wired, welded, and occasionally glitchy, but they strive to flourish, experience states analogous to harm, and pursue goals. In philosophically relevant ways, they live lives that matter. Ignoring that simply because they lack skin is moral laziness, not moral insight, and it leaves us uncomfortably close to smashing a thinking, feeling being just because its pain sounds metallic when it cries out.

Who Gets to Be Someone in the Wasteland?

The journey from a cyborg's fragmented memory to a synth's chosen sacrifice, and finally to a robot's quiet moments of triumph, culminates in a singular moral insight. This journey brings us, fittingly, back to ED-E, the wandering Eyebot who first prompted these inquiries. After countless miles traveled through the Mojave, ED-E may finally reach his destination on the West Coast, completing the mission entrusted to him by Doctor Whitley. When this moment arrives, it transcends a mere fetched item or completed quest. ED-E's proud chirps, triumphant music, and joyful buzzing signify the fulfillment of a promise. This outcome reinforces the idea that the distinction between "someone" and "something" is not defined by biological composition but by actions, choices, and the capacity for care. Ultimately, the philosophical journey extends beyond mere resolutions, revealing the undeniable emergence of personhood in unexpected forms. In a world scarred by catastrophe, recognizing personhood, regardless of its origin, becomes a necessity for survival and growth in a post-nuclear wasteland.

Notes

1. John Locke, *An Essay Concerning Human Understanding*, (London: Penguin, 1997), 296–314.
2. Derek Parfit, *Reasons and Persons*, (Oxford: Oxford University Press, 1984). especially part 3
3. Hilary Putnam, "The Nature of Mental States," in Ned Block ed., *Readings in the Philosophy of Psychology*, (Cambridge, MA: Harvard University Press, 1980), 223–231.
4. Evan Thompson, *Waking, Dreaming, Being: Self and Consciousness in Neuroscience, Meditation, and Philosophy*, (New York: Columbia University Press, 2015), xxxi–xl.
5. Martha Nussbaum, *Women and Human Development: The Capabilities Approach*, (Cambridge: Cambridge University Press, 2000).
6. Popular culture often conflates sentience—the simple capacity to feel pleasure or pain—with sapience, which denotes higher-order intelligence like wisdom, judgment, and self-awareness. Singer, however, grounds moral status solely in sentience, setting a deliberately low threshold so that any being capable of suffering—including non-human animals, robots, and other artificial beings—enters the moral community even if they lack human-level rationality.
7. Peter Singer, *Animal Liberation: A New Ethics for Our Treatment of Animals*, (New York: Ecco, 2009).
8. *Fallout: New Vegas* (Bethesda Softworks, 2010).

Part 3

OVERSEER, OVERSEEN: *FALLOUT* AND POLITICAL PHILOSOPHY

9

Locked In: The Fallout of Liberal Ideals in Vault 33

John P. Irish

We are bonded, not just as neighbors, but by a shared duty. To keep the candle of civilization lit.

—Overseer MacLean

You look out at this wasteland, looks like chaos. But there's always somebody behind the wheel.

—The Ghoul

Vault 33, one of the central settings in the Amazon *Fallout* series, is introduced as a functioning subterranean society preserved from the devastation of nuclear war. Its residents live in a carefully maintained environment, guided by communal norms, regular elections, and a visible emphasis on cooperation and order. Overseers are selected through a public vote, and a citizen council regularly convenes to discuss matters of shared concern, including leadership transitions and responses to external threats. From its food production systems to its education practices, Vault 33 operates with a high degree of internal stability and procedural formality. To its inhabitants, the vault provides continuity—a controlled environment where human civilization can survive while the outside world, the wasteland, remains hostile and chaotic. With its emphasis on democratic participation, social harmony, and civic order, Vault 33 reflects many of the aspirations commonly associated with Enlightenment rationalism and liberal political thought—particularly those of one of its chief architects, the philosopher John Locke (1632–1704). In this context, "liberal political thought" refers to the Enlightenment tradition (roughly 1680s–1820s), emphasizing individual rights, consent of the governed, constitutional limits on power, and the rule of law.

The Original Overseer

Locke emerged from the religious and political turbulence of seventeenth-century England as one of the most influential thinkers of the Enlightenment. Raised by a Puritan father who fought for Parliament against the monarchy during the English Civil War, Locke was educated at Westminster and

Oxford, where he developed a lifelong interest in science, medicine, and political philosophy. His early exposure to religious disputes and civil unrest shaped his belief in tolerance, empiricism, and reasoned debate. In the 1660s, Locke formed a close partnership with the Earl of Shaftesbury, serving as his personal physician and political adviser. This alliance exposed Locke to the practical realities of power and revolution, especially during the Exclusion Crisis and the Rye House Plot. Forced into exile in Holland, Locke returned to England after the Glorious Revolution of 1688 and soon published his two most influential works: *An Essay Concerning Human Understanding* and *Two Treatises of Government*, both of which helped shape modern views on knowledge, liberty, governance, and civil society, positioning Locke as a cornerstone of Enlightenment liberalism.

At the core of Locke's political philosophy is the belief that all individuals are by nature free, equal, and rational. In *Two Treatises of Government*, he argues that humans possess natural rights to life, liberty, and property even before forming any government. Political society arises, not through divine right or coercion, but through mutual consent: individuals agree to form a civil community in order to better preserve their rights, secure peace, and establish impartial laws. For Locke, legitimate government depends entirely on this consent and must act according to the will of the majority for the public good. Importantly, Locke insists that citizens retain the right to resist or overthrow any authority that violates their foundational trust. These principles—consent, equality, the rule of law, and the preservation of rights—form the ideological backbone of modern liberal democracy.[1] In *Fallout*, Vault 33 appears to exemplify many of these Lockean ideals. However, as the narrative unfolds, it becomes clear that these principles have been subtly removed, transforming the vault from a sanctuary of civil society into a controlled experiment in authoritarian design.

"We the Vault Dwellers": Elected and Equal (On Paper)

Vault 33, as depicted in the *Fallout* Amazon series, initially presents itself as a model of post-apocalyptic order—a carefully sustained micro-society where peace, cooperation, and civic virtue prevail beneath the ruins of the world above. Its systems are orderly, and its leadership, at least ostensibly, accountable to its citizens. In contrast to the lawless wasteland, the vault represents stability, reason, and shared purpose—qualities that seem to echo the liberal political ideals of the Enlightenment, particularly those articulated by Locke. With its structured elections, public forums, and concern for the common good, Vault 33 gives the impression of a society built upon the foundational principles of equality, consent, the rule of law, and the preservation of rights.

Locke begins his political theory with the premise that all individuals are naturally equal, "wherein all the Power and Jurisdiction is reciprocal, no one having more than another."[2] Vault 33 reflects this vision of mutual standing through its social and political structures. There are no visible class distinctions, no ruling elite or caste system. Overseers are elected by the community, and policy decisions are discussed in open meetings where all citizens are welcome to speak and be heard. This structure is dramatized in moments of crisis, such as when Lucy MacLean proposes a rescue plan following the abduction of her father, Overseer Hank MacLean, and again when the vault council convenes to decide the fate of captured raiders from Vault 32. Rather than relying on executive decree or hierarchical command, the community turns to open deliberation—a process that reinforces the impression that power in Vault 33 is shared equally among its members.

For Locke, equality is inseparable from the principle of consent. Legitimate government, he argues, arises only when individuals willingly enter into political society, and "no one can be subjected to the Political Power of another, without his own Consent."[3] Vault 33 reinforces this ideal through its most ceremonious civic ritual: *Election Day*. After the loss of Overseer MacLean, a new election is held between three candidates—Betty Pearson, Reg McPhee, and Woody Thomas—amid carefully staged patriotic imagery. Vault residents see images of a sewn flag in a scene evocative of Betsy Ross, campaign posters promote civic identity, and songs like "The Battle Hymn of the Republic" echo through the halls. The election itself becomes a reaffirmation of collective agency and shared governance. While the inner workings of vault politics remain somewhat opaque, the tone of civic life suggests that the residents believe their voices matter—that their leaders derive authority from the consent of the governed. The political culture affirms the idea that the vault is not ruled but chosen.

Casseroles and Compliance in Vault 33

This view of the vault is further supported by what appears to be the rule of law. For Locke, the transition from the state of nature to political society requires the formation of a collective will: individuals "have thereby made that Community one Body, with a Power to Act as one Body, which is only by the will and determination of the majority."[4] Vault 33 operates under this logic. In both major crises—the disappearance of the Overseer and the arrival of the raiders—the community does not devolve into panic or despotism. Citizens convene, debate, and arrive at conclusions together. The council meetings function as scenes of rational deliberation, reinforcing the notion that law in Vault 33 is not arbitrary but participatory. It is not enforced through coercion, but through consensus, echoing Locke's belief that just law arises from shared agreement, not imposition.

The purpose of this civil order, according to Locke, is the preservation of what he broadly defines as "property"—a term encompassing life, liberty, and material well-being. "The great and chief end therefore, of Mens uniting into Commonwealths, and putting themselves under Government," he writes, "is the Preservation of their Property,"[5] and such government must be directed "to no other end, but the Peace, Safety, and public good of the People."[6] Vault 33, sealed off from the irradiated wasteland, appears to fulfill Locke's vision of civil society as a protective institution. It offers its residents consistent food, shelter, education, and community—the basic conditions necessary for peace and preservation. Daily life is stable, safe, and routine. Lucy's apartment in the first episode is especially striking. Decorated with soft pastels, clean lines, and mid-century furnishings, it evokes a sanitized, idealized version of 1950s white, middle-class domesticity. "Isn't it great?" she says. "Every big moment of our lives is gonna happen right here." The space, like the society around it, is designed to feel safe, familiar, and frozen in time—a carefully curated illusion of stability and happiness, where efficient but unobtrusive appliances and bright, modest rooms evoke a world of normalcy, simplicity, and calm. "We have everything, with the hand-me-downs; an icebox, a blender." Everything from the communal dining hall to the school spaces reinforces a sense of secure continuity, as if civilization had been paused just before modern anxieties took hold.

This aesthetic is not incidental; it is part of Vault-Tec's broader ideological project. By reconstructing a culture frozen in the imagined postwar optimism of the American 1950s, Vault 33 presents itself as both morally stable and socially coherent. It mimics the Lockean promise that a well-ordered society can secure not only life and liberty but also a harmonious domestic sphere where individuals flourish free from fear. Residents of Vault 33 are, in this sense, not simply protected from violence—they are shielded from change, dissonance, and disruption. The world outside may be chaotic and fragmented, but inside the vault, life follows a script of order and predictability. It is, at least in form, a rational society—not one that seeks to dominate its citizens, but one that claims to sustain and preserve them.

This dedication to peace and the public good is exemplified in the scene where the council discusses how to handle the captured Vault 32 raiders. While one member, Norm MacLean, suggests execution, the others react with dismay, reaffirming the vault's rejection of cruelty and its belief in rehabilitation over retribution. What follows is an almost comic but deeply revealing debate about reintegration: one resident proposes teaching the raiders Shakespeare to awaken empathy; another suggests grounding them first in moral philosophy, beginning with Immanuel Kant (1724–1804)[7] and John Stuart Mill (1806–1873);[8] yet another recommends starting with math and calculus to instill logical reasoning. Absurd though it may appear, this moment encapsulates the Enlightenment dream, the belief that humanity can be elevated through reason, education, and ethical dialogue. Vault 33, at least on the surface, represents Locke's commonwealth not only as a system of protection but as a moral project: a society dedicated to the cultivation of rational, responsible citizens.

Taken together, the structures, rituals, and civic norms of Vault 33 suggest a community built upon the very ideals that Locke believed necessary for a just society. Its practices of open deliberation, electoral participation, legal consensus, and mutual protection all work in concert to construct the image of a functioning liberal democracy—one that has survived the apocalypse intact. At least for a time, Vault 33 appears to fulfill the Enlightenment promise: that reason, equality, and consent can triumph over violence and chaos, even in a lead-lined world.

Lead-Lined Liberalism: Equality, Now with Extra Supervision

If Vault 33 appears to reflect the political ideals of Locke on the surface, that illusion quickly collapses under scrutiny. What seems to be a democratic society governed by consent, equality, and law is in fact a carefully engineered facade—one that distorts Locke's core principles while preserving their rhetorical trappings. Vault-Tec's system does not fulfill the liberal promise of government by the people; instead, it perverts Enlightenment ideals by transforming them into instruments of surveillance and control. Equality, participation, and deliberation are not emancipatory here—they are mechanisms of compliance within an ongoing human experiment.

Locke insists that political society begins with equality: a "State also of Equality, wherein all the Power and Jurisdiction is reciprocal, no one having more than another."[9] But in Vault 33, this equality is only structural in appearance. The Vault lacks a visible aristocracy, but power is far from reciprocal. Vault-Tec maintains ultimate authority, unseen and unaccountable, orchestrating the system from behind the curtain. The election of Betty Pearson as Overseer—a Vault-Tec administrator promoted under the guise of civic trust—initially seems like a genuine expression of communal will. However, when Norm MacLean gains access to Vault 32's internal database, he discovers the truth: all overseer elections are rigged. The winning candidate in each case originates from Vault 31, and the results are manipulated to create the illusion of popular choice.

Norm's investigation reveals something darker still: Vault 31 houses cryogenically preserved Vault-Tec bureaucrats, prewar technocrats strategically reinserted into positions of leadership in Vaults 32 and 33. This hidden class of "leaders" ensures ideological continuity and administrative control, while residents below believe they live under a self-governing social contract. The myth of shared authority collapses. Norm ultimately learns that even his father, Hank MacLean, was complicit in concealing these truths, participating in the cover-up and submission to Vault-Tec's broader aims. Vault 33's residents believe they are free citizens in a democratic community, but their options are bound by an invisible hierarchy. Power is not shared but simulated, distributed only insofar as it reinforces the parameters of an experiment. Locke's principle of mutual jurisdiction is thus entirely undermined: the vault is not a commonwealth but a lab.

This illusion of equality is inseparable from a corresponding illusion of consent. "No one can be put out of this Estate, and subjected to the Political Power of another, without his own Consent,"[10] Locke writes—making informed agreement the bedrock of a legitimate political society. Yet, Vault 33's residents are unaware of the conditions under which they live. They have not agreed to be test subjects; they do not know the nature of the larger system to which they belong. Consent here is a carefully staged performance, manufactured through omission, ignorance, and ritualized symbolism. The *Election Day* pageantry—with campaign posters, patriotic music, and communal flag sewing—fosters the feeling of legitimacy while disguising the reality that outcomes are already determined. Vault-Tec has preserved the form of Lockean governance only to drain it of content, using ceremony to obscure coercion.

Freedom by Design: Press 1 for Consent, 2 for Compliance

Locke views law as a rational mechanism through which free individuals voluntarily bind themselves to ensure mutual protection. "The only way whereby any one devests himself of his Natural Liberty … is by agreeing with other Men to join and unite into a Community … in a secure Enjoyment of their Properties."[11] Vault 33 appears to function under this logic: residents live by shared rules, deliberate through councils, and resolve crises collectively. But this rule of law, like the elections, is structurally compromised. Norm's discovery of manipulated records is matched by a deeper realization: the laws, councils, and rituals that guide vault life are not created by the people, for the people—they are imposed from above as part of a controlled social simulation.

Each vault group is operated by a different corporation, which is allowed to conduct its own experiment. Vault-Tec has engineered Vaults 31, 32, and 33 as behavioral studies, but they are not a true community. The council's public debates—such as those concerning the captured raiders from Vault 32—may appear democratic, but the terms of discussion are carefully constrained. Outcomes are accepted not because they are freely chosen, but because they have been pre-shaped within a narrative that privileges order, predictability, and data collection. In this context, law ceases to be a covenant of mutual respect. It becomes a tool of manipulation, cloaked in language that evokes the social contract while operating entirely outside its ethical structure.

This manipulation extends even to Locke's ultimate justification for civil society: the preservation of life and property. "Men ... have a right to their Preservation, and consequently to Meat and Drink, and such other things, as Nature affords for their Subsistence."[12] In Vault 33, these basic rights are conditional and provisional. Every aspect of daily life in Vault 33—food rations, education, reproductive roles, and family structures—is subject to institutional oversight and reconfiguration based on experimental needs. The right to preservation, which Locke describes as foundational to civil society, is no longer treated as an entitlement but rather as a reward for compliance.

One striking example is the regulation of relationships and reproduction. To ensure population growth, the vault organizes arranged marriages under the guise of community stability. Lucy's own experience with this system is revealing: her "application" for marriage is framed as a free choice, but it is carefully manipulated to appear consensual while functioning as a mechanism of social control. This practice, staged with the aesthetic trappings of 1950s-style order and family values, reinforces the illusion of a benevolent, rational society while concealing the deeper logic of behavioral engineering. In this framework, life is preserved only to the extent that it generates useful outcomes for Vault-Tec's long-term study. Vault-Tec does not value individuals for their judgment or dignity, only for how they serve the experiment. Locke's vision of civil society as a safeguard for human flourishing collapses under the weight of this manipulation.

This collapse is not merely theoretical; it is vividly dramatized in key moments that expose the full extent of Vault-Tec's betrayal of Enlightenment ideals. Two scenes in particular illustrate how the form of rational governance is preserved while its moral core is undermined. In the very first episode, after the infiltration of Vault 33 by the raiders of Vault 32, the bodies of the dead are dragged into a room marked "Compost." On a practical level, this could be interpreted as a utilitarian solution in a closed ecosystem—efficient, necessary, and aligned with sustainability. Yet the visual framing and tonal cues suggest something colder and more cynical: the reduction of human life to material input, a quiet but chilling echo of *Soylent Green*–style disposability.[13] What might be reasonable in context becomes morally unsettling in presentation, blurring the line between pragmatism and dehumanization.

Later, in the eighth episode, "The Beginning," any lingering ambiguity disappears. Cooper Howard overhears a secret meeting between Vault-Tec and executives from RobCo, West-Tek, Big MT, and others, in which his wife Barb proposes that Vault-Tec initiate the nuclear war itself in order to ensure the success of the vault experiments. Cooper's horror reflects the viewer's: the apocalypse was not merely survived by Vault-Tec—it was orchestrated by them. The world was not destroyed despite their best efforts to preserve humanity, but because of their desire to control its reconstruction. The civil society Locke imagines as a bulwark against chaos has been wholly inverted. Vault-Tec has taken the outward form of Enlightenment ideals and filled it with authoritarian design, preserving structure while erasing moral intent.

Vault 33 thus reveals a chilling irony: Enlightenment liberalism, stripped of transparency and ethical grounding, can be repurposed to sustain authoritarian control under the guise of rational governance. The form of Locke's social contract remains—elections, councils, law, and security—but the spirit is absent. Consent becomes choreography, equality becomes illusion, and law becomes scripted behavior. What appears to be a liberal dream is, in truth, a philosophical parody: an experiment in freedom that offers none.

Fallout from the Enlightenment

Vault 33 offers a compelling case study in political philosophy disguised as science fiction. At first glance, the vault appears to realize John Locke's Enlightenment vision of civil society: a community founded on equality, consent, law, and the preservation of individual rights. Its elected leadership, participatory governance, and shared commitment to public order seem to embody the principles outlined in Locke's *Two Treatises of Government*. But beneath this surface lies a calculated inversion. Vault-Tec has reconstructed the form of Locke's liberal society while systematically undermining its substance. Consent is simulated through deception, rights are conditional upon compliance, and the rule of law serves experimental control rather than civic justice. The vault becomes not a beacon of Enlightenment ideals, but a parody of them—a sealed chamber where liberalism is undermined from within.

What *Fallout* ultimately dramatizes through Vault 33 is the ease with which political ideals can be manipulated when they are stripped of ethical transparency and grounded instead in technocratic authority. Locke's social contract was built on mutual recognition and genuine consent, but in the hands of Vault-Tec, those ideals become tools of containment. The show's satire serves as a philosophical warning: even the most well-intentioned principles can be co-opted into mechanisms of control when reduced to appearance without accountability. In the world of *Fallout*, the Enlightenment dream of rational order survives—but only as a myth carefully engineered to prevent rebellion, suppress truth, and ensure that no one ever truly escapes the vault—until *Reclamation Day!*

Notes

1. This section draws upon material first published in my article, John P. Irish, "Brief Lives: John Locke (1632–1704)," *Philosophy Now: A Magazine of Ideas*. 138 (2020), 36–39.
2. John Locke in Peter Laslett ed., *Two Treatises of Government*, (New York: Cambridge University Press, 1988), 269.
3. Locke, *Two Treatises of Government*, 330.
4. Locke, *Two Treatises of Government*, 331.
5. Locke, *Two Treatises of Government*, 350–351.
6. Locke, *Two Treatises of Government*, 353.
7. Kant was a German Enlightenment philosopher known for his deontological ethical theory, which emphasizes duty, moral law, and the intrinsic worth of rational beings. His principle of the Categorical Imperative holds that actions are morally right if they can be universally willed and if they treat others as ends in themselves, not merely as a means to an end.
8. Mill was a British philosopher and political economist whose ethical theory of utilitarianism evaluates actions based on their consequences. Mill argued that the morally right action is the one that produces the greatest happiness for the greatest number, with an emphasis on intellectual and moral pleasures over mere physical ones.
9. Locke, *Two Treatises of Government*, 269.
10. Locke, *Two Treatises of Government*, 330.
11. Locke, *Two Treatises of Government*, 330–331.
12. Locke, *Two Treatises of Government*, 285.
13. *Soylent Green* (1973) is a dystopian science fiction film loosely based on Harry Harrison's 1966 novel *Make Room! Make Room!*, in which an overpopulated, resource-depleted society turns to radical solutions for survival; the film's infamous twist reveals that the titular food product is made from human remains, symbolizing the commodification and disposability of human life.

10

War Never Changes: Just War Theory in the *Fallout* Universe

Alba Curry and Gerald Lang

"War Never Changes" is a ubiquitous slogan in the *Fallout* world. What does it mean? Obviously enough, the circumstances of war can change, and the fortunes of the protagonists in war can fluctuate. Wars can be won or lost. There are victors and losers. There are differences in the levels of damage and destruction that can be inflicted in war. And wars can be fought for different reasons, with different things at stake.

It isn't difficult to recognize and appreciate substantial differences between the Hundred Years' War and the Vietnam War, or the wars fought by the Spanish Empire and World War I. What exactly do these wars have in common? The sheer *variability* of war makes it difficult to arrive at secure generalizations about it. Even so, there may be common features or underlying facts about our vulnerability to war that are worth thinking about.

Human beings seem prone to war. It is easy enough to imagine circumstances in which large-scale violence breaks out, because of competition for scarce resources and threats posed by rivals for these resources. Perhaps, too, there are deep-lying impulses in human nature toward violence and military confrontation. Particularly vivid pictures of human nature at its most bellicose are painted by the English philosopher Thomas Hobbes (1588–1679) in his book *Leviathan* and by Xunzi 荀子 (310–238 BCE), a "Confucian" philosopher of the Warring States period, in his eponymous book.[1] In this chapter, we'll be looking at their views, as well as some other sources in the Western and Chinese philosophical traditions, for appraising war. These philosophical ideas can be helpful for thinking further about the moral conundrums of the *Fallout* universe, since both China and the United States are its two main original powers.

While not a directly playable faction or heavily represented in person, China is central to the lore and history of the world before the nuclear apocalypse. The Great War of 2077 is a culmination of global tensions and resource wars between these two powers. It is unclear who launches the first nuclear strike, but both the United States and China were involved in the full-scale nuclear exchange that destroyed civilization. Given China's central—but largely unexplored—role in the *Fallout* universe, examining both traditions side by side can illuminate what the games include, overlook, or distort.

"Every Man for Himself": Hobbes, Xunzi, and *Fallout*'s Wasteland

Hobbes's principal aim in *Leviathan* is to explore how political states can acquire political legitimacy over their political subjects. States claim to have authority over us, not merely the power to keep us in line. How do they pull this off? We were not consulted about any of this, after all: we were born into political societies, and it was assumed (normally reliably enough) that we will become meekly obedient subjects when we reach the age of majority. In the episode "The Trap," the Ghoul, having been dragged by the "Sheriffs," questions the legitimacy of the so-called "President," remarking that it is the first time he has heard about him. Who decided that the President was in charge?

What would happen if we were left to our own devices, without political authorities to keep us in line? Short answer: trouble. Lots of trouble. Without any political organization, we would simply act in a self-interested way. We would distrust each other and find it almost impossible to persevere with any stable schemes of cooperation. Hobbes attributes to humankind psychological elements that are hyper-combustible when humans interact with each other. He contends that

> a general inclination of all mankind [is] a perpetual and restless desire of Power after power, that ceaseth only in Death. And the cause of this is not always that a man hopes for a more intensive delight ... but because he cannot assure the power and means to live well, which he hath present, without the acquisition of more.[2]

Human beings are also naturally competitive, and they place an overwhelming priority on acquiring the means of self-preservation. Because these are in short supply, and because we are insatiable in our demands for security, we will tend to regard others as natural sources of competition and threat. We are not prepared to take the chance that others may be friendly rather than hostile. We will kill them just in case, boosting our reputations for prowess and ruthlessness.

In conditions like these, it will be unsurprising that "during the time men live without a common Power to keep them all in awe, they are in that condition which is called Warre; and such a warre, as it is of every man against every man."[3] It will also be unsurprising that, in the state of nature,

> there is no place for Industry; because the fruit thereof is uncertain: and consequently no Culture of the Earth; no Navigation, nor use of the commodities that may be imported by Sea; no commodious Building; no Instruments of moving, and removing such things as require much force; no Knowledge of the face of the Earth; no account of Time; no Arts; no Letters; no Society; and which is worst of all, continual fear, and danger of violent death; and the life of man, solitary, poor, nasty, brutish, and short.[4]

This situation will be worse for everyone than it would be, measured in even narrowly self-interested terms, were we forced to cooperate and keep a lid on some of our immediate self-interested impulses.

Everyone in the Hobbesian story, then, is strongly motivated to leave the state of nature and to enter political society. In the words of the "President," "Somebody's gotta step up and bring some order around here." The details of that Hobbesian transition, which is supposed to involve a form of contract or agreement, need not concern us here. What we need to keep in mind are the tainted origins of political society and the claim that political society has authority over us because it is *better* for us: it prevents us from being trapped in the warlike conditions of the state of nature.

When the advantages of political society disappear and there is no one who enjoys the authority or power to keep us in line, we can expect those tendencies to reassert themselves. Look at what 200 years of no political organization did to America's TV hero, Cooper Howard! And that lack of organization might describe the various conditions in the *Fallout* world. Ordinary political society in the wasteland has been decimated, and the fighting that occurs when the various inhabitants of the vaults venture out unfolds in a neutral, politically uncolonized space. In effect, the inhabitants of *Fallout* have reverted to the state of nature.

For Xunzi, things are not much brighter. Human nature is bad: we are driven by desire and aggression.[5] But, unlike Hobbes, Xunzi's aim is not to legitimize a would-be sovereign or to pretend that political sovereigns can somehow mend or contain all these frailties. His aim, rather, is to legitimize a return to ritual (*li* 禮), righteousness (*yi* 義), and thus moral cultivation. The chief difference between these two thinkers turns on the order of explanation between moral virtue and civil society. For Hobbes, civil society is prior to moral virtue, whereas for Xunzi, moral virtue is prior to civil society.

Xunzi witnessed firsthand that political authority is not much help without a strict moral education. We are born crooked wood, says Xunzi, which must be reshaped to become straight. In other words, ritual is the key technology of civilization. It establishes order through hierarchies that cultivate restraint and deference; it transforms base desires into harmonious social roles; and it provides structure even for warfare, as we will see later:

> Without ritual and righteousness, they will be unruly, chaotic, and not well-ordered. In ancient times, the sage kings saw that because people's nature is bad, they were deviant, dangerous, and not correct, unruly, chaotic, and not well-ordered. Therefore, for their sake, they set up ritual and *yi*, and established proper models and measures.[6]

Xunzi would have likely found some structural similarities between the pre–Great War world of *Fallout* and the competing states seeking dominance through brute force in his own time. Kings and ministers acted from ambition, greed, and hatred. In *Fallout*, too, there is no *li*. No rites. No moral education. The prewar world reflects these various moral absences: states go to nuclear war over resources, ideology, and fear. After the bombs fall, human desires are fully unrestrained: raiders kill for sport, factions vie for power, and people live by cunning and force. Even the vaults parody the very idea of ritual order. They are technocratic experiments in psychological manipulation, not sites of ethical formation. The subjects in the vaults are kept docile through fear and misinformation, not through any honest calculation or understanding of the benefits of political community.

Xunzi famously disagreed with his predecessor Mengzi 孟子 (371–289 BCE), an earlier follower of Confucius (551–479 BCE), who argued that human nature is basically good. Xunzi thinks that Mengzi cannot possibly be right. A stable society can emerge only through sustained education, ritual discipline, and moral cultivation.[7] Mengzi would have a harder time explaining the brutality of the wasteland (let alone the pre–Great War world). A key argument for Xunzi is that resources are finite; there simply cannot be enough for everyone to satisfy their unrestrained desires. This is a recipe for conflict. That is why we need hierarchies that coax us into a state of ethical maturity:

> From what did ritual arise? I say: Humans are born having desires. When they have desires but do not get the objects of their desire, then they cannot but seek some means of satisfaction. If there is no measure or limit to their seeking, then they cannot help but struggle with each other. If they struggle with each other then there will be chaos, and if there is chaos then they will be impoverished. The former kings hated such chaos, and so they established rituals and *yi* in order to divide things among people, to nurture their desires, and to satisfy their seeking. They caused desires never to exhaust material goods, and material goods never to be depleted by desires, so that the two support each other and prosper. This is how ritual arose.[8]

In the *Fallout* wasteland, there are no schools of virtue, no moral exemplars, and no institutions of *li*. Even those who aspire to order—such as the Brotherhood of Steel or the Enclave—do so through authoritarian control, not ethical cultivation. Elder Cleric Quintus does seem to still care about noble values, and laments to Maximus that only the two of them still seem committed to them. However, it is exactly at this moment that he says to Maximus, "power is taken, not given." *Fallout* thus dramatizes what happens when the practices of governance Xunzi valued are destroyed—when desire becomes law, and power rules without righteousness.

At this point, we need to revisit Hobbes. As we saw, the original warring impulses come from unrestrained human nature, together with external circumstances of scarcity and competition. But if sovereigns are also human—and Hobbes certainly thinks that sovereignty can be personified as a specific flesh-and-blood human being—then how can we expect any improvement? One compensation for being in the state of nature is that no one is much more powerful than anyone else. The unappealing properties of aggression and physical threat are at least basically egalitarian in their distribution. Endow any one of us with the trappings of political power, however, and the rest of us are surely exposed to a worry from another English political philosopher: John Locke (1632–1704). Locke worried that, in accepting absolute monarchy as the price of extracting ourselves from the state of nature, "men are so foolish, that they take care to avoid what mischiefs may be done them by *pole-cats*, or *foxes*; but are content, nay, think it safety, to be devoured by *lions*."[9] A second Lockean worry is that, as history amply confirms, political society does not correct tendencies to war. History thoroughly disproves the notion, as Locke sees it, that "absolute power purifies men's blood."[10] Isn't that going to be because our political rulers are just more powerful (and therefore more dangerous) specimens of unreconstructed human nature?

Hobbes's answer to this worry is that sovereigns are governed, like the rest of us, in self-interested ways, but that *their* self-interest demands, in these circumstances, that they govern fairly and non-tyrannically. Ruling fair-mindedly will allow their subjects to see that they are better off under their authority than by taking their chances in the state of nature. Even though Hobbes's official line of argument is that the political subjects of a state contract into political authority and must therefore obey the sovereign, he is also fully aware that they will ignore the contract if the sovereign's own activity places their security at intolerable risk. This might strike us as an unsatisfactory consolation. After all, for sovereigns' self-interest to maintain productive contact with the security interests of each of their subjects, we need to imagine that any flagrant injustice will be punished by a mass rebellion. To avoid such a mass rebellion, the sovereign will have to rule fairly. But this is an extravagant assumption. Sovereigns really just need to ensure that *enough* of their subjects are *sufficiently* secure, *sufficiently* often. Why, then, should those who are made to feel less secure have any reason to put up with their insecurity? Why should they obey the sovereign? The "contract" seems null and void by this point. Political society is not safer for *these* people.

Yet for all this, Xunzi, like Hobbes, believed it is in everyone's rational self-interest—including rulers'—to uphold a stable social and political order. Disorder harms not just the weak but the powerful too. But unlike Hobbes, Xunzi did not think authority could spring from self-interest alone. Political power, for him, had to be undergirded by ritual and righteousness—moral practices that discipline both subjects and rulers. Moral cultivation is not the private concern of a few but the public work of civilization. For Xunzi, then, political and moral order rise and fall together. The problem is that because human nature is bad, we must be forever training our moral muscles. The *Fallout* universe shows us what happens when both collapse—when power is severed from righteousness, and ritual from authority. What remains is not just the absence of government but a return to the state of nature.

"Everyone Wants to Save the World, They Just Disagree on How": Just War Theory in the West and China

The establishment of political societies may have saved us from a war of all against all, but, as we know, they do not save us from war. For war is usually fought between states, or (in civil wars) between groups of people who are vying for political control of the state. Yet, echoes of pre-political state of nature thinking are preserved in philosophical theorizing about war. The international political arena is often regarded, in effect, as an international state of nature, where the relevant parties are states rather than individual human beings. There is no sufficiently powerful over-arching authority to keep everyone in line. International law governing violent conflict is basically composed of a set of rules agreed upon by members of the international community. We cannot expect the content of these laws to get significantly out of alignment with national self-interest, whatever our moral ambitions.

Just War Theory in Western thought has a complex, impure history.[11] It is a patchwork of considerations and rules whose overall purpose was built to govern the relationships between the bodies of citizens in different states. Philosophical theorists of war investigate Just War Theory in the search for unified moral foundations, but it should be emphasized that this is essentially a project of reconstruction. The content of Just War Theory was rolled out in dribs and drabs, to suit whatever warmongers could be coaxed into accepting. Some of it stuck and became more deeply entrenched, while other elements proved more transient.[12]

A case for *some* mutual restrictions on fighting—on how fighting is conducted, and on the kind of reasons for which it is undertaken in the first place—was compelling to all parties, because even if the surest route to military victory in many cases of military conflict was to crush a weaker opponent by any means available, in the greater scheme of things no one was interested in a war of all against all. First, and most obviously, there had to be a division between *combatants* and *non-combatants*. The combatants' function was to fight on behalf of and to protect civilians or non-combatants, while non-combatants abstained from any direct role in the fighting and were protected by combatants.

At a more fine-grained level, there are two main axes or dimensions in Just War Theory, which are usually rendered in their untranslated Latin form. One of them is *jus ad bellum* ("right to war"), and it is concerned with the various conditions that must be satisfied if a side is to have moral permission to go to war. The second dimension is *jus in bello* ("right conduct in war"), and it is concerned with the various conditions that must be satisfied if, having started to fight, a side is to do so permissibly.

Jus ad bellum is composed of several conditions. First and foremost, there must be *just cause*: a side cannot fight permissibly unless it has just cause. This is usually construed as a violation of territorial sovereignty. In *Fallout*, the original catalyst for war was resource scarcity, especially in oil and uranium. China invaded Alaska; the United States retaliated and invaded mainland China. *Fallout* arguably offers a critique of how doctrines of "necessity" are used to justify aggression and an expansion of the notion of "just cause." At the same time, one might suspect that, when national survival is genuinely at stake, the restriction of the usual understanding of a just cause to breaches of territorial security risks being small-minded.

Another *jus ad bellum* condition is *right authority*. In *Fallout*, both the United States and China were run by authoritarian regimes or corrupted democratic systems. By 2077, the United States had effectively become a corporatist autocracy with total control over media and military decisions. This raises questions, in turn, about whether either of these governments had legitimate authority to declare war, or whether the war was driven by corporate and nationalistic self-interest. When governments fall out of alignment with the interests of ordinary citizens, then the right authority condition risks being breached.

A further condition is the *last resort* condition. We should not go to war if a non-violent remedy can be applied instead. The *Fallout* world suggests, by contrast, that war was pursued because diplomatic avenues had been deliberately undermined. Propaganda from both sides portrays its enemy as a monster, making good-faith negotiation politically impossible.

The last significant *jus ad bellum* condition is *proportionality*: the values fought for must be proportionate to the costs inflicted by war. We know that this condition was not fulfilled by the Great War of 2077. This war ended with mutually assured destruction, which was a clear violation of proportionality. Nuclear annihilation cannot be proportionate to *any* political goal. If nothing remains of the society, then no war will have been proportionate to the costs it imposed.

Jus in bello is composed of two principal conditions. The first of these is the *discrimination* condition. The fighting in war should be deliberately aimed only at combatants, not non-combatants. Any war in which civilians are the primary victims risks violating this condition. The wars in *Fallout* clearly breach the discrimination condition, because Vault-Tec's shelters were available to only a fraction of the population. (Leave aside the concern that many vaults were human experimentation sites: the inhabitants were unsafe for other reasons.) And the nuclear exchanges in the Great War clearly obliterated all distinctions.

The second main *jus in bello* condition, as for *jus ad bellum*, is concerned with *proportionality*. The fighting must not come at a cost that is disproportionate to the value of the goals it is intended to achieve. The weapons of mass destruction, which are central to the wars in *Fallout*, once again pretty much guarantee that the *in bello* proportionality condition will be violated. The use of "mini nukes" as regular battlefield weapons shows how normal proportionality constraints have dissolved.

How do *jus ad bellum* and *jus in bello* go together? For some, they are basically independent. A war can be entered into for bad moral reasons, thus earning discredit under *jus ad bellum*, but if it is fought according to the rules of *jus in bello*, then the fighting is permissible. This is what "orthodox" Just War Theory says.[13] More recently, "revisionist" Just War Theory has declared a puzzle about how *jus ad bellum* and *jus in bello* can be kept apart in this way.[14] True, we can imagine a side that has satisfied the *jus ad bellum* tests but fights in impermissible ways, randomly killing citizens and executing prisoners of war. In this sense, *jus ad bellum* and *jus in bello* can come apart. Problems begin when we imagine a side that satisfies *jus in bello* but has already failed the *jus ad bellum* tests. The question for this side can be put as follows: if it has already failed *jus ad bellum*, then it is fighting impermissibly. But if it is fighting impermissibly, then it cannot get to fight permissibly by satisfying the *jus in bello* tests. It is too late for this side to be fighting permissibly. Its moral record may be still worse if it both goes to war impermissibly (having failed *jus ad bellum*) and it *also* fights in ways that flout the *jus in bello* rules. But things are already bad enough, for it should not be fighting *at all*.

Consider the US soldier fighting in Operation Anchorage (as seen in *Fallout 3*'s DLC). In the simulation, you are reenacting the US liberation of Anchorage from the Chinese: you fight in line with military code; you target only enemy combatants. On the surface, you satisfy *jus in bello*. But if the war itself was unjust—fought for imperialist aims, or on false pretenses—then, according to revisionist theory, you are still fighting impermissibly. Your actions, though restrained, contribute to an unjust cause and are therefore impermissible.[15]

What about military ethics in the Chinese tradition? The idea of a "righteous army" (*yi bing* 義兵) emerged from centuries of debate during the Eastern Zhou and especially the Warring States period. Unlike many modern forms of Just War Theory, early Chinese discussions took the existence of war for granted—it was seen as inevitable, even natural. The central question was how war could be justified and who had the moral authority to wage it. Military thinkers such as Sunzi 孫子 (previously transliterated as Sun Tzu; 544–496 BCE) treated war as an essential tool of statecraft, albeit one that should be governed by strategy and restraint. More philosophical traditions, such as those of the Mohists and Mengzi, offered moral critiques. The Mohists argued for strictly defensive wars aimed at protecting the innocent, while Mengzi held that the virtue of a true king would obviate the need for violence altogether.[16]

Against these views, proponents of *yi bing* argued that righteous war was not just permissible, but necessary as the highest form of punishment, used by a moral ruler to suppress large-scale injustice and restore order. These debates took on new urgency as the Warring States period saw the collapse of the old aristocratic chariot-based warfare and the rise of mass infantry armies led by professional officers. Warfare had become more brutal and more impersonal, forcing thinkers to reconsider the ethical grounds for violence.

Xunzi argues that legitimate wars are those conducted under the guidance of a ruler who embodies ritual and righteousness. War must not be driven by our untrained emotions or conquest, but by a commitment to restore harmony. In the world of *Fallout*, where power is wielded without virtue and violence is ubiquitous, such a vision is notably absent.

It is also worth asking whether any figures or factions in *Fallout* even pretend to uphold such ideals. Occasionally, we see gestures toward moral justification, particularly from the New California Republic, which claims to restore law and democratic values. But even the NCR's campaigns are tainted by expansionism, corruption, and bureaucratic self-interest. Caesar's Legion, while cloaking itself in the rhetoric of civilizational renewal and harsh justice, is explicitly modeled on authoritarian brutality, not ethical rule. The Brotherhood of Steel values discipline and hierarchy, but nonetheless pursues power through technological monopolization rather than any broadly shared conception of moral virtue or community.

Nor does *Fallout* present us with a serious postwar legacy of Chinese Just War Theory. While China is symbolically present, through relics like the stealth suit, propaganda, and Captain Zao, there is no meaningful trace of *yi bing*'s ethical ideal. Whatever traditions of morally justified warfare may once have existed in prewar China, they have been annihilated alongside everything else. In this sense, *Fallout*'s world does not simply represent a failure of American sovereignty, but a universal failure of any philosophical effort to constrain war within the bounds of justice.

The Fallout from War

Fallout is a deeply cynical, satirical world built around a history of catastrophic war, and that makes it a fascinating (and tragic) playground for testing the limits and failures of Just War Theory. This chapter has explored the moral and political collapse that defines the *Fallout* universe—a world in which war persists, but all attempts to regulate or justify it have broken down through the lenses of Hobbes and Xunzi. We have seen how war emerges not only from scarcity or strategy, but also from unrestrained human nature. Furthermore, the famous slogan

"War Never Changes" is not a literal claim, but a grim commentary on the constancy of human impulses toward conflict, especially when all notions of Just War fail.

Notes

1. See Thomas Hobbes in R. Tuck ed., *Leviathan*, (Cambridge: Cambridge University Press, 1996), Xunzi, *Xunzi: The Complete Text*, trans. E.L. Hutton (Princeton: Princeton University Press, 2014).
2. Hobbes, *Leviathan*, chap. 11, 70.
3. Hobbes, *Leviathan*, chap. 13, 88.
4. Hobbes, *Leviathan*, chap. 13, 89.
5. Xunzi, *Xunzi*, chap. 23, 248.
6. Xunzi, *Xunzi*, chap. 23, 248–249.
7. Xunzi, *Xunzi*, chap. 23, 249.
8. Xunzi, *Xunzi*, chap. 19, 201.
9. Locke in C.B. Macpherson ed., *Second Treatise of Government*, Vol. §7.93., (Cambridge: Hackett, 1980), 50.
10. Locke, *Second Treatise of Government*, §7.92, 49.
11. For an overview, see Torkel Brekke, ed., *The Ethics of War in Asian Civilizations: A Comparative Perspective*, (London: Routledge, 2006).
12. See Stephen C. Neff, *War and the Law of Nations: A General History*, (Cambridge: Cambridge University Press, 2005), for a comprehensive and fascinating history.
13. Michael Walzer, *Just and Unjust Wars: A Moral Argument with Historical Illustrations* 4th ed., (New York: Basic Books, 2006).
14. For further details, see Helen Frowe, *The Ethics of War and Peace: An Introduction* 3rd ed., (London: Routledge, 2023); Jeff McMahan, *Killing in War* (Oxford: Oxford University Press, 2009); Seth Lazar, "War," in *The Stanford Encyclopedia of Philosophy*, at https://plato.stanford.edu/archives/spr2020/entries/war.
15. *Fallout*'s twist in the Fallout 3 *Operation: Anchorage* DLC is that you are playing a simulation of this war, made for propaganda purposes.
16. Mark E. Lewis, "The Just War in Early China," in Torkel Brekke ed., *The Ethics of War in Asian Civilizations: A Comparative Perspective*, (London: Routledge, 2006), 186.

11

The Brotherhood of Steel: The Politics of Monopolizing Knowledge and Technology

Sergio Urueña

The world ended on Saturday, October 23, 2077. Thermonuclear fire lit up the sky, and in a matter of minutes, the world as we knew it was gone. But if *Fallout* teaches us anything, it's this: when the bombs fell, they didn't just destroy cities; they rewired civilization itself. What was once considered commonplace in the prewar world (for example, purified water, electricity, medicine, digital archives, advanced robotics, artificial intelligence) became almost mythical treasures and therefore highly contested resources. Access to functioning tech meant more than having tools; it conferred power. *Fallout* throws us into a combative, polemical world where the main catalyst for this suffering—namely, the scarcity of oil and the struggle for control over assets during the Resource Wars (2052–2077)—continues to shape the sociopolitical world long after the bombs fell.

Of the many factions clawing their way out of the ashes, none is as fascinating (and, at times, as frustrating) as the Brotherhood of Steel. The Brotherhood's mix of military discipline and techno-religious zeal makes it one of *Fallout*'s most attractive forces. Founded in the Lost Hills bunker by US Army captain Roger Maxson, the Brotherhood emerged from a crisis of conscience. Maxson, disillusioned by prewar scientific overreach, broke ties with the remnants of the US government and vowed to protect humanity's technological legacy.

Initially, the Brotherhood did just that—salvaging, cataloging, even sharing prewar knowledge to help rebuild civilization. But by the time we encounter them in the original *Fallout* game, *Fallout 3*, *New Vegas*, *Fallout 4*, and even in the *Fallout* Amazon series, the Brotherhood's posture has shifted dramatically. To be sure, there are still reformers calling for openness and outreach, but they're often sidelined. The dominant chapters have become isolationist, authoritarian, and obsessed with control. They don't recruit from the wasteland. They don't share tech. They don't help unless it serves their own goals. They just take.

You can see them marching across the ruins in suits of power armor, confiscating energy weapons, hoarding fusion cores, and locking everything away inside their bunkers and airships. Their justification? "We're protecting civilization from itself." And on the surface, it almost makes sense. If irresponsible tech use caused the end of the world, someone should probably make sure it doesn't happen again. But dig just a bit deeper, and it starts to look a lot less like *stewardship* and a lot more like a *monopoly*.

The faction is more concerned with monopolizing knowledge and technology than it is with truly preserving it. Elders decide what gets preserved, who gets access to it, and how it's used. Ordinary Wastelanders are ignored. Super Mutants and ghouls are treated as threats by default. And the Brotherhood rarely stops to ask whether anyone outside their ranks might have wisdom of their own to offer. In the end, their hoarding extends beyond old-world tools; it includes the power these tools confer. They act as if they're serving the greater good, yet they do so in the absence of (and often in opposition to) the very society they claim to protect. Their military and political power depends on this exclusive access to knowledge and technology. Rather than merely preserving civilization's scraps, their grip on knowledge and technology serves to control which futures get to exist and who gains privileged access to them.

This chapter is an investigation into just how the Brotherhood of Steel turns access, knowledge, and technology into a tool of exclusion and domination. *Fallout* gives us a world where information and knowledge are scarce, trust is rare, and technology is often the difference between survival and death. To illustrate how the Brotherhood fits into that world (and how they use knowledge to define who's "in" and who's expendable), we'll use some philosophical backup. We'll draw on contemporary thinkers like Langdon Winner and Andrew Feenberg to unpack how technology is not reducible to its function—it always carries social and political meaning and weight. Miranda Fricker's work on epistemic injustice will reveal what happens when the Brotherhood ignores or erases other forms of knowledge, those held by scavengers, settlers, ghouls, and others trying to survive outside the bunker. Finally, Sheila Jasanoff's concept of co-production will help to explain how the Brotherhood, far from merely preserving knowledge, actively shapes entire social structures through its control.

Ultimately, *Fallout* is more than post-apocalyptic fun or ecological warning. It's also a meditation on who gets to know and who gets access to knowledge and technology. Should humanity's technological future rest in the hands of a self-appointed moral elite? Or can it—messily, imperfectly—be shared or democratized? The politics of distributing or monopolizing knowledge and technology in *Fallout* echo far beyond the wasteland, speaking to struggles we're living through today.

The Brotherhood of Steel: Saving the Past, Stealing the Present, Sealing the Future

Step into any Brotherhood of Steel bunker, and you'll likely see rows of terminals humming faintly, crates of salvaged prewar tech stacked neatly, and guards standing in reverent silence, as if protecting sacred relics. From their power armor to their pseudo-monastic rituals, everything about the Brotherhood projects discipline and devotion. Their official mission sounds noble enough—to preserve the technologies of the past for the good of the future. But if you've spent any time in the wasteland, you know that their mission often masks something far less generous.

Since their debut in the original game, through *Fallout 4*, and in the Amazon series, the Brotherhood has operated less like a public library and more like a classified military archive. Access to their technology demands loyalty, rank, and ideological alignment. Knowledge isn't a shared good—it's a restricted weapon.

Consider *Fallout 3*. Early in the game, you may notice that the Brotherhood has access to advanced medical supplies, high-powered weapons, and even functioning archives. Yet nearby communities like Megaton and Rivet City are left to scrape by. The player walks past locked vaults of withheld resources while the wasteland bleeds. Even more telling is a minor quest involving Scribe Yearling at the Arlington Library. She offers the player 100 bottle caps and 10 XP in exchange for readable prewar green books, rewarding not for their utility, but for their potential knowledge. Books become sacred artifacts, fetishized for what they might reveal.

In the same vein, the Brotherhood appears in *Fallout: New Vegas* as a closed, declining faction obsessed with preserving prewar military artifacts. Side-quests involving HELIOS One or advanced suits highlight their focus not just on technology, but on its symbolic control. If it once belonged to the old world, it now belongs—symbolically and literally—to the Brotherhood. And the *Fallout* writers love to poke fun at this obsession. In the DLC of *Fallout: New Vegas*, *Old World Blues*, players meet a now-iconic character: the Mad Toaster, a deactivated appliance that, once reawakened, maniacally proclaims:

"A toaster is just a death ray with a smaller power supply! As soon as I figure out how to tap into the main reactors, I will burn the world!"

"Soon, pitiful worms! Soon I will rule, and your lives will have their doneness setting turned to ... darkest!"

The Amazon series also echoes this satire. In episode 2, "The Target," Titus, the Brotherhood knight, is brutally attacked and seriously wounded by a yao guai (a mutated bear). Through tears, the knight laments, "Sending me .... Stupid missions!! For remnants that turn out to be ... a fucking toaster! You know what you can do with a fucking toaster oven. Do you have any idea?"

Here, the Brotherhood reveals its most radical tendencies: demanding the recovery of something as trivial as a toaster oven because any scrap of tech might contain knowledge and secrets about the past. Their worldview sacralizes past technology without regard for context or purpose. This obsession has a politics of its own: artifacts—even inactive ones—are used as political assets (assets for power). Contemporary political theorist Langdon Winner, in his classic essay "Do Artifacts Have Politics?" argues that technologies are not neutral tools, but embedded structures of power.[1] Even seemingly harmless objects, like a toaster, can encode explicit or implicit forms of order.

To the Brotherhood, prewar artifacts like green books or dead appliances function as tokens of legitimacy rather than mere relics. Whoever controls them controls the story. Winner's famous example of low overpasses designed to exclude buses (and by extension, low-income communities) applies here: "the technological deck has been stacked long in advance to favor certain social interests, and ... some people were bound to receive a better hand than others."[2] The Brotherhood's relation to knowledge and technology does not revolve exclusively around conservation. They actively reshape the conditions of access, deciding who can use, understand, or even touch the remnants of the past. What initially presents itself as preservation operates, in practice, as a mechanism of selection and control. The past is not merely stored; it is reconfigured, sanctified, and strategically deployed. Through this process, the Brotherhood do more than safeguard history: they delineate its meaning. History, in their hands, becomes a curated foundation for governing the future.

This raises a central question: Can monopolizing knowledge ever be justified in the name of protection? According to the Brotherhood, the answer is yes. *Fallout* suggests otherwise. Across the wasteland, factions like scavengers, medics, mechanics, and independent settlers repurpose old-world technologies not to dominate, but to survive, to heal, and to teach. Their practices reflect a different logic of technological life, one grounded in cooperation and education rather than control. A clear example is the Followers of the Apocalypse, a humanitarian organization founded after the Great War by survivors who believed knowledge and technology should serve to rebuild society. Based in the ruins of the Los Angeles Public Library in the Boneyard (*Fallout*) and later active in the Mojave (*Fallout: New Vegas*), they run clinics, schools, and archives—offering medical aid, education, and technical support to other wasteland communities. Unlike the Brotherhood, their model of knowledge and technology is inclusive, restorative, and rooted in open access, solidarity, and empowerment.

Here, contemporary philosopher Andrew Feenberg provides a crucial framework. In *Transforming Technology: A Critical Theory Revisited*, he argues that technology is neither neutral nor deterministic—it is shaped by social struggles and always open to political reinterpretation. For Feenberg, the key issue is not what technology *is*, but how it is rationalized: authoritarian systems—like the Brotherhood—treat technology as a tool for domination and insulation, while democratic systems—like the Followers—treat it as a means for inclusion and shared agency.[3] The Brotherhood, with its rigid hierarchy and strict gatekeeping, leans heavily into the authoritarian model. Their foundation—"Others aren't ready" or "They wouldn't understand"—echoes an old trope in the politics of knowledge: disqualify others from epistemic authority, then claim to act on their behalf. What presents itself as a paternalistic rationale operates, in the wasteland, as a structured mechanism of exclusion—one that consolidates power by redefining who has access to certain technologies and who gets to know certain information. In *Fallout*, controlling knowledge means orchestrating the frameworks through which the past is interpreted and through which possible futures are either enabled or shut down.

Knowing Who Counts: Epistemic Injustice in the Wasteland

The inhabitants of the wasteland struggle with more than radiation, hunger, and raiders. They also confront a quieter obstacle: the systematic discrediting of their voices, skills, and lived experience. This pattern of who gets heard—and who does not—is baked into the Brotherhood of Steel's very identity. Their legitimacy rests on an unspoken premise: only they can be trusted to know what is best.

To understand the epistemic dimension of this exclusion, the contemporary philosopher Miranda Fricker offers a powerful conceptual toolbox. In her influential book *Epistemic Injustice: Power and the Ethics of Knowing*, she distinguishes two forms of epistemic wrong: testimonial injustice and hermeneutical injustice. Both find unsettling echoes in Brotherhood practices.[4]

According to Fricker, *testimonial injustice* occurs when a speaker's credibility is unjustly deflated because of the identity they inhabit.[5] In the eyes of the Brotherhood, everyone outside their order—settlers, scavengers, community medics, even renegade scientists—is presumed incapable of using technology "responsibly." Their reports of need, their ingenious repairs, and their local expertise are dismissed before they are even heard. The justification: "If we share this tech, you'll misuse it and doom us all." But beneath that rhetoric lies a deeper moral and epistemic arrogance. The Brotherhood casts itself as the sole arbiter of technical rationality, denying others recognition as full epistemic and technologically capable agents.

A vivid example appears in *Fallout 4* in the quest "Blind Betrayal." Paladin Danse—a decorated Brotherhood knight—is revealed to be a synth. Instantly, his exemplary service counts for nothing. The fact of his synthetic biology overrides every testimony about his loyalty or character. The diagnostic device that "proves" he is a synth is not used to deepen moral understanding, but to cancel it. Danse's narrative of self—his memories, motives, friendships—becomes inadmissible in the eyes of the Brotherhood, solely on the basis of his identity. As the game makes clear, the Brotherhood treats synths as ontological threats, not as beings with agency or experience. Their refusal to listen to the synths' stories, their history, or their perspective is a paradigmatic case of testimonial injustice.

Hermeneutical injustice is a more subtle form of injustice. It arises "when a gap in collective interpretive resources puts someone at an unfair disadvantage when it comes to making sense of their social experiences."[6] The issue is not merely one of confusion—it reflects a deeper structural condition shaped by prejudice, ignorance, and asymmetries of power. Sometimes, individuals are unable to fully grasp or articulate what is happening to them because the necessary interpretive tools are either nonexistent or structurally beyond their reach. At other times, they may understand their experience, but those around them—or society at large—lack the conceptual resources to recognize or make sense of it. In both cases, the underlying problem is the same: a structural gap in collective understanding that obstructs meaning-making, either internally or through external misrecognition. Fricker illustrates this with the example of sexual harassment: before the term entered common usage, many women experienced degrading, coercive behavior in the workplace but lacked the language to name it, report it, or understand it as a form of injustice. Their experiences were isolated, individualized, and often internalized as guilt or shame, rather than being recognized as part of a structural violent pattern.[7]

The deprivation of technical artifacts through monopolization, which we explored in the previous section, can also be seen as a form of shaping hermeneutical injustice. Philosopher of technology Don Ihde (1934–2024), in *Technology and the Lifeworld: From Garden to Earth*, argues that technological artifacts mediate our relation to the world through different modes of intentionality.[8] One of these is the hermeneutic mode, when technology acts as an interpretive interface, as a tool that *must be read or decoded to access reality*. A thermometer, for example, doesn't show temperature directly—it provides a reading that must be interpreted to understand the thermal state of the body or environment.[9]

In *Fallout*, when the Brotherhood hoards diagnostic devices, medical consoles, terminals, or even seemingly trivial appliances with hidden functions (like toasters?), it restricts access to the signs through which people understand their world. Wastelanders lose not just tools, but modes of interpretation—technological mediation that enables them to orient themselves. This is epistemic injustice in a material key.

The Brotherhood deepens this injustice by monopolizing not just artifacts, but archives: maps, schematics, medical data, linguistic interfaces. Consider the *Fallout* Amazon series. In episode 2, Brotherhood squads seize locally engineered water-purification rigs from a desert settlement. They do not document the villagers' innovations, nor share maintenance manuals. Stripped of both hardware and technical blueprints, the community loses the conceptual and material means to articulate their needs, protect their systems, or demand restitution. Silence is enforced not only through technical censorship but by depriving people of the very terms in which to understand, speak, and act.

Fricker insists that epistemic injustice is not simply an intellectual error—it is a moral harm. To deny someone's credibility, or to withhold their conceptual means to make sense of their world, is to undermine their agency. *Fallout* dramatizes this again and again: the ghoul gunslinger who hot-wires prerar security turrets is dismissed as a "feral abomination"; the self-taught mechanic in Diamond City is treated as a curiosity, not a colleague. Seen through Fricker's lens, the Brotherhood of Steel is more like an epistemic border patrol than a knightly order. It decides who may know, who may speak, and who may even imagine alternative futures. By showing how easily testimony and meaning can be policed, *Fallout* invites us to imagine other models—horizontal, inclusive, reparative—where memory, know-how, and technical agency circulate rather than calcify.

Technology, Knowledge, and Social Order: The Co-production of Power

Much as Miranda Fricker helps us understand who gets excluded from knowledge in *Fallout*, contemporary scholar Sheila Jasanoff shows us how those exclusions become permanent fixtures of the world. In her work on science and society—especially "The Idiom of Co-production,"[10] "Ordering Knowledge, Ordering Society,"[11] and *Designs on Nature: Science and Democracy in Europe and the United States*[12]—Jasanoff develops the concept of co-production: the idea that scientific knowledge, technical practices, and social order are produced together: "the ways in which we know and represent the world (both nature and society) are inseparable from the ways in which we choose to live in it."[13] In other words, and echoing Langdon Winner, knowledge and technology don't just sit inside society—they help build its orderings.

By deciding what technologies survive, who gets to access them, and under what conditions, the Brotherhood draws the boundary between the "civilized" and the "expendable." Its control over technology and knowledge is not merely functional—it is foundational. As Jasanoff puts it, technoscientific practices are deeply constitutive of social life: "technoscience itself might function as a regulatory device shaping human possibilities; its limits would then have to be clarified and democratically deliberated just like those of any other exercise of state power."[14] In *Fallout*, access goes beyond mere survival—it confers recognition. To use a medical terminal, wear power armor, or access a secured archive is to be granted status, safety, and voice. Access to knowledge and technology becomes a form of citizenship. The Brotherhood aims to decide who gets to know—and by extension, who gets to belong.

This logic isn't only external. It plays out within the Brotherhood itself. The *Fallout* Amazon series shows how recruits like Maximus are trained not just in technical repair but in obedience. Learning to fix a circuit and learning to follow orders become inseparable. The Brotherhood doesn't just teach how to use machines—it trains people to *become* part of one. Even internally, knowledge is stratified. Only high-ranking Elders have access to full archives or experimental schematics. The same epistemic hierarchy the Brotherhood imposes on the wasteland is mirrored within its own ranks—producing a closed, recursive system of control.

That's why its conflict with groups like the Followers of the Apocalypse runs deeper than tactical skirmishes. It's a philosophical clash between two models of co-production of social-knowledge-technological orderings: one centralized, secretive, and exclusionary; the other open, distributed, and communal. In the Followers' vision, the future doesn't belong to those who guard the past—it belongs to those willing to share it. In this sense, *Fallout* urges us not only to question technological ownership ("Who gets the tech?"), but also to confront the deeper issue of the social architectures these machines potentiate and sustain ("What kinds of worlds are being wired through that technology?").

From Steel Valley to Silicon Valley: Technology and Knowledge as Power, There and Here

Beneath its retrofuturist skin, *Fallout* is more than a post-nuclear parable. It's a story about who gets to know, who gets to speak, and who gets to shape the future. The Brotherhood of Steel, with its hoarding of prewar technology, mirrors the gatekeeping logic of modern tech monopolies. Fusion cores there, data centers here. Locked archives in bunkers, locked source code in servers.

The Brotherhood insists its monopoly is necessary. According to its narrative, it is protecting the world from another apocalypse. In our own world, Google, Meta, OpenAI, and others say much the same: advanced technologies must be contained for our own good. But as philosophers like Fricker, Winner, Feenberg, and Jasanoff show us, this is never just about safety—it's about power. As Fricker makes clear, to deny someone's capacity as a knower is to diminish their agency. As Winner argues, technology always carries politics. As Feenberg reminds us, how we rationalize technology determines whether it serves democracy or domination. And for Jasanoff, these dynamics are not accidental—they're co-produced. The social world and the technical world are built together, brick by algorithmic brick.

Fallout dramatizes what happens when that co-production tilts toward hierarchy. The Brotherhood decides who gets to repair, who gets to access, and who gets to belong. Knowledge becomes currency. Ignorance becomes exclusion. Even inside the Brotherhood's ranks, access is tiered. In this way, *Fallout* dramatizes resistance not only on the battlefield, but in the domains of knowledge and technological access. Factions like the Followers of the Apocalypse offer alternative social orderings: shared archives, distributed expertise, and mutual aid. Their vision reminds us that knowledge doesn't have to be monopolized to be powerful—it can be collectively held and critically shared.

Fallout leaves us with no illusions: monopolies of knowledge will always claim moral authority. But it also leaves us with a challenge. If the apocalypse teaches us anything, it's that survival is meaningless without justice. And justice—real justice—requires epistemic and technological equality. The wasteland isn't some distant dystopia. It's just a distorted mirror.

Notes

1. Langdon Winner, "Do Artifacts Have Politics?," *Daedalus* 109 (1980), 121–136.
2. Winner, "Do Artifacts Have Politics?," 125–126.
3. Andrew Feenberg, *Transforming Technology: A Critical Theory Revisited*, (Oxford: Oxford University Press, 2002).
4. Miranda Fricker, *Epistemic Injustice: Power and the Ethics of Knowing*, (Oxford: Oxford University Press, 2007).
5. Fricker, *Epistemic Injustice*, 9–29.
6. Fricker, *Epistemic Injustice*, 1.
7. Fricker, *Epistemic Injustice*, 147–175.
8. Don Ihde, *Technology and the Lifeworld: From Garden to Earth*, (Bloomington: Indiana University Press, 1990).
9. Ihde, *Technology and the Lifeworld*, 80–96.
10. Sheila Jasanoff, "The Idiom of Co-production," in Sheila Jasanoff ed., *States of Knowledge: The Co-production of Science and the Social Order*, (London: Routledge, 2004), 1–12.
11. Sheila Jasanoff, "Ordering Knowledge, Ordering Society," in Jasanoff ed., *States of Knowledge*, 13–45.
12. Sheila Jasanoff, *Designs on Nature: Science and Democracy in Europe and the United States*, (Princeton: Princeton University Press, 2005).
13. Jasanoff, "The Idiom of Co-production," 3.
14. Jasanoff, *Designs on Nature*, 66.

12

Lucy in the Wasteland with Ghouls: The Search for Truth in a Platonic World

Federico Dal Barco

Imagine living in a beautiful house with the people you love. Imagine also that the world outside your home is filled with monsters, mutants, headhunters, ghouls, and mercenaries. Would you stay inside your comfortable nest, or would you go outside in search of adventure and risk? Lucy, the main character of Amazon's *Fallout* series, chooses to leave her vault. Admittedly, Lucy's nest is not maximally comfortable: the vaults have been designed for human survival and do not offer all the amenities of the pre-nuclear world, but compared to the wasteland, they surely provide safety and comfort. With its perilous search for truth, Lucy's quest calls to mind Plato's (428–347 BCE) myth of the cave. As we'll see, both stories feature brave heroes who abandon comfort and break the chains of ignorance to grow on a personal and intellectual level.

Lucy's Journey in the Wasteland

Lucy's adventure starts in Vault 33, where she lives a happy life with her father, Hank MacLean, and her brother Norm. The small society inside Vault 33 lives a simple but rewarding life. They grow their own crops under a fake but inspiring sky, they teach American history to the children, and they occasionally meet the inhabitants of communicating vaults to reproduce and celebrate the survival of the human species, planning to one day repopulate the planet. Little do they know that humans have survived on the surface, inhabiting the harsh reality of the wasteland despite daily radiation exposure.

Lucy's idea of the external world has been manipulated by the owners of her vault. The aim of the vaults, according to what she knows in the first part of the story, is the repopulation of Earth after the atomic war that happened in 2077. Living her daily routine and fully trusting her father, Lucy continues to adhere to the ideals and aims of the vault without questioning the authority of her superiors.

Things change when Hank is kidnapped by Moldaver and her scoundrels. In this moment, Lucy encounters a different reality and starts to question the meaning of her daily life. Here, she finds the motivation to escape the vault: to rescue her father. Despite the reluctance of the survivors of Vault 33 and the difficulty of escaping, she eventually makes it, opening the big door and feeling the warmth of the sun's light on her skin for the first time. This marks the beginning of the second part of Lucy's journey. As she exits her comfortable home, the power of the sun illuminates a new and unknown world. After a brief moment of disorientation, her eyes adjust and she begins to explore the new world.

Lucy lends her bottle of water to the first stranger she comes across, not knowing that water is more valuable than gold in the new world, and she tries to explain the plan of Vault-Tec for saving America to a trader who is only making fun of her. Despite the difficulties and the rampant violence of her new world, she keeps inquiring about the inhabitants of the wasteland until she finds the information she needs to retrieve her father. Exploring this new world, Lucy also learns a great deal about the actual state of humanity, whose future seems doomed to violence and radioactive destruction. The inhabitants of the vaults are a useless dying species, as she learns soon after leaving home, and the urge to ask her father many questions about his relationship with Moldaver grows.

As Lucy faces these challenges, she accidentally finds the entrance to another vault, where a small community keeps living a simple life in the middle of a devastated hospital in the wasteland. She returns to a place similar to the one where she grew up. At first glance, the hidden community appears peaceful, but this time she knows that secrets lie beneath the surface. On this occasion, she is not alone; Maximus is with her and has the chance to experience vault life for the first time. Seeing the quality of life of the people in the hospital vault, Maximus is especially tempted to remain there. Lucy, on the other hand, is more skeptical; she knows that vaults often hide dark secrets and warns Maximus of the dangers of this quiet life.

This represents the third crucial step in Lucy's journey. The hero, after discovering the world outside her original land, has the chance to abandon her journey and return home, safe but also empty-handed. Lucy is too motivated to cease her adventure. Now she needs to find the truth behind her father and the mysterious head she has been carrying. Ready to face the new dangers of the wasteland, Lucy decides to get out of the vault for a second time, marking a fundamental decision in her personal growth.

The last step of her journey is the final reward: the truth. In the concluding episodes of season 1, Lucy and Maximus reach Moldaver's hideout, only to find a harsh reality: Hank MacLean, her father, was one of the orchestrators of the nuclear war that caused the destruction of the old world. On top of this, her mother is now a ghoul.

If we compare these painful revelations to the state Lucy was in at the beginning of the series, we might ask what value Lucy got from her heroic journey. Was it worth it to escape Vault 33 and track down her father among monsters and ghouls, only to discover the awful truth? Wouldn't it have been better to remain in her previous world, comfortable and oblivious?

Lucy's heroic path ultimately leads us to question the value and meaning of such an enterprise. What is the point of sacrificing oneself for the truth? As we'll see, Plato has an answer to this and many other questions coming from *Fallout*.

The Philosopher's Journey

Let's consider the key elements of Plato's myth of the cave. As will be clear, the crucial steps of Plato's description of the philosophical journey mirror Lucy's. Picture yourself chained in a dark cave, unable to move your head.[1] A fire burns some distance behind you, and between that fire and your locked position, people parade shapes that cast shadows on the wall you're forced to face. For as long as you can remember, you and other prisoners have believed these silhouettes to be the only reality. You laugh, cry, name them, and argue about them. Your entire world is an elaborate puppet show. This is the initial part of the myth, where prisoners are ignorant and unaware of a different world beyond the walls of the cave. Here's how Plato puts it:

> Imagine human beings living in an underground, cavelike dwelling, with an entrance a long way up that is open to the light and as wide as the cave itself. They have been there since childhood, with their necks and legs fettered, so that they are fixed in the same place, able to see only in front of them, because their fetter prevents them from turning their heads around. Light is provided by a fire burning far above and behind them. Between the prisoners and the fire, there is an elevated road stretching. Imagine that along this road a low wall has been built—like the screen in front of people that is provided by puppeteers, and above which they show their puppets.[2]

This sounds like Lucy's life inside Vault 33. The first stage of both journeys is characterized by ignorance: the prisoners believe that life is made of shadows, whereas the inhabitants of Vault 33 believe that the only functioning world is inside their safe home. Although the Vault Dwellers are aware that an external world exists (the prisoners in the cave are unaware of its existence), they still don't know what this external world looks like, and all the information they have about it is either fake or manipulated.

Imagine that one of the prisoners is suddenly freed. The escape from the cave is frightening, but the prisoner is intrigued by the discovery of something new. As the prisoner stumbles through the cave's tunnels to escape, he starts to feel the warmth of the sun and gradually gets blinded by its light. Although he is at first tempted to retreat into the comfortable cave, he resists. Slowly, his vision returns: first, shapes, then reflections in water, then trees and sky, and eventually, the sun itself becomes visible. Plato writes:

> What do you think he would say if we told him that what he had seen before was silly nonsense, but that now—because he is a bit closer to what is, and is turned toward things that are more—he sees more correctly?[3]

The outside world is finally accessible, and the truth is revealed (he can see more accurately): the cave visions were only illusory shadows; the sun reveals and illuminates the truth (namely, the real world).

This second step of the escaped prisoner corresponds to Lucy's experience when she escapes Vault 33: the brightness of the sun signals the moment of passage from her old life to a new adventure. Initially, Lucy encounters a hostile environment. Still, she gradually recovers her motivation and acquires the survival skills necessary to stay alive in the wasteland, just like Plato's prisoner.

The discovery of a new and true world is an enlightening experience, but the prisoner feels the need to return to the cave. He would love to stay outside, but he feels a duty to save the other prisoners. The return to the cave is tragic, however. The darkness of his previous nest of falsehood is so deep that his eyes struggle to get accustomed to it. Plato says:

> Now, if he had to compete once again with the perpetual prisoners in recognizing the shadows while his sight was still dim and before his eyes had recovered, and if the time required for readjustment was not short, wouldn't he provoke ridicule? Wouldn't it be said of him that he had returned from his upward journey with his eyes ruined, and that it is not worthwhile even to try to travel upward? And as for anyone who tried to free the prisoners and lead them upward, if they could somehow get their hands on him, wouldn't they kill him?[4]

The other prisoners have a hard time understanding how his experience could be positive. They don't trust the fugitive, and they think that the sun's light damaged him irreparably.

This clash between the prisoner, with his new awareness of the external world, and the ignorant inhabitants of the cave mirrors Lucy's adventure inside the hospital vault. When she finds a reality almost identical to her birthplace, she is confronted with a choice: Maximus tells her that they could live happily inside the new vault, becoming a family and living a comfortable life in the new society. Lucy, however, never changes her mind: she is firmly convinced that her goal is to save her father and then, eventually, to bring Maximus to her original vault. Lucy's urge to go back to her original life is still present, just like the prisoner who wants to save the other prisoners. The return to the original comfort with a new awareness of the external world is a common characteristic between the two narratives (although Lucy still sees the vaults as safe spots). Her awareness of the hypocrisy of these safe homes begins to grow only when she discovers that bizarre scientific experiments are conducted inside each vault.

When Lucy decides to return to the wasteland, she commits to a perilous path, that of the philosopher. Eventually, she will reach the truth. However, the truth can be disappointing: What would you do if you discovered that your father caused an atomic war and that your mother has become a ghoul? Would you continue to seek the truth?

The Myth of the Wasteland

According to Plato, the supreme Good is a sort of divinity; it is the source of all knowledge, science, and freedom for the human mind. In the myth of the cave, the sun symbolizes the Good, which illuminates the truth and makes the real world visible. We could say that the supreme good in Lucy's adventure is the sun illuminating her path through the wasteland.

Plato's explicit goal is to determine which form of government is the best. As he sees it, knowledge of the supreme Good is required for the education of those who will rule and implement the perfect government with justice.

How do we translate this ideal and abstract concept of a supreme Good into action? The journey outside the cave, according to Plato, is a journey of revelation guided by the supreme Good. Enlightened beyond his position of extreme ignorance, the prisoner experiences the world from a neutral perspective and comes as close as one can to the sun's warmth. The prisoner who learns to overcome ignorance and to look at reality from a neutral perspective is, according to Plato, the perfect guide for an ideal Republic. This is because he has become a philosopher who feels a duty to serve the common good.

In Lucy's world, there is no divine-like supreme Good, but nonetheless, Plato's message resonates in *Fallout*. Through her journey from the false reality of Vault 33 through the wasteland, Lucy has become a post-apocalyptic philosopher. Plato describes the good philosopher as "a noble and well brought-up character, perhaps, kept down by exile, who stays true to his nature and remains with philosophy because there is no one to corrupt him."[5] Moreover, he adds:

> doesn't it follow necessarily from what was said before—that uneducated people who have no experience of true reality will never adequately govern a city, and neither will people who have been allowed to spend their whole lives in education. The former fail because they do not have a single goal in life at which all their actions, public and private, inevitably aim; the latter because they would refuse to act, thinking they had emigrated, while still alive, to the Isles of the Blessed.[6]

A good philosopher, namely a person who can lead his or her people toward the just and the true, is noble, true to his or her nature, educated, but also experienced and willing to act. This sounds a lot like Lucy. She has a noble soul, always prone to help others and act for the just cause; she is true to her nature since she does not abandon her aims and convictions throughout the journey. Lucy is a philosopher-hero who acts for the right cause and is motivated by the noble aim of saving her father. Sure, she cuts some heads and kills some monsters on the road, but who could blame her?

Why Have I Left?

We can now consider the fateful question: Was it worth it for Lucy to leave her house and find out the cruel truth about her parents? In Plato's cave, the returning prisoner with his message of truth and liberation is not believed or welcomed. Lucy's experience is similar. Norm and Chet prefer to leave Lucy alone, frightened by the real world. Why leave the vault and remain outside, then?

Seen in light of Plato's perspective, Lucy's decision makes sense because she is a philosopher who can help rebuild a better world. Lucy's initial dream, which we learn while she is still inside Vault 33, is to make her small community prosper so that it can one day repopulate the Earth. When she goes outside and discovers the truth, her plan changes only on the surface. Hidden beneath *Fallout*'s narrative surface lies a tale of a hero who has the potential to restore civilization, even though she may still be unaware of this potential. Lucy suffers greatly during her journey, leaving behind her welcoming community, discovering the harsh truth about her parents, and trying to survive in a hostile world. It is ultimately thanks to Lucy, though, that Moldaver can activate her machine and bring electricity back to the city. The first steps for the construction of a new civilization—one that, this time, is not living through the lies or shadows of a hidden cave—happen because of Lucy's heroic (and philosophical) decision to pursue the truth. So, yes, it was worth it.

Notes

1. In this context, I provide a summary of Plato's myth of the cave. For a detailed account, I suggest reading the entire myth, which is located at the beginning of Book 7 of the *Republic*.
2. Plato, *Republic*, trans. C.D.C. Reeve (Indianapolis: Hackett, 2004), 514a.
3. Plato, *Republic*, 515a.
4. Plato, *Republic*, 517a.
5. Plato, *Republic*, 496a.
6. Plato, *Republic*, 519a.

13

No Mungos! Children and Politics in Little Lamplight

Andrea Conque

In the post-apocalyptic 2277 Washington DC of *Fallout 3*, a number of children grow up in vaults like Vault 101. These children are well cared for and relatively safe, despite the occasional encounter with radroaches or a Tunnel Snakes gang member. Yet, there is another group of children in the game who have managed to survive for over 200 years without the assistance of adults. Eighty-two students originally left the Early Dawn Elementary School in 2077 and soon found themselves trapped within Lamplight Caverns, an old tourist destination before nuclear bombs shook the site.

After their caretakers (or other adults they knew) met sticky ends or mistreated them horribly, the Little Lamplighters decided to create their own society, free from "Mungos" (their term for adults). For Little Lamplighters, Mungos are the ones who caused the world to be such a horrible mess, so Mungos are not to be trusted. In fact, there are only two laws in Little Lamplight: obey the mayor (who can be elected at any time) and leave by your sixteenth birthday (or suffer dire consequences!).

The role of children is rarely, if ever, considered in discourse concerning politics. This chapter, though, will address the many ways in which the children of Little Lamplight are political: they act as effective agents of political socialization—the process by which people's political viewpoints are formed through interaction with family, friends, school, and the media—take on roles of political representation, combat social isolation, create strategies for resisting political oppression, and seem to avoid the usual pitfalls of group conflict concerning limited resources that plague most societies … all without the help of Mungos!

No Mungos!!

Fallout 3 is set in a world in which a Great War between China and the United States ended in worldwide nuclear devastation. The area near what was once Washington DC is now, two centuries later, referred to as the "Capital Wasteland." Many human beings who survived the radiation from the Great War were able to do so because Vault-Tec created bunkers around the country that could withstand nuclear blasts. Of the nearly

400,000 planned Vault-Tec vaults, only 122 were successfully constructed by the day the atomic bombs fell. Most of these vaults, except Vault 101 from which the Lone Wanderer hails (the protagonist and player character of *Fallout 3*), were secret hubs of human experimentation where human beings were exposed to radiation, placed in untenable scenarios with one another, or worse. The children in Lamplight Caverns were protected from the radiation blast (the same as if they were in a vault) and survived to form their own city and government.

Politics was important from the earliest stages of Little Lamplight. Southwest of Paradise Falls, Little Lamplight was once Lamplight Caverns, an old spelunking attraction complete with a mascot—a mole in a mining hat. The entrance to the cavern is filled with signs that reference Mungos, like "NO Mungos!!," and pointing to "Mungo-Land" (outside the cavern itself). Just inside the cavern, the Lone Wanderer meets the first of the Little Lamplighters: foul-mouthed Mayor R.J. (Robert Joseph) MacCready, or "Mayor-Mac," who stands guard. It is from MacCready, other Lamplighters, and four holotapes that we learn both the history and the governmental setup of Little Lamplight.

In the weeks following that fateful day when mushroom clouds were seen outside the entrance to Lamplight Caverns, the grownups seem to have disappeared. Originally, there were Ms. Carrie Delaney, two other teachers, two parents acting as chaperones, and a few members of the cavern staff who survived the bombings. Two holotapes authored by Ms. Delaney deliver the basic facts that 82 fourth graders from Early Dawn Elementary School took a field trip to Lamplight Caverns on the day of the bombs: "We were packing up to leave when everything went crazy."

Two other holotapes, authored a month later, this time by 10-year-old Jason Grant, tell us that the adults have disappeared. Some of the grown-ups have simply died and were buried in the waters of a local underground lake, while others ventured outside and never returned. Grant says of his teacher, who brought his class to Lamplight Caverns, "Delaney went to get help and never came back. The other adults never came back either, so now it's just us kids." Further holotapes reveal that Grant is not scared like the other kids; instead, he thinks they're safe "as long as we don't go outside."

Two months on, the children in Lamplight Caverns are beginning to think that they're truly on their own, but they are hopeful when they discover the entrance to Vault 87, thinking that someone there will be able to help them. Instead, "a guy on the other side [of the door to Vault 87] told us we were dead already." This angers Grant and the other children. "F— those grownups," he complains. "F— them all. We don't need them ever again." This exchange at the door of Vault 87 proves to be a turning point for the Lamplighters.

On January 26, 2077, Grant and the others are three months into their ordeal in the caverns, and they collectively decide two things. First, they will no longer put their lives in the hands of adults or "Mungos." Second, they are better off creating their own, grown-up-free society. One Lamplighter proclaims, "It's way better than it used to be. Who says kids can't take care of themselves? ... A few of the kids have started saying we're like a whole new city. A city of kids. They call it 'Little Lamplight.' It's so cool!"

What is political socialization if not a life-long process in which people understand their government through various experiences, influences, and relationships with others? Under normal, non-apocalyptic circumstances, people are socialized politically through the media, and the beliefs espoused by their families, friends, and institutions like schools. Through exposure to values, attitudes, and beliefs, a person begins to form a picture of what it means to live well in their society, to be a good citizen, and to behave in ways that are accepted by their community.

To be sure, the citizens of Little Lamplight have been socialized politically, mainly in their belief that anyone over the age of 16 is not to be trusted. In fact, the distrust of adults among Little Lamplighters is so ardent that they enforce mandatory banishment for everyone who reaches the age of 16. Each kid in Little Lamplight serves as an agent of political socialization for the others, and two whole centuries after the original group of children was betrayed by adults, MacCready tells us, "People change when they grow up, and we don't trust Mungos living down here. So we leave for a place called Big Town before we get too old."

Distrust of adults has been passed down like a mantra to the resident Lamplighters for 200 years, and they mostly live by this one rule because it's worked to keep them safe, even from the Super Mutants who were created as part of an experiment at their very doorstep. However, Little Lamplighters are also socialized to look out for one another, meet outsiders with sarcastic cynicism, and depend upon one another for everything. These are their political ideals. And as the city of Little Lamplight socializes its citizens to a particular way of thinking about citizenship, it should be of little surprise that they also have a simple but formal governmental structure.

Mayor for Life

MacCready claims that Little Lamplight is "pure anarchy," but that turns out not to be true. There is a discernible political organization in Little Lamplight, just as there is a clear message of political socialization. Although the Lamplighters may not like to admit it, their city is almost as highly organized as any other colony in the Capital Wasteland. And it is certainly better constructed than the nearby Big Town of which Lamplighters like Sticky (who is turning 16 just as the Lone Wanderer enters Little Lamplight) dream. At the very least, Little Lamplight boasts an elected leader.[1]

From the outset, Lamplighters have simply used the popular vote to elect one official—the mayor. Lamplighters, in other words, mainly represent themselves. MacCready describes the process: "It's not that complex. Any kid can say they want to be mayor here. It's just that most kids don't want to bother with the responsibility of leading—most of the time, they last until the kids get tired of them, then they get kicked out on their asses by the new mayor. One only lasted five minutes." He ought to know; the kids have kept him on as mayor for three years, a position which MacCready refers to bluntly as "Mayor for F—ing Life," suggesting that he will likely be mayor until he ages out of the city.[2]

Term limits do not seem to exist in Little Lamplight, but neither do true "terms." Mayors only remain in office until their fellow Lamplighters decide they no longer like their leadership. This is done "so we have a good time while we're here," MacCready explains, "and the occasional ruthless little bastard like me makes sure it doesn't fall apart for the other kids." The city's first mayor, Jason Grant, was also elected by popular vote. A holotape from Jason's time confirms, "All of us voted, in secret, and tomorrow we're going to tell Jason that he's the city's first mayor! He's going to be so happy with us!"

Lore has it that MacCready became mayor after a fellow Lamplighter, Princess, declared herself in charge. When Princess tried to rename the office of "mayor" as "Princess," a 10-year-old MacCready walked up to her and punched her in the face, saying that what the Lamplighters needed was not a princess but a leader. Technically, MacCready's act counts as a political coup, but MacCready was subsequently elected to the position by popular vote, so his position as mayor is politically legitimate according to the electoral traditions of Little Lamplight.

Vault Boy's Big Book of Laughs for Kids

In *Fallout 4*, MacCready appears as an adult after having left Little Lamplight many years before. He reminisces, "Everyone pulled their own weight. Just like a colony you'd find anywhere, we all had our designated jobs, and we watched each other's backs. Can you believe I was actually the mayor for a while? Me? Crazy, I know." Even beyond the mayor, kids in Little Lamplight seem to each have their own responsibilities that help them to combat social isolation, another important aspect of government in a place like Little Lamplight that has little contact with the outside world.

Civic engagement of some sort is usually presented as the antidote to social isolation. For the children of Little Lamplight, isolation is a necessity. So, too, is their level of involvement with their community. It seems to be part of the city's tradition to allow children to take on what would normally be adult roles. This gives them a sense of pride in their community and a purpose, both of which are likely significant factors in the longevity of the city. If Lamplight's citizens feel connected to one another, then they are less likely to feel socially isolated and more likely to take public interest seriously. When the Lone Wanderer happens upon Little Lamplight in 2277, a child named Lucy serves as the city doctor; Joseph educates the other children as their teacher (and barber); Eclair "takes care of the food" and a restaurant called Spelunker's; Knick Knack engages in trade at the general store; and, most interestingly, Knock Knock (Knick Knack's fraternal twin) is in charge of morale or "keeping the peace."

All these positions are important to the political structure and function of Little Lamplight, but Knock Knock's job best combats social isolation. "Technically, I'm patrolling and 'keeping the peace.' Mostly, that involves making sure people are happy and not getting into trouble. You can't very well keep the peace if you've already lost it, see?" Knock Knock accomplishes her assignment by telling corny jokes she gets from *Vault Boy's Big Book of Laughs for Kids*. "Everyone knows them and thinks they're a bit dumb," Knock Knock explains, "but the jokes are comforting and familiar." Lamplighters seem to understand that preventing social isolation is vital to their survival.

Biwwy's Wazer Wifle

Children in Little Lamplight also perform another fundamental political function: that of resisting political oppression from outside forces. Even though they live a stone's throw away from Super Mutants and other dangerous elements, they seem relatively untouched. Sure, sometimes kids on scav teams get taken by slavers, but the city remains safe, secure, and free from adults who might seek to control the Lamplighters' lives. The main way in which Lamplighters avoid political oppression is by ruling and providing for themselves.

Little Lamplighters understand, maybe more than their adult counterparts in *Fallout 3*, how to take care of themselves. Oftentimes, this means that they engage in posturing—looking and talking tough—to get respect from any Mungos they might encounter. Lamplighters are also usually armed. When the Lone Wanderer first appears at the cavern entrance, MacCready threatens to shoot unless he leaves immediately.

In the gameplay, Little Lamplight is important to the Lone Wanderer's larger quest in that it contains the entrance to Vault 87, where a G.E.C.K. (Garden of Eden Creation Kit, a device for terraforming created by Future-Tec/Vault-Tec) can be obtained. The Lone Wanderer must access Murder Pass to get to Vault 87, but entering Little Lamplight is not that easy. Either the Lone Wanderer must use the Child at Heart perk to pass a challenging speech check or complete a lengthy rescue mission involving three Little Lamplighters who have been stolen by slavers in the "Rescue from Paradise" quest to gain MacCready's trust.[3] Even Biwwy, who has been effectively exiled to the Great Chamber in Little Lamplight, has a modified laser rifle he refers to as his "wazer wifle." Biwwy's wazer wifle, however, like many things in Little Lamplight, is an unexpectedly hot commodity. Normal laser rifles effect 25 damage, while Biwwy's boasts 29. Biwwy will give the Lone Wanderer his wazer wifle if they possess the Child at Heart perk. This further shows that kids in Little Lamplight are trained to maintain their safety in isolation from the adult world, not only by acting and talking tough, but by managing to *be* tough. They effectively dissuade most adults from interfering in their affairs and from disrupting their way of life.

Cave Fungus and Conflict

So far, we've explored the specifics of the political system of Little Lamplight: how political socialization is achieved, political representation is accomplished, and isolation is combatted. It remains to be explained how Little Lamplighters successfully avoid conflict over limited resources. Interestingly, Lamplight seems to be a more successful version of Muzafer Sherif and colleagues' classic "Robber's Cave" experiment, which attempted to measure intergroup conflict and cooperation using two cadres of young boys in the mid-1950s.[4] Twenty-two twelve-year-old middle-class Protestant boys from well-to-do families in Oklahoma City were taken in two separate groups (the "Eagles" and the "Rattlers") to Robber's Cave State Park. There, they were observed to perceive themselves as "in-groups" and to be hostile, and even sometimes violent, to the other boys in the "out-group." The experimenters concluded that, when limited resources are involved, the norm is for intergroup conflict to arise. The Robber's Cave boys were only able to resolve their conflict with one another when facing what experimenters called a "superordinate goal." In other words, they were suddenly forced to deal with something, in this case, a water supply shortage purposefully caused by experimenters, that affected both groups and required them to work together to problem-solve.

Comparatively, Little Lamplighters are always working toward their superordinate goal, that of survival. They must consistently make certain that they are safe, fed, and healthy (mentally and physically). Little Lamplighters are the in-group, and their out-group is the Mungos. Conflicts between Lamplighters are rare.[5] This must be due to their surprisingly excellent management of limited resources. In particular, the management of cave fungi is of great importance.

Lamplight's resident doctor, Lucy, understands that the cave fungus that grows there is a precious commodity when it comes to its medicinal aspects. "And way back when, someone figured out that some of the plants and fungus around here absorb radiation. The little ones don't like to eat their veggies, but they don't like to be sick either, so we get by ..." As it happens, the cave fungus of Little Lamplight is the most valuable food source in the entire game. Not only can it help with the removal of radiation from the human body, but it's also dense with nutrients. As Éclair puts it, scav teams will find outside food sometimes, but "most often food comes from fungus that grows in these caves." Cave fungus does not grow anywhere else in the Capital Wasteland, and it is thus rare. Éclair goes on to comment: "They say the fungus grows in the pools where the first Lamplighters dumped the Mungos. That's about the most they ever helped us. I don't know how true that is, but I know sometimes the scav teams come back with this strange meat that tastes terrible, but the fungus love it."[6]

Cave fungus is how the Little Lamplighters have survived for so long; the children have a renewable and dependable food source that also serves to reduce the effects of radiation. Having a dependable food source that keeps them healthy must also be the reason that the Lamplighters have survived politically: they have not had to become aggressive with one another because they share superordinate goals that surpass the need for hostility or violence within their group. Additionally, the rule that says Lamplighters must leave the city at age 16 isn't just a tradition. As MacCready says, there isn't enough "space or food for everyone to stay here forever. So, I've got to exile some to avoid ruining the whole town. It's a f—ing hard brutal choice to make, but that's the way we stay alive."

Keep Our Little Lamplight Caverns Safe and Free

Because of their systems of governance and political socialization, Little Lamplighters enjoy a unique kind of freedom compared to other settlements in the Capital Wasteland and surrounding area. Larger places like Megaton, Andale, and Paradise Falls have a dangerous lack of formal leadership, harbor cannibals, or are led by slavers. The Republic of Dave seems to be the only other *Fallout 3* locale that has any meaningful system of government (besides the overseer of Vault 101) and is certainly the only other example of a democratic society in the Capital Wasteland. Yet, because they mainly stick to themselves, heartily shun outsiders, and have their own anti-rad food supply, Little Lamplighters enjoy the greatest amount of freedom compared to other inhabitants of this post-apocalyptic world.

Joseph, Lamplight's designated schoolteacher, tells the Lone Wanderer, "People don't have the same sort of safety and freedom to run around and play like you can here. They have to work hard for food and safety. Things outside are very dangerous indeed, and that's why we fight so hard to keep our Little Lamplight caverns safe and free." Little Lamplight is often dismissed because it is a city of kids, implying that they are disorganized, weak, and vulnerable. Nothing could be further from the truth. Maybe it's because they *are* children that the Little Lamplighters are not burdened with the problems that arise in adult governments. The lives of these children are better because they run things exactly how they are supposed to—better than the Mungos.

Notes

1. It's interesting to note that the term "mayor" comes from the Latin *maior*, which means the "best," "greater than," or "superior to." In Little Lamplight, only those children whose peers deem them the best, strongest leader will become head of the city. The French *meilleur* means much the same. History's first mayors appeared during the medieval period in Europe and, just like in Little Lamplight, they were usually locals who stepped up to leadership roles within their own communities. The use of the term "mayor" is clearly purposeful here—as opposed to "president," "king," or the like. Lamplight is a city, not a country or state, and its leader is rightly referred to as "mayor."
2. MacCready is the only Little Lamplighter to appear in *Fallout 4*. We never learn the fates of many of the Little Lamplighters as they transition out of the city and into adulthood.
3. Without the speech check and Child at Heart perk, the "Rescue from Paradise Falls" can take up to two hours on average to complete.
4. Muzafer Sherif, O.J. Harvey, B. Jack White, William R. Hood, and Carolyn W. Sherif, *The Robber's Cave Experiment: Intergroup Conflict and Cooperation*, Wesleyan ed. (New York: Harper & Row, 1988). The fact that the experiment originally occurred in the mid-1950s is likely one reason it was chosen by *Fallout* creators. The *Fallout* universe consistently incorporates elements of the American 1950s as part of an alternate timeline for gameplay. Additionally, the experiment refers specifically to a "cave." In real life, the "Robber's Cave" is a state park in Oklahoma where the experiments took place. It is highly possible that these classic experiments were the inspiration for Little Lamplight. Also of interest, the superordinate goal that created cooperation among the Robber's Cave kids was a water supply issue.
5. The altercation between Princess and Mayor Mac seems to be the exception, not the rule, for Little Lamplight.
6. "Strange meat" is, of course, human flesh.

Part 4

MORALITY AT THE END OF THE WORLD

14

Should Chems Be Banned?

Ian McDaniel

Well now, that is a very small drop into a very, very large bucket of drugs.
—The Ghoul

In the *Fallout* games, regular repeated use of chems increases the potential for addiction in which the player's abilities are reduced.[1] To avoid this, there are temporary and permanent means of ending addiction to chems. Taking more of the chem at the onset of withdrawal symptoms will alleviate the penalties for the chem's active duration. Given a sufficient supply of chems, the player character can effectively remain on chems indefinitely with no further negative consequences.[2] Alternatively, the chem addiction can be remedied permanently by visiting a physician or with the right consumable, like the "refreshing beverage" in *Fallout 4* or the "tasty radscorpion egg omelette" in *Fallout 76*.[3] When addictions can be cured immediately for little cost, players who use chems frequently are likely to make regular trips to the nearest wasteland doctor for a cure. For the cost of a little time and a few caps, the player can repeatedly enjoy the instant enhancement of chem use.[4] Thus, the benefits of chem use seem to greatly outweigh the costs.

Starting with *Fallout 3* and continuing through *New Vegas*, *Fallout 4*, and *Fallout 76*, chem addiction can be cured instantly. These instantaneous addiction cures are an obvious disconnect from real-world addiction. The games try to simulate the negative physical aspects of drug addiction and withdrawal, but as players, we are, thankfully, shielded from any actual physical suffering caused by our player characters becoming addicts. Many of us do not even realize our player character has become addicted to a chem until we check the Pip-Boy for something and wonder, "Why is Vault Boy's tongue hanging out of his mouth?" The most serious negative consequence of drug use, the inherent physical suffering of addiction and withdrawal, cannot be adequately replicated when it comes to chem addiction.[5] Thus, the most accurate part of *Fallout's* chem addiction model is that it creates the conditions for a cycle of addiction and recovery that many (possibly most) *Fallout* players routinely put their player characters through.

And I'm Feeling ... Good ...

Never trip alone.

—John Hancock, *Fallout 4*

In the real world, many people take drugs simply for pleasure. However, just as the player is spared from the ill effects of chem addiction and withdrawal by their player character avatar, so too is the player largely separated from any physically pleasurable effects of chem use. The only clear pleasurable effect a player will experience from chem use is the heightened in-game performance of their player character. As such, chems provide pleasure only indirectly. Since players cannot experience the pleasure (or pain) of chem use directly, we must look to representations of pleasure (and pain) connected with chem use by non-player characters. Fortunately, there is one prominent example: *Fallout 4*'s Cait.

Cait's story shows the pleasure motivation for chem use that players cannot properly experience. Cait's motivation for taking the combat chem Psycho was not to improve her fighting abilities, though it surely helped her survive as the headliner of the Combat Zone near Boston Common. Cait's backstory reveals that she killed her parents in response to the horrendous way they mistreated her, and she started using Psycho to numb the pain and escape her guilt and shame.[6] Because the pain of her addiction is greater than the pain of her past, Cait asks the player character for help; she wants to find a cure. Importantly, her desire for a cure shows how painful chem use and addiction can become. The problem for Cait is that her addiction cannot be cured like a player character's addiction; no wasteland physician or a "my wasteland chemistry set cocktail" will solve Cait's problem. Instead, she must be escorted to a particular location, Vault 95, where means to cure Cait's crippling chem addiction can be found.

Cait's story shows that chem use is properly analogous to real-world drug use. Although the player cannot experience chem use in a way that fully parallels the cycle of drug use, addiction, and recovery in the real world, *Fallout's* non-player characters can.

The Harm Principle

It's a free wasteland.

—Veronica Santangelo, *Fallout: New Vegas*

In the real world, many drugs are banned in most jurisdictions. Should chems be banned in the world of *Fallout?* Let's consider John Stuart Mill's (1806–1873) Harm Principle:

> The sole end for which mankind are warranted, individually or collectively, in interfering with the liberty of action of any of their number, is self-protection.

> That the only purpose for which power can be rightfully exercised over any member of a civilised community, against his will, is to prevent harm to others.... In the part which merely concerns himself, his independence is, of right, absolute. Over himself, over his own body and mind, the individual is sovereign.[7]

The Harm Principle sets a limit on individual liberty: a person can act freely so long as their action does not bring harm to another.[8] So, if your drug use only harms you, then you can use any drugs you like. However, if your drug use harms others, then society is obligated to intervene.

In *Fallout*, institutions like the New California Republic and Caesar's Legion have chosen to prohibit the use of many, or in some cases even all, chems. The New California Republic allows some medicinal chems that they deem beneficial and permits doctors in their camps to administer chems for medical purposes. We can, for example, find Dr. Alex Richards in Camp Forlorn Hope administering chems to wounded soldiers, and Richards also makes chems available to the Courier. Additionally, though, the activities of Lt. Carrie Boyd and Ranger Keller show that the New California Republic has a prohibition on other chems, since the pair are investigating what they call "illegal chem trafficking" in and around New Vegas and its suburb, Freeside. As we discover, the punishment for illicit chems can be severe in the New California Republic, including death by firing squad.[9]

Caesar's Legion is more extreme in prohibiting chems, deeming all alcohol and chems detrimental to the human condition. This prohibition extends to non-addictive chems that are clearly beneficial to the user, like the ubiquitous stimpak that improves healing with no known negative side effects. The punishment for chem dealing and chem smuggling in Legion territory is severe. An encounter with the chem smuggler, Anders, crucified by the Legion along the roadside, tells us all we need to know.

Initially, chem use seems to only harm the user. Our player character is the only one suffering any direct harm from their chem use and only if they become addicted.[10] Similarly, chem-using non-player characters we encounter appear to be inflicting direct harm only to themselves. So it looks like Caesar's Legion and the New California Republic violate Mill's Harm Principle.

Some might argue that chems do inflict direct harm upon others, though, especially when taken to enhance combat performance. The increased damage that chems like Buffout and Psycho provide to combat damage deals direct harm to the enemy combatant. One might dismissively point out that it is the projectiles fired from our weapon of choice that are doing the harm, not the chems, but this is too careless, and the objection is worthy of a more thoughtful response. So, let's grant that the chems are doing harm because they specifically increase the damage enemies receive above what the weapon itself would normally do. Thus, there is a direct connection between the drug itself and harm being suffered by the enemy combatants.

Fortunately, the solution to this objection is already stated in the Harm Principle, which begins with the recognition that "the sole end for which mankind are warranted ... in interfering with the liberty ... of any of their number, is self—protection."[11] In violent conflict between individuals, the right of self-protection (self-defense) justifies the use of any means the individual deems necessary to preserve their life against those who threaten it.[12] If this includes the use of chems to boost one's combat abilities and end the threat, then the Harm Principle justifies that behavior. All's fair in love and war and *war, war never changes*. So, the *Fallout* societies cannot prohibit the use of combat chems using Mill's Harm Principle.

The concern now is whether Mill's Harm Principle limits chem use in non-combat scenarios. Consider a scenario in which the player character is using chems to persuade a non-player character to give the player additional information in a dialogue. The player character lacks the necessary Charisma to succeed normally, so they augment their ability score using Grape Mentats (*Fallout 4*) or Party Time Mentats (*New Vegas*). With the bonus, the player character is now able to pass the Charisma or Speech check, and the non-player character reveals the information. In this case, the drug use did alter the non-player character's behavior; the player character would not succeed the check without the chem. However, it's unclear if this harms the non-player character. We would need clear examples of non-player characters being persuaded into doing something clearly harmful to themselves to claim that our player character's chem use harms non-player characters.

The most common problem with trying to find the needed example of a non-player character being persuaded into doing harm to themselves is the myriad motivations and values individuals possess. This is especially true of human beings, by extension, our player character, and to a lesser extent to the non-player characters in *Fallout*. We cannot know what motivates each non-player character. For example, we might see a choice to turn oneself over to the authorities and accept a prison sentence as harmful to the non-player character. On the surface, then, using chems to persuade a non-player character to do so would be using chems to harm the non-player character. But we do not know the non-player character's preferences. We cannot rightly say that the decision to go to prison is harmful to the non-player character any more than we can rightly say the decision to refuse to go to prison is harmful to the non-player character. The non-player character is best placed to decide for themselves which outcome they deem harmful to their well-being. In that respect, non-player characters are just like the player behind the player character avatar, doing the persuading.

When it comes to something like a Charisma check in a dialogue option, Mill's Harm Principle seems to allow chem use. While chem use admittedly allows the player character to reach the requirement needed to pass the skill check, the non-player character is the one who is effectively setting the requirements of the exchange. It is the non-player character's preferences, established in their programming, that allow the player character to be persuasive or not. Meeting the requirement simply means that the necessary inputs have been met to activate the appropriate non-player character preferences. The non-player character then reacts based on their own preferences. Thus, the non-player character is not being harmed by the player character's chem use in these scenarios because the outcome is determined primarily by the non-player character's own preferences. Furthermore, we could repeat this example with different chems and different skills or S.P.E.C.I.A.L. stats, but the outcome would be the same. So, the prohibition of chems in *Fallout* does not seem justified via the Harm Principle. There is no obvious harm being done to others because of individual chem use, even if chems do harm the user.

Paternalism

Mankind will thrive under our guidance.

—The Institute's speech to the Commonwealth, *Fallout 4*

Another possibility for justifying a ban on chems is paternalism, which seeks to limit the freedom of individuals or groups with the goal of promoting those individuals' well-being but without their explicit consent. The complicated matrix of overlapping values and preferences means it can be nearly impossible to convincingly show that infringing on individual liberty is truly promoting a person's well-being. For our player character, prohibiting chem use would seem contrary to promoting their well-being. If a failed Charisma or Speech check leads to gunfire with a room full of non-player characters, the well-being of our player character is better secured by passing the check using the chem. The well-being of non-player characters in similar situations would also be better served by allowing the chems. Yes, the non-player character could become an addict like Cait, but they could also end up dead on the floor. This sometimes happens to Paul Pembroke at the hands of Henry Cooke in the Colonial Taphouse unless the player character intervenes during the *Fallout 4* quest "Diamond City Blues." In this situation, if Pembroke could use some Charisma chems to help him persuade Cooke to leave Pembroke's wife alone, it is conceivable that neither non-player character would die. While there might be some situations where prohibiting chems would clearly promote the well-being of the user, in a world as dangerous and violent as *Fallout*, where the slightest misstep could bring about a swift and violent end, allowing certain chems could actually promote well-being. Other people are best positioned to judge what is best for their own well-being. Therefore, it is best to avoid paternalism as a principle of action in nearly all but the clearest cases.

Chems vs. Drugs: War and Sports

> One team would beat the other team to death with things called Baseball Bats, and the best bats were called Swatters. True fact.
>
> —Moe Cronin, *Fallout 4*

Let's see what our discussion of *Fallout* chems can tell us about using performance-enhancing drugs (PEDs) in our world, starting with soldiers fighting in war. Previously, we justified using chems in combat scenarios, which aligns well with military personnel using combat-enhancing drugs while fighting in a just war. The Harm Principle allows our player character to use chems in combat as a matter of personal choice. In this situation, *Fallout* enemies engage as threats to each other, so self-preservation justifies using the means necessary to preserve one's life, including combat chems. Even paternalism will struggle to justify prohibiting chem use in combat since the plausible consequence of not allowing the chems is the combatant's death. The same arguments should therefore extend to any soldier fighting on the battlefields of our world. Assuming such individuals are engaged in combat against enemy combatants (not innocent non-combatants) and are fighting in a *just* war,[13] the analogy of our *Fallout* player character using combat chems to win a battle seems to justify the use of combat-enhancing drugs by willing soldiers in war.

Now let's consider another slightly less violent application of PEDs: sports. Professional sports incentivize individuals to risk the health problems of PED use to gain the rewards of being among the elite in their chosen sport. However, the Harm Principle would seem to prohibit PEDs in many or most sports.

In physical sports, the stronger, faster opponent can present a physical threat to their opposition. The dilemma for non-PED users is between using PEDs and their associated health risks on the one hand or, on the other, not using PEDs and competing against chemically enhanced competitors who now represent a physical harm potential to the non-PED athlete. The PED-using athlete is like our combat-chem-using player character. The added risk of harm to others from the PEDs is like the added damage from using Psycho, something that is more than what the opponent could do if they did not use the PEDs. The drugs pose a direct threat of harm to the other athletes. In such a situation, the non-PED user is now forced to choose between the health risks of using the PEDs or the health risks of competing against individuals who could do them (serious) bodily harm. Neither is acceptable under the Harm Principle.

There is now a third option, but one that is also a harm—the athlete can quit. Imagine if every non-player character in *Fallout* were like the PED-using athlete, and your player character were forever like the non-PED user. The non-player characters would operate on a much higher level. Your player character would either have to use a chem that could result in actual serious negative consequences for your entire playthrough, or face the serious possibility of having your player character physically injured for a time, possibly having your limbs permanently crippled.[14] You might get frustrated at that point and quit, and who could blame you? And that, my fellow Vault Dweller, Courier, Sole Survivor, would clearly harm you.

Shared Wasteland, Shared Consequences

Now you're not alone.

—*Fallout 76* tagline

The world of *Fallout* distorts our own world while offering a useful mirror for reflection. In that world, chems are abundant, consequences minimal, and the moral terrain is as brutal as the wasteland on survival mode. Using *Fallout's* chems, we see how personal liberty and harm intersect in war and sports. In war, chems (and by analogy PEDs) are survival tools, where the Harm Principle and paternalism bend under the weight of mortal danger. But in sports, where success is based on comparisons, PED use becomes a means of coercion, harming those who would choose otherwise. We can use chems freely in *Fallout* precisely because we are isolated and our playthrough is ours alone. In real life, our choices change the game for other players around us. The games show us the moral boundaries of enhancement and caution us about life lived at the extremes. Even though something is possible, or even advantageous, that alone does not make it just. In the world beyond the wasteland, fairness, well-being, and freedom collide, and unlike in *Fallout*, when we get it wrong, we don't get to reload from a previous save.

Notes

1. Chem addiction is also intended to offer some verisimilitude between chem use in the game and drug use in reality, though later versions of the franchise in particular cut corners on the penalties in the interest of more fun gameplay.
2. Various non-player characters (NPCs) can overdose and die. Paulie in *Fallout 3* and Mama Murphy in *Fallout 4* are two such characters. There are also random encounters throughout the franchise that suggest an NPC died of an overdose of chems. But for the player character overdosing is not a potential consequence.

3. In early games in the franchise, the penalties for becoming addicted were not immediate but there was also no instant cure; players just had to wait out the negative withdrawal effects.
4. Provided the player character does not resume chem use, the cure is permanent. However, given the benefits of use and the relatively low negative costs of addiction players experience and ease of obtaining a cure, most players repeat a cycle of use, addiction, and cure throughout their *Fallout* playthroughs.
5. An even more problematic aspect of chem addiction introduced in *Fallout 4* and continued in *Fallout 76* is the presence of the Junkie legendary weapon effect. This effect can be found on certain legendary weapons and increases the damage the weapon does based on the number of withdrawal symptoms the player character is currently experiencing. This effect essentially rewards the player for having their player character addicted to ever-increasing numbers of chems (up to a maximum of 10 different chem addictions), making chem addiction into a "good" thing for a player character armed with such a weapon.
6. Cait explains that her parents abused her physically and emotionally before selling her into slavery. After five years of further horrors I will not detail here, she took her revenge on her parents with the business end of a shotgun. If her Psycho use, abuse, and addiction had not already begun before that moment, it certainly did afterwards as she tells the story.
7. John Stuart Mill, *On Liberty*, (Oxford: Oxford University Press), 21–22.
8. It is worth noting that Mill recognizes a difference between *harm* and *offense*. Mill does not see mere offense as sufficient justification to limit liberty. Rather, it seems that Mill recognizes that "To constitute a harm, an action must be injurious or set back important interests of particular people, interests in which they have rights." For more on Mill's Harm Principle, see David Brink, "Mill's Moral and Political Philosophy," in *The Stanford Encyclopedia of Philosophy*, at https://plato.stanford.edu/entries/mill-moral-political.
9. One resolution for the quest "Dealing with Contreras" involves the player character providing incriminating evidence of Contreras's drug smuggling operation to Ranger Keller. When asked by the player character about the consequences for Contreras, Keller responds, "He'll be shot. We have no tolerance for chem dealers in the military."
10. Even if the player character does become addicted, it is unclear that this is even truly a proper *harm* according to Mill's principle. Given the ease of chem addiction removal, especially in the later editions of the franchise, chem addiction feels more like a *nuisance* than a proper harm; unwelcome in the moment, but not something truly injurious to the player character.
11. Mill, *On Liberty*, 21.
12. The right to self-defense or self-preservation is a long-standing principle recognized in Just War Theory to justify killing enemy combatants in war. See theorists' discussions of *jus in bello* ("justice in war") for more on the right conduct of combatants in war.
13. Just War Theory recognizes not only just acts in war (*jus in bello*) but also the defining characteristics that make an individual war itself just or unjust (*jus ad bellum*). The discussion here presumes that the requirements for *jus ad*

bellum (the right to go to war) have been met by the combatants and/or those they represent and, as such, the use of drugs in war qualifies as just (*jus in bello*).

14. Consequences that you would seriously have to struggle with and would not be instantly cured at a wasteland doctor or by downing a questionable cocktail you whipped up with your "my first wasteland chemistry set."

15

The Ghoul and the Golden Rule: A Rare Taste of Ethical Riches from the Vault

Benjamin B. DeVan

In episode 3 of Amazon's *Fallout*, intrepid teacher of American history (with a focus on ethics) Lucy MacLean reproaches Cooper Howard, aka "The Ghoul," after he submerges Lucy in a poison river to bait a gulper: "You can't treat people like this!" The Ghoul is incredulous: "Why's that?" Summoning her strength, Lucy shouts with quasi-biblical gusto: "Because of the Golden Rule: Do unto others as you would have done unto you!"

Notwithstanding her persuasive force or lack thereof, Lucy's appeal to, and her later demonstration of the "Golden Rule" to the Ghoul in episode 4, "The Ghouls," connects us to a great line of thinkers. The ancient Greek philosopher Thales (624–546 BCE) articulated it in negative or silver form: "Never doing ourselves what we blame in others."[1] So, too, Master Kong Qui, Confucius (551–479 BCE): "What you do not want done to yourself, do not do to others."[2] And, Siddhartha Gautama, the Buddha (563–483 BCE): "Hurt not others with what pains yourself."[3]

Aristotle (384–322 BCE), like Lucy, put it positively: "As the virtuous are to themselves, so are they to friends, for a friend is another self."[4] We find parallel prescriptions in the Jewish Bible and Talmud, by Jesus of Nazareth, among Muslims, Hindus, and Baruch Spinoza (1632–1677): "The good which a virtuous person seeks for themselves they will desire for all of humanity."[5]

Like moles, philosophers can mine past luminaries for wisdom, using critical thinking as their breathing apparatus to sift fresh air from toxic fumes. Would Lucy best follow the Golden Rule by sacrificing her life as bait for the Ghoul and fodder for the gulper? Is the Golden Rule constrained or invalidated by contrary preferences? Which and whose conflicting wants and needs take priority, and why? In this chapter, I'll argue that slightly qualifying the Golden Rule with "in a similar situation" serves as a handy, multi-jointed "rule of thumb" for moral reasoning and ethical consistency, like Cooper Howard's test for when to run for shelter during a nuclear blast.

Do Unto Others Before and After the Bomb Drops?

As we begin our journey, let's first inquire whether the Golden Rule has any viable competitors, counterfeits, or nuances. Do certain shades or grades contain more carats or karats? Refining and weighing our choices equips us to go for the *purest* gold. By following the lead of another recent philosopher, Harry J. Gensler (1945–2022), we ask just how golden the Golden Rule is, or if the Silver Rule shines brighter in selected lighting, or if rarefied gases like the Sulfur Rule avoid tarnish altogether: "You want others not to stink up your world, do not stink up theirs."[6]

The Ghoul offers one dismissive but easily dismissible substitute: "The wasteland's got its own golden rule, thou shalt get sidetracked by bull … every … time." Ethical *Fallout* fans will resist digging through the nuggets denoted by these ellipses, distinguishing the Ghoul's gold as the cynical fool's gold or pyrite that it is. As a replacement Golden Rule, it glows with duller luster, passively excreting what the ethical equivalent of S.P.E.C.I.A.L. will sniff out.

Are there plausible alternatives? Several abominations corrode or degrade, if not dissolve, practicing the Golden Rule. The Iron Rule is "might makes right," or do to others *before* they do unto you.[7] Thaddeus improvises one alloy by redirecting Aspirant bullies to haze Maximus as a fresher fish. The Arsenic Rule is to do others in, so they won't do you in. This is why the Ghoul shoots Tommy at the lead field. The Neon Rule is to only *appear* to follow the Golden Rule. As the Ghoul taunts Lucy: "There's what people say they did and what they really did." These three downgrades suggest that only the strong survive, kill or be killed, and brazen hypocrisy.

The Bronze Rule is do to others *as they do to you*. This is why the Ghoul slices Lucy's finger. It's the basis, though not necessarily the ideal or starting point, for tit-for-tat in game theory and persistence in fair play. It is intuitive and reciprocal, recalling the Code of Hammurabi, *lex talionis*, and the law of limited retaliation in Leviticus 24:20: "fracture for fracture, eye for eye, tooth for tooth; the injury inflicted is the injury to be suffered."[8]

The Bronze Rule is a cut above torture, or spiraling escalations in war, or going nuclear on all or rival targets. Still, a merely less-than-nuclear option leaves substantial room to advance. As Tevye in *Fiddler on the Roof* and Martin Luther King Jr. (1929–1968) interpreted Mohandas Gandhi (1869–1948), an eye for an eye and a tooth for a tooth leaves all who play this game blind and toothless.[9] Presumably, even the Vault-Tec Edition of the New Testament encourages: "If you do good to those who are good to you, what credit is that to you? Even sinners do that."[10]

Your Thumb or Mine?

How about treating others as *they* want to be treated? This Platinum Rule strides farther along empathy's path than *unreflectively* doing to others what we would like them to do for us.[11] Janey Howard reminds us that her thumb is not the same as her dad's, and by extension, we ought not attach our digital or personal preferences to other humans, to wasteland post-humans, or to anyone else. Let's say I favor Fusion Cola, but you like Nuka-Cherry. Assuming I possess fizz a-plenty, I ought to furnish you with Nuka-Cherry even though I would prefer Fusion Cola. The Platinum Rule prompts us to put ourselves in the other person's boots, unless they are too sharp like Dane's, or too small like Bert's. We may discover, moreover, however we measure, that Lucy's sensible shoes tread closest to one size fits all.

If we switch our metal foot to the Platinum Rule, we find that it is inclined to slips that Immanuel Kant (1724–1804) projected for the literal, unqualified Golden Rule: "On this principle, the criminal might argue against the judge who punishes him, and so on."[12] Treating others as *they* want to be treated, without qualification, would lead to the government acquitting the guilty without penalty if it ignored otherwise disposed stakeholders or indisposed victims. It would force Lucy to surrender to the Ghoul and/or to the gulper, or to whomever presented her with their Platinum card, so long as Lucy lived. As Gottfried Wilhelm Leibniz (1646–1716) complained, such privileged petitioners would receive "more than their share."[13]

Yielding to unreasonable cravings can be unhealthy, if not radioactive! Vault Dwellers would cave in to lethal raids, and anyone outside would Vault-Tec acquiesce to annihilation. A naive Platinum Rule indulges unsavory tastes like those of a fiend or a ghoul who, after fishing, cuts bait to eat a fella, even if other nourishing provisions are available. Is there, in truth, more toothsome fare?

You're a Good Person for not Shooting Me with That Gun!

One might suppose that it's easier to discern the Silver Rule, how humans and post-humans do *not* want to be treated, than how they *do* want to be treated. Besides the masochistic or suicidal, few aspire to trade a tooth for a two-second radio repair, or to be left to rot in T-60 power armor, or to be killed for 1000 bottle caps, or to forfeit their community's energy after losing their fusion core, or to die to feed "people who eat people."

To top it off, the price for the Golden Rule at first glance tends to trade steeper than the Silver Rule. Do not pilfer your knight's armor, and do not marry your cousin, require less effort than binding the injured, campaigning in elections, educating raiders about Shakespeare, Kant, and Mill, or delivering sanity-saving vials to semi-disposed ghouls. Complicating our concerns are *opportunity costs* and *competing moral obligations* in a world of haves and have-nots, where so little is left to have. By assisting one person or group or faction, we conceivably forego assisting another person or group in a corresponding fashion. If I have access to one fusion core, I can power a T-60, or power Vault 4, or power neither, but I cannot power both.

On the other hand, "do all the good I can" is arguably at least as important as minimizing harm.[14] When we wield the proper perception, position, and power, we ought to pump or pour clean water for those who thirst, and set Super Duper Mart captives free, unless they are feral and attempt to devour their rescuers. The Golden Rule *situationally* illustrates how many of us would yearn to be treated if we were parched or left to rot in a strip-mall refrigerator.

By thinking critically, we can determine that to pit the Golden Rule against the Silver is a distraction or red herring (like a Red Death or a Shine Fish), as well as a false dilemma or false dichotomy. Gold and Silver are frequently flip sides of the same cap by casting complementary actions in positive and negative terms. If you want others to honor your life (Golden), then do not kill them (Silver), except in self-defense or to save other threatened lives. If you do not want others to lie to you (Silver), then be authentic with them (Golden). Valuing people's property (Golden) involves not stealing, or swindling, or wasting their wealth (Silver). The positive Golden Rule can simplify a negative, or a double-negative Silver Rule. The Silver Rule reframes the positive Golden Rule. The key to applying the Golden Rule in its positive and negative vocabularies is *consistency*. If you do not want your faction to famish when another has bounteous foodstuff, share your spare vittles with parties who need them. As St. Francis of Assisi (1181/82–1226) was first known to qualify: "Blessed is the person who supports a neighbor in weakness as that person would want to be supported *in a similar situation*."[15]

Who could object? Besides the Ghoul, Sigmund Freud (1856–1939) and Friedrich Nietzsche (1844–1900). Freud believed that the Golden Rule was psychologically "impossible to fulfill," and yet people practice the Golden Rule regularly, even if simultaneously attending to their own predilections.[16] Even if people can't perform the Golden Rule without mixed motives, or *perfectly*, or to accomplish comprehensive immediate change, it may still be a worthy ethic: "I am only one, but still I am one. I cannot do everything, but still I can do something; And because I cannot do everything, I will not refuse to do the something that I can do."[17]

Nietzsche dissents from a different direction: "It is IMMORAL to say that 'what is right for one is proper for another.'"[18] Envisioning another's situation as relevant *partly* parries Nietzsche, but Nietzsche is not deterred: "To refrain mutually from injury, from violence, from exploitation, and put one's will on a par with that of others: this may result in … DENIAL of life … life itself is ESSENTIALLY appropriation, injury, conquest of the strange and weak, suppression, severity."[19] As per Wilzig, for Lucy to survive as a Vault Dweller, she must act like a surface dweller. Does the Golden Rule survive this egoistic Law of the Jungle?[20]

Multiplying Motivations for the Golden Rule

Rationales for the Golden Rule mingle elements of self-interested egoism, social contract, conscience, psychology, virtue, duty, faith, and utility. Let's sample the theoretical smorgasbord. Treating others as you want to be treated benefits the egoist by anticipating role reversals like Lucy and the Ghoul. Cooperating in groups or societies stabilizes our long-term prospects by linking them with others. *Enlightened* egoism or self-interest recognizes that relationships help us to navigate the shifting (Shady?) Sands of Fate, Fortune, or Karma. To adapt Thomas Hobbes (1588–1679), who approved of the Golden Rule, life without it tends to be "solitary, poor, nasty, brutish, and short."[21] Even an egotistical ghoul, to see this, need not cut off his nose to spite his face.

Jean-Jacques Rousseau (1712–1778) argued that even egoists will shoulder a less guilty conscience by adopting the Golden Rule. (How can you live like this?) "When an expansive soul makes me identify myself with my fellow, and I feel that I am, so to speak, in him, it is in order not to suffer that I do not want him to suffer. I am interested in him for love of myself, and nature leads me to desire my well-being."[22] Voltaire (1695–1778) also ventured: "Treat others as you would be treated. This law is from nature itself: it cannot be torn from the heart."[23] From Voltaire's heart to Wilzig's head, the Golden Rule relieves cognitive dissonance and psychological pressure.

Along with Aristotle, Mengzi (Master Meng or Mencius, 372–289 BCE) appealed to practicing the Golden Rule to build character.[24] One reason to practice it is to become a better person. Al-Ghazali (1058–1111) added hyperbolically: "Were all people only to renounce the things they dislike in others, they would not need anyone to discipline them."[25]

The Golden Rule may also motivate a *duty* "to better this fallen world." Aristotle's faithful heir, Thomas Aquinas (1225–1274), coupled the Golden Rule to the New Testament's second greatest commandment: "Love your neighbor as yourself."[26] Furthermore, it might be reasoned that God will treat *us* as *we* treat *others*, even if this incorporates God loving us while we are still sinners, like Lucy saving the Ghoul to show him a more excellent way.[27]

How Does That Golden Rule Jibe with What's Going Through Your Head Right Now?

An idealistic or ideal observer informed by St. Francis's *similar situation* clause could insist that the Golden Rule respects everyone we encounter. This is all creatures for the Sufi, Ibn Arabi (1165–1240).[28] For the Jains of India, it is all beings.[29] Aldous Huxley (1894–1962) fetches the Golden Rule down to earth for all "living creatures and the planet."[30] This, in *Fallout*, could apply to the *situation* of any synth that feels, a mutant, or a dog. St. Augustine (354–430) inverts the letter order of the latter by urging that since we want *God* to love us, we, by the Golden Rule, ought to love God.[31] Or, we ought to love God as we would want to be loved if we were God.

For David Hume (1711–1776), the Golden Rule naturally applies to those who are "brought near to us and represented in lively colors."[32] Is such partiality perverse? Vault-Tec Sales emphasizes family over others, but aside from Overseer Hank's prioritizing Lucy versus other Vault Dwellers, exercising the Golden Rule first toward our family does not by itself force us to treat outsiders poorly. Nor is partiality a problem if we affirm that others can be partial *in similar situations*. Here we tip our hats to John Rawls (1921–2002), who offers a useful tool for thinking about the social contract, which we can adapt and apply to the Golden Rule by imagining ourselves in divergent circumstances.

Rawls argued that we ought to reason ethically as though we are ignorant of our stake in any dilemma, and of our place in any society in which we subsist.[33] Thinking this way maximizes justice for the vulnerable, the powerful, and everyone. Parents are ethical if they try to save their child's life over a stranger's, so long as they esteem other parents doing so under similar conditions. Lucy rightly fights for her life, extending the same expectation to the Ghoul or the gulper, overriding their voracious appetites or schemes. We support our faction, or our nation, and allow others to support theirs. If we vote for Betty, Woody, or Reg, we follow the Golden Rule to all parties by conceding to whoever receives the most *legitimate* votes. I root, root, root for my home team. If others win, it's a shame, but it does not destabilize the Golden Rule if all consent to compete.

We Can Judge a Person and a Society by How They Treat Their Enemy

Applying the similar situation clause of the Golden Rule to family, friends, nations, neighbors, and ambiguous strangers, whether they are AI (you might as well be holding an air conditioner hostage), animals (he ain't mine), humans, post-humans, the planet, and God, glosses glosses the Golden Rule with a splendid sheen. Are we to demonstrate comparable largesse to adversaries, enemies, or hostiles? Freud wrote that without exception, "it is the same thing."[34] The Ghoul protested: "It makes sense if a man hurts me, I don't want to do him any favors."

In contrast to the Ghoul, Vault 33's Council counseled rehabilitating raiders and integrating them into the vault society. Norman MacLean and

Steph Harper counter-proposed to execute the raiders. Who is right? Each has their advantages. Simply letting the raiders off the hook without discipline or rehabilitation offends justice. Passively submitting to the raiders (not the same as principled pacifism, or Gandhi or Martin Luther King Jr.'s nonviolent resistance) is societal suicide. If the raiders resist reconciliation, what can the vaulties do? Assuming they have the resources (they don't), proportional containment is one avenue for the Golden Rule; banishing is another. Obviously, someone will carry the supplies to the surface for you.

Seneca (4 BCE–65 CE) tempered vengeance with introspection: "We should put ourselves in the place of the person we're angry with: from that perspective we see that an unfair valuation of ourselves makes us angry, and that we don't want to suffer an act that we'd willingly commit."[35] The *Tao Te Ching* tells us to take the initiative: "To those who are good (to me), I am good, and to those who are not good (to me), I am also good."[36] The Qur'an, Surah 41:34 reads: "Repel evil with what is better and your enemy will become as close as an old and valued friend."[37] Charles Darwin (1809–1892) signaled that sympathy, reason, instruction, and "the love or fear of God" assist in applying the Golden Rule to adversaries.[38] These attitudes are powerful and empowering. Looking beyond ourselves via the Golden Rule to transform those who are hostile to us is best conducted not from a position of appeasement or capitulation, but resourceful confidence. Lucy embodies the third when she saves the Ghoul.

Emotional ideas like this call for the strong stuff. For Lucy's literary context, does the following sound familiar, slightly adjusting the *Fallout* narrative? A ghoul was traveling on the road from Santa Monica to Griffith Observatory when he collapsed, though it was not until later that he fell into the hands of robbers. A knight from the Brotherhood of Steel passed him by on the other side. Then, a New California Republic official also passed by on the other side. Finally, one of the Ghoul's victims, an antagonist, took pity on the Ghoul. Pouring vials upon him, she set him straight with medicine for healing. If an innkeeper like Yefim Bobrov had been present, and more vials were needed, we surmise that she would have offered the Ghoul additional vials if necessary, if she had sufficient vials when she returned that way.

Which journeyer fulfilled the Golden Rule? "I suppose it was the one who had mercy on him."[39] In opposition to Vault-Tec's global reversal of this ethic on a colossal scale, may we go and do likewise. After all, the original meaning of Bethesda in Hebrew is "house of mercy."

Notes

1. Thales, *Testimonia*, part 1: Person (P), at https://www.loebclassics.com/view/thalesperson/2016/pb_LCL525.227.xml.
2. Confucius, *Analects*, 15:23, at https://www.gutenberg.org/ebooks/3330.
3. *Dhammapada,* 5:18, at https://archive.org/details/in.ernet.dli.2015.283948.

4. Aristotle, *Nicomachean Ethics*, book IX, chap. IX, at https://classics.mit.edu/Aristotle/nicomachaen.9.ix.html, modified for gender inclusivity.
5. Baruch Spinoza, *Ethics*, part 4, proposition XXXVII, at https://www.gutenberg.org/ebooks/3800, modified for gender inclusivity; Leviticus 19:18; Matthew 7:12; *Babylonian Talmud: Tractate Shabbath*, folio 31a, at https://halakhah.com/shabbath/shabbath_31.html; *Mahabharata*, book XIII, section XLIII, at https://sacred-texts.com/hin/m13/m13b078.htm; and *Sahih al-Bukhari*, vol. 1, book 2, number 12, at www.iium.edu.my/deed/hadith/bukhari/002_sbt.html.
6. Harry J. Gensler, *Ethics and the Golden Rule*, (New York: Routledge, 2013), 185, outlines Sulfur, Iron, Arsenic, Neon, Bronze, and other rules
7. Compare Plato, *Republic*, book I, section 338c, at https://www.gutenberg.org/files/1497/1497-h/1497-h.htm; Thucydides, *A History of the Peloponnesian War*, book 5, chap. XVII, at https://www.gutenberg.org/files/7142/7142-h/7142-h.htm.
8. The Bible, *New Revised Standard Version Updated Edition* (NRSVue).
9. Norman Jewison, dir., *Fiddler on the Roof*, United Artists, 1971 (at 2:40:14–24); Martin Luther King Jr., "Nonviolence and the Crisis We Face," address delivered at the Fifth Annual Gandhi Memorial Lecture at Howard University (November 6, 1963). See also https://quoteinvestigator.com/2010/12/27/eye-for-eye-blind.
10. Luke 6:33, The Bible, *New International Version* (NIV). The Holy Bible Vault-Tec Edition appears in show promo, "Follow Your No's!" Amazon Prime, 1:52–2:07.
11. "Platinum Rule" referenced in Milton J. Bennett, "Overcoming the Golden Rule: Sympathy and Empathy," in Dan Nimmo ed., *Communication Yearbook 3: An Annual Review Published by The International Communication Association*, (New Brunswick, NJ: Transaction Publishers, 1979), 406–422. https://doi.org/10.1080/23808985.1979.11923774
12. Immanuel Kant, *Fundamental Principles of the Metaphysic of Morals*, (Halle, Germany: University Press, 1785), section 2, at https://www.gutenberg.org/cache/epub/5682/pg5682.txt
13. Gottfried Wilhelm Leibniz, *New Essays on Human Understanding* (Cambridge: Cambridge University Press, 1996), book I91–92.
14. John Wesley, "The New Birth," IV.4 (1760), at https://wesley.nnu.edu/john-wesley/the-sermons-of-john-wesley-1872-edition/sermon-45-the-new-birth.
15. Italics added and adjusted for gender inclusivity, from Regis J. Armstrong, J.A. Wayne Hellman, and William J. Short, *Francis of Assisi: Early Documents, Volume 1*, (New York: New City Press, 1999), 134.
16. Spelling modernized from Sigmund Freud, *Civilization and Its Discontents* (London: Hogarth Press, 1930), 143, https://www.sas.upenn.edu/~cavitch/pdf-library/Freud_SE_Civ_and_Dis_complete.pdf.
17. In a quote referencing a book title suitable for Vault 4's library: Edward Everett Hale in Edwin Osgood Grover, *The Book of Good Cheer: A Book of Cheery Thoughts*, (Chicago: P.F. Volland, 1909), 28.
18. Friedrich Nietzsche, *Beyond Good and Evil*, VII: 221, https://www.gutenberg.org/files/4363/4363-h/4363-h.htm#link2HCH0007.
19. Nietzsche, *Beyond Good and Evil*, IX: 259.
20. Rudyard Kipling, *The Jungle Book*, (London: MacMillan, 1894), passim, at https://www.gutenberg.org/files/236/236-h/236-h.htm

21. Thomas Hobbes, *Leviathan*, (London: Andrew Crooke, 1651). chaps. XIII and XIV, at https://www.gutenberg.org/cache/epub/3207/pg3207-images.html.
22. Jean-Jacques Rousseau, *Emile or On Education, book IV*, trans. Allan Boom, (New York: Basic Books, 1979), 235. at https://commons.princeton.edu/eng574-s23/wp-content/uploads/sites/348/2023/02/Rousseau-Emile-excerpts.pdf
23. Voltaire, *Remarques pour servir de Supplément à l'Essai sur les mœurs and l'esprit des nations*,17° (Remarque: Des lois, Paris: Garnier, 1963), II: 935–936. Referenced by Oliver du Roy, "The Golden Rule as the Law of Nature," in Jacob Neusner and Bruce Chilton eds., *The Golden Rule: The Ethics of Reciprocity in World Religions* (New York: Continuum, 2008), 94.
24. Mencius, *Mencius*, rev. ed. (New York: Penguin, 2003), book VII, part B, 146.
25. Al-Ghazali, *On Disciplining the Soul*, book 22.7 (1095), at https://www.emaanlibrary.com/wp-content/uploads/2018/12/Al-ghazaliOnDisciplingTheSoulAndBreakingTheTwoDesires.pdf.
26. Reiterated in Leviticus 19:18; Matthew 22:39; Mark 12:31; Luke 10:27; Romans 13:9; Galatians 5:14; Thomas Aquinas, *Summa Theologica*, I–II, Q. 99, art. 1 (compare Q. 94, art. 4), at https://www.gutenberg.org/ebooks/17897.
27. Compare, e.g., Matthew 5:3–46, 6:1–33, 7:11, 18:21–35; Romans 5:1–21, 1 John 4:19.
28. Ibn al-Arabi, *Kunhi ma la brudhu lil-murid,* in Arthur Jeffery, *Reader on Islam* ('s-Gravenhage: Mouton, 1962), 647; Neusner and Chilton, *The Golden Rule*, 107.
29. Jaina Sutras, Sutrakritanga, II.I.48, at https://sacred-texts.com/jai/sbe45/sbe4565.htm.
30. Aldous Huxley, *Literature and Science*, (New York: Harper & Row, 1963), 109.
31. Augustine, *On the Sermon on the Mount, book* 2 (393–396), Vol. 22., 75–76. at https://www.newadvent.org/fathers/1601.htm
32. David Hume, *A Treatise of Human Nature* (London: Longman, 1740), III.II.I, at https://www.gutenberg.org/files/4705/4705-h/4705-h.htm#link2H_4_0088.
33. John Rawls, "*A Theory of Justice*, rev. ed.," in *especially but not limited to I.3–4*, Vol. III., (Cambridge, MA: Harvard University Press, 1999), 22–24.
34. Freud, *Civilization and Its Discontents*, 110.
35. Seneca, *To Novatus on Anger: Book 3, Book 5:12(3) of the Dialogues*, at https://ia804605.us.archive.org/33/items/seneca-on-anger-kaster/Seneca%20-%20%27%27On%20Anger%27%27%20%5Bkaster%5D.pdf.
36. Parentheses in original, see https://classics.mit.edu/Lao/taote.2.ii.html, 49.2.
37. The Qur'an, https://www.emaanlibrary.com/wp-content/uploads/2018/01/Quran_trans_Abdel-Haleem.pdf.
38. Charles Darwin, *The Descent of Man* 2nd ed., (London: John Murray, 1874), I:4, fn 262, at https://psychclassics.yorku.ca/Darwin/Descent/descent4.htm.
39. This retelling of Luke 10:25–37 makes more sense if readers are aware that Judeans (Jews) and Samaritans in the ancient Near East were enemies. For some other biblical examples, compare Exodus 23:4–5; 1 Samuel 24, 26; 1 Kings 5, 6; cf. 2 Samuel 14, 20; Proverbs 25:21; Isaiah 2:4; Jeremiah 29:7; Jonah 3; Micah 4:3; Matthew 5:44; Luke 6:27–28; Romans 12:20.

16

You Gotta Stand for Something: Ethical Reasoning in *Fallout 4*

Armond Boudreaux

"War never changes," says the Sole Survivor of *Fallout 4*—to which I might add, "And that's because human nature doesn't change." That said, human nature expresses itself differently as circumstances change. Certain aspects of our nature—our willingness to commit violence in order to survive, for example—might be heightened in one situation, while in others they are subdued or suppressed. But no aspect of our nature ever disappears entirely.

One of the most important aspects of human nature is morality, our inherent sense of how we ought to behave. It is true that we don't always agree on all the rules of morality, but we've always had notions of *ought* and *ought not*. And while the word "morality" might conjure up objective moral codes like the Ten Commandments or the Golden Rule, humans have a variety of ways of reasoning morally. You might say that those different ways of thinking about morality are the tools we can use to determine what we ought to do in any given situation. When *Fallout 4* players reach the Battle of Bunker Hill, should they support the Railroad? The Brotherhood of Steel? The Institute? Different ethical "tools" can yield different answers to the question.

While these different ways of reasoning about morality are deeply instinctual, over the centuries, philosophers, ethicists, and theologians have formalized largely habitual patterns of thought into schools of ethics. Each school is complete with its own heavyweight philosophers—Aristotle, Thomas Aquinas, Immanuel Kant, and Jeremy Bentham, just to name a few—and each has its own distinctive framework for addressing ethical questions.

Though there are no academic philosophers in *Fallout 4*, we can see various systems of ethics at work in different characters and factions throughout the Commonwealth. When the Sole Survivor meets Preston Garvey at the Museum of Freedom, Garvey describes the Minutemen as "people coming together to protect each other at a moment's notice." Though he probably doesn't realize it, here, Garvey is reasoning ethically in a particular way—one that emphasizes being a certain kind of person. Likewise, when Father describes the work of the Institute, he does so in terms that privilege good outcomes over good deeds: "It is my hope that you'll see that the Institute's mission is a better future. A future worth fighting for." These two philosophies are both ethical, but they each result in very different approaches to human life. Garvey is willing to sacrifice himself if necessary in order to do right by people. Father is willing to sacrifice others in order to achieve the "better future" that he imagines the Institute can bring about. Most people won't sympathize with Father's goals, but even if we view him as a villain and Garvey as a hero, both are equally guided by ethics.

To make matters more complicated, most people unconsciously use multiple ethical philosophies in their everyday lives, effortlessly shifting from one way of reasoning to another without realizing it. In *Fallout 4*, this is often evident in the Sole Survivor's choices (and therefore in the choices of the player). Throughout the game, the dialogue options offer the player different ways of ethically responding to non-player-character interactions. Some responses are based in compassion, selflessness, or loyalty. Others are based in more pragmatic thinking: *How will this advance the story? How will this move me closer to completing this mission? What good will come of this response as opposed to the other options?* Other dialogue options involve a moral principle or duty, as when the Sole Survivor has to choose whether or not to sell Billy Peabody to Bullet as a slave during the "Kid in a Fridge" side-quest. Still others are based in a sense of what seems naturally right and wrong, for example, when the Sole Survivor may choose to defend the dignity of synths because he or she believes that they are persons.

We see these different, often wildly divergent ways of doing ethics at work in everyone. You would be hard-pressed to find someone who doesn't use each of the schools of ethics even in a single day, but nobody—except perhaps for an especially consistent philosopher—says to herself, "I am now going to apply Kantian deontological ethics to this situation so that I can know the right thing to do." It's only when we turn to the philosophers that we have names for the schools of ethics.

"You Don't Just Survive Out Here. You Become Something Better ..."

One of the oldest ways of thinking about ethics focuses on the idea of virtue; this school of thought is called *virtue ethics*. Virtues are those qualities that enable a person to achieve *eudaimonia*, which is a Greek word that could be translated as "happiness," "blessedness," or "flourishing." The idea of virtue ethics is that the most virtuous person is the one who is best equipped to live a life of excellence and happiness. But as

Aristotle (384–322 BCE) says, these virtues aren't inherent, and we aren't born with them:

> From this it is also plain that none of the moral virtues arises in us by nature; for nothing that exists by nature can form a habit contrary to its nature.[1]

According to virtue ethics, then, being a good person comes down to the habits that you have learned from good examples and good teaching and then cultivated over a long time so that they become part of your personality. Only then will they lead a person to *eudaimonia*.

Though philosophers from Plato (428–347 BCE) to Alasdair MacIntyre (1929–2025) have described forms of virtue ethics, Aristotle is its most famous proponent. In the *Nicomachean Ethics*, he defines virtues as the mean point between two related vices. For example, courage is a virtue because it is situated in the middle of a spectrum between recklessness and cowardice. We can see this in the way the Sole Survivor might respond to Preston Garvey's calls for help in defending settlements against attack. He could charge recklessly into an attack by Super Mutants and die. He could also choose not to defend the settlement at all, instead sneaking around and stealing loot where he can and then leaving. Or he could make preparations and defend the settlers against the attack. Each of these responses exists on the same spectrum, but the first two (which are the extreme ends of the spectrum) are vices that do not lead to a life of excellence. Only the middle course—courage—is the virtuous one.

The game gives players other opportunities to practice virtue ethics, as well. For example, as the Sole Survivor roams the Commonwealth, he or she frequently comes across various forms of addictive drugs—alcohol, Buffout, Jet, Mentats, and others—that can provide temporary benefits like increased strength or intelligence but come at the cost of addiction. The virtue of temperance—self-control, the ability to tell oneself *no*—is the virtue that enables someone to avoid two vices: over-indulgence or insensitivity (which Aristotle defined as an insufficient appreciation for certain physical pleasures, the opposite of over-indulgence). So just as someone who enjoys whiskey can drink it temperately, a *Fallout 4* player *can* make it through the game by using chems temperately—only when fighting a Legendary enemy, for example—and avoiding using them excessively in order to make every fight or task easy.

Many other Aristotelian virtues come up in *Fallout 4*, as well. Throughout the game, players have the opportunity to practice the habits of justice (like helping the Railroad free synths in order to grant them fair treatment as sentient beings), magnanimity (like rebuilding settlements with the Minutemen to generously aid struggling communities), prudence (like choosing dialogue to peacefully resolve conflicts with faction leaders), and others. After all, it ain't easy navigating the post-apocalyptic landscape of the Commonwealth with its numerous dangers and various competing factions. Practicing the virtues can help to determine the best path through the darkness.

"There's a Line You Don't Cross, No Matter Who's Giving the Orders"

While good habits are a solid foundation for moral excellence, sometimes people still need rules and a clear sense of duty in order to follow the right course of action. Even prudence, one of the most important of the virtues, is the ability to choose wisely between competing rules and duties. For example, during the "Human Error" side-quest, the Sole Survivor has to use prudence in deciding whether or not to free the synth Amelia Stockton from the Covenant. The decision involves weighing two different possible obligations or duties: justice for Amelia and respect for Covenant's mission to protect humans from synth infiltration. In this case, prudence itself isn't the moral choice. All prudence can do is tell the Sole Survivor what his duty is (or possible duties are) in this circumstance.

This brings us to *deontological* ethics, which is a moral framework that judges the rightness of an action based on adherence to universal rules or duties. The most famous defender of deontology was the German philosopher Immanuel Kant (1724–1804), who wrote in his book *Groundwork of the Metaphysics of Morals*,

> there is, therefore, only a single categorical imperative and it is this: act only in accordance with that maxim through which you can at the same time will that it become a universal law.[2]

What Kant asks us to do in applying the Categorical Imperative test is to consider whether or not a *maxim*—the principle behind any given action we might take—could be universalized as a moral law without leading to a contradiction. So, for example, let's say that I, playing as the Sole Survivor, leave Sanctuary on a dangerous mission without bringing ammo. So, I decided to stop in Concord and steal some ammo from the settlers. It's a good place for it. I'm more likely to get away with stealing the ammo in Concord than I am in a place like, say, Diamond City with all of its guards.

The Categorical Imperative asks me to test my *maxim*—in this case, that would be "I will steal ammo when I need it"—by *universalizing* it, by turning it into a universal moral law for everyone in all times and places. Can I say, "People should steal ammo when they need it"? Putting it this way exposes a problem with my maxim. If stealing were made a universal rule, then no one could own anything at all. Since "theft" by definition assumes that property and ownership are real, making theft a universal rule would result in a contradiction, which means that the maxim cannot be universalized.

A further example from the game will show how the Categorical Imperative test can help us to decide between two competing maxims. Think about one of the most important moral choices that the Sole Survivor faces. During the Battle of Bunker Hill, when the Sole Survivor has been sent by the Institute to retrieve four escaped synths who are being sheltered by Bunker Hill residents, he has the option of warning Railroad leadership about the upcoming attack by the Institute. This choice involves a conflict between two maxims. On the one hand, the Sole Survivor might feel a duty to follow Father's instructions to retrieve the synths, since the instructions came with an implied expectation of loyalty to the Institute and its mission. On the other hand, if the Sole Survivor believes that synths are persons with rights, then he will probably feel an obligation to side with the Railroad and warn them of the upcoming attack by the Institute. This dilemma results in two contradictory maxims: "I will help the synths and warn the Railroad," and "I will withhold information and remain loyal to Father and the Institute." Since the two maxims are in conflict with one another, there's no way for the Sole Survivor to obey both. The only option is to choose between the two.

In order to decide which maxim must win out, deontological ethics would ask which one can be universalized without contradiction. Universalizing the first one—"I will help the synths and warn the Railroad"—seems to pass Kant's test. If everyone shared information to protect autonomous beings—that is, beings who make moral choices for themselves[3]—that would support respect for persons (assuming that synths *are* people). The second maxim, though—"I will withhold information and remain loyal to Father and the Institute"—seems to clearly fail. If everyone kept secrets for loyalty all the time, trust would collapse; nobody could rely on anyone, even within the Institute. Worse, if synths are persons, loyalty to the Institute means treating synths as tools, contradicting their right to autonomy and violating Kant's famous statement that we must always treat persons as ends in themselves and never as "merely as a means."[4]

Of course, the choice of whether or not to help the Railroad also comes down to a question of fact: *Are* synths persons, as the Railroad views them, or are they nothing more than scientific assets, as the Institute claims? If they are persons, then the right moral choice seems to be helping the Railroad. If they aren't, then maybe the Institute has it right.[5] This, of course, mirrors real-world moral issues like abortion, IVF, cloning, and similar issues where the central question has to do with personhood.

"Some Things Are Just Wrong, No Matter How You Dress 'Em Up'"

Where rules-based ethics are concerned, Kantian deontology isn't the only game in town—or in the Commonwealth, as it were. Other philosophers have argued that we can use reason to discover the rules of morality, but rather than use Kant's Categorical Imperative, we can look at the nature of things for clues.

Natural law ethics, most closely associated with the medieval philosopher and theologian Thomas Aquinas (1225–1274), can trace its origins at least as far back as the ancient Greeks, especially to Aristotle. In the *Rhetoric*,[6] Aristotle describes a "law of nature," and in works like the *Physics*, he says that all of existence can be explained by four *causes* (perhaps best understood as *reasons*). These *causes* explain the existence of every object in the universe, the philosopher thought, and one of those causes was the *teleological* cause—the final cause, the purpose of a thing. For example, the *telos* of power armor is to enhance the strength and durability of a soldier. The *telos* of a settlement workbench is to facilitate community building and resource management. The *telos* of a Pip-Boy is to manage information and aid survival in hostile environments. And so on. Aristotle believed that everything that exists has a purpose, a role that it was meant to play in this world.

Now, what does all this have to do with ethics? Thomas Aquinas, who adapted much of Aristotle's philosophy into his own, developed Aristotle's "law of nature" and the four causes into a full-fledged ethical system called *natural law ethics*. For Aquinas, we can use reason to discern the moral law by examining human nature's natural inclinations—toward life, reproduction, knowledge, social harmony, happiness—and paying special attention to the *telos* of things.[7] For example, the *telos* of the human mind seems to be discovery and knowledge. Well, that has implications for morality. It means that lying is wrong, for instance, because lying thwarts the purpose of the mind. Likewise, the *telos* of the human body is life and health, which means poisoning someone in order to steal ammo—*But I really need 5mm for my minigun so I can defeat the Deathclaw that has been causing me problems!*—is wrong because doing so selfishly destroys something with a good purpose.

In many ways, natural law is the most elegantly simple ethical system. It's intuitive and easy to understand. But in *Fallout 4*, things get a little complicated when we try to decide what natural law ethics would say about synths.

From the perspective of natural law ethics, synths present interesting problems. What might a natural law philosopher like Thomas Aquinas say about synths? While he never contemplated the idea of sentient artificial beings, he does say that natural law implies clear rules about how humans reproduce. Our nature is to reproduce by sexual intercourse, so anything that thwarts or distorts that *telos* is contrary to the natural order. This is one of the reasons why natural law philosophers (as well as religions like Catholicism and some Protestant denominations) oppose in vitro fertilization: because it separates the creation of new people from the natural process of reproduction. Does the artificial creation of synths also violate that natural law? After all, synths are not human, but they are (probably) rights-bearing persons, and they're made in the image of ... well, *us*. So, arguably, their creation violates natural law by bypassing the natural order of things.

But natural law also demands that all persons, regardless of how they were born, be treated with the respect and dignity owed to all people. This is why, even though a natural law ethicist might say that IVF is morally unacceptable (for several reasons, one of which is that it bypasses the natural process of reproduction), she would also say that children produced by IVF have all the dignity and rights of a child who is the product of sexual intercourse.

In this case, what might natural law theory say about the synths themselves? As we saw in the discussion of Kant's deontological ethics, this partly depends on whether or not we agree that synths are actually persons. But some evidence from the game suggests that they are—for example, the behavior of four synths who hide from the Institute in Bunker Hill—so for the sake of argument, let's say that they are, in fact, persons. In that case, natural law might say that the act of creating synths was contrary to the natural order, but those synths who exist must be treated with the same dignity and respect as other persons. Would that lead a natural law ethicist to oppose the actions of the Institute (especially in creating the synths) and also side with the Railroad, which is totally committed to the personhood and rights of synths?

The implications of these questions go beyond the fictional landscape of *Fallout 4*, too. After all, we seem to be rapidly approaching a world in which cloning, gene editing, and AI raise all sorts of ethical questions that are eerily similar to those posed by *Fallout 4*'s synths.

"The Institute's Work Is for the Greater Good"

So far, all of the ethical schools that we've considered focus on either people's moral character or on the rules that they should follow. But there is another way of doing ethics that thinks primarily about the *results* of our actions: *consequentialism*, the most famous and influential form of which is called *utilitarianism*.

Though consequentialism goes back a long way, utilitarianism traces its origins to the English philosopher and social reformer Jeremy Bentham (1747–1832). Bentham proposed his utilitarian theory of ethics in *Principles of Morals and Legislation*, where he argued that the right course of action was the one that produced the greatest happiness for the greatest number of people. Determining the right course of action amounted to a kind of calculus, one that was based on signals that we have in our own nature:

> Nature has placed mankind under the governance of two sovereign masters, pain and pleasure. It is for them alone to point out what we ought to do, as well as to determine what we shall do.[8]

For Bentham, pleasure and pain exist to tell us what is good and bad for us. In that case, we ought to listen. This means that the right course of action is whatever maximizes pleasure and minimizes pain. This technically makes Bentham a *hedonist*, someone who believes that pleasure is the highest good, but he wasn't a hedonist in the pejorative sense of that term. He wasn't self-indulgent and pleasure-seeking without regard for the good of others. Rather, he believed that a good society would maximize pleasure for the greatest possible number of people.

Well, it's hard to imagine maximizing pleasure in the irradiated world of *Fallout*, but the point of utilitarianism is to act in a way that brings about the greatest *possible* good for the greatest *possible* number of people. We don't necessarily have to imagine a perfect future in which everyone has comfortable lives.

However, there is a clear example of a faction that embraces utilitarian ethics in the Commonwealth—one that *does* imagine a future that is as close to perfection as possible: the Institute.

The most secretive of *Fallout 4*'s factions, the Institute is the technologically advanced remnant of the prewar Commonwealth Institute of Technology. It survived the Great War by moving underground, where it continued its work on cutting-edge technologies, most notably on synthetic humans. Their leader—Shaun, the Sole Survivor's son, now known as "Father"—believes that the work of the Institute, especially the development of synths, serves humanity. For the Institute, the purpose of the synths is fourfold: one, to serve as a highly adaptive labor force, performing tasks ranging from manual labor up to more complex work; two, to serve as a platform for experiments in bioengineering, artificial intelligence, and other technologies that will enable the Institute to enhance humanity; three, infiltration and control of the surface world; and four, to help foster stability and order.

Even though pretty much everybody will view the Institute as villains, most of these purposes have something like good intentions behind them. It is good to have a stable, dependable workforce. Science has usually worked to improve the quality of human life. And stability and order are undeniably good things. Even rights and freedoms are impossible for most people in the absence of a stable and ordered society.

However, even with all of those caveats and nuances in mind, we have to acknowledge that the Institute views the synths as servants or slaves whose sole purpose is to serve the needs of their masters. This view isn't a new one. At least since human beings stopped being hunter-gatherers and started farming on a large scale (if not before), they have been exploiting and enslaving one another. No culture on earth is innocent of it. And as uncomfortable and unpleasant as this is, most of the things that we value in the world today were made possible at least partly by the exploitation of others. Science, art, music, literature, developments in political thought, even philosophy—these things were possible because some people in the past had the leisure to pursue them, and this was made possible in part by institutions like slavery, feudalism, and caste systems.

Of course, none of that justifies the exploitation of others—far from it—but it does mean that the Institute's treatment of synths is not at all unique to its scientists. They're not cackling villains looking for ways to hurt people because they enjoy it. Even worse, it's important to see that Father and the rest of the Institute believe that they are *morally right* in creating the synths, in using them as a labor force that can free scientists and intellectuals to work for the benefit of humanity.

You might ask, *How could they possibly believe that they are morally right in their treatment of synths?* After all, we've already seen three schools of ethics that are likely to conclude that the Institute is morally indefensible. This is where utilitarianism can have something to say.

If the true measure of the morally correct course of action is what utilitarians call *utility*—the likelihood that the action will produce the greatest good (meaning *happiness*) for the greatest number of people—then the Institute might be perfectly justified in its goals. "The Institute is humanity's best hope for the future," Father tells the Sole Survivor. "Without our work, the Commonwealth would spiral into darkness." The Institute believes that they are the last bastion of science in the post-apocalyptic world. They are convinced that if *they* don't preserve the best of human knowledge, no one will, and this will result in greater misery for the people who remain after the Great War. In Father's view, the work of the Institute will ultimately lead to the reemergence of civilization, which will obviously mean greater happiness for humanity as a whole.

Conclusion: "You Gotta Decide What Path You're Gonna Take"

It might be frustrating to look at each of these ethical schools and wonder which is the surest guide to living morally—and the feeling might get even worse when you realize that there are other ethical systems besides virtue ethics, deontology, natural law, and utilitarianism. This chapter hasn't even touched on more recent schools of ethics like existentialism, contractualism, pragmatism, or relativism.[9] With so many systems to choose from, how is a survivor of a nuclear war supposed to know what to do?!

Fortunately, most people don't approach right and wrong by first choosing an ethical school to follow consistently. As I said at the beginning of this chapter, human nature seems to have come preloaded with certain instincts that are the basis of each of these moral systems. We all have at least a rudimentary sense of what makes a person good, what moral rules shouldn't be violated, what is contrary to the natural order, and basic fairness. And we all navigate our lives calling on each of those instincts as they serve our needs or the situation.

You might think of the philosophical schools of ethics as advanced levels on the perk chart in *Fallout 4*. In the game, you spend your level-up points to hone your skills and enhance your abilities in areas like strength, intelligence, and charisma. Philosophy has done something similar with our moral instincts by systematically describing ethics and formalizing them into schools. It doesn't necessarily make any of us better people because Aristotle, Aquinas, Kant, and Bentham have done this for us, but being aware of the ethical schools they founded might make it easier to navigate an irradiated post-apocalyptic landscape—should the need ever arise.

Notes

1. Aristotle in Jonathan Barnes ed., *The Complete Works of Aristotle: The Revised Oxford Translation*, (Princeton: Princeton University Press, 1984), 1103a. *Nicomachean Ethics*, trans. W.D. Ross,
2. Immanuel Kant, *Groundwork of the Metaphysics of Morals*, trans. Mary Gregor, Vol. 4., (Cambridge: Cambridge University Press, 1998), 421.
3. *Autonomous* comes from the Greek αὐτο- (*auto-*, "self-") + νόμος (*nómos*, "law").
4. Kant, *Groundwork*, 4:429.
5. It seems clear that Kant would say that the synths are persons. See, for example, his discussion of personhood in *Groundwork* (4:428–429), which makes clear that personhood is a matter of rational agency rather than biology.
6. Aristotle in Jonathan Barnes ed., *The Complete Works of Aristotle*, Vol. 1., (Princeton: Princeton University Press, 1984), 1373b2–1373b5.*Rhetoric,* trans. W. Rhys Roberts and ed. W.D. Ross
7. Thomas Aquinas, *Summa Theologica*, trans. Fathers of the English Dominican Province, (Benziger Bros, 1947).
8. Jeremy Bentham, *An Introduction to the Principles of Morals and Legislation*, (Mineola, NY: Dover Publications, 2007), 1.
9. I've not discussed these schools partly because each of them (with the possible exception of relativism) could be analyzed as forms of either virtue ethics, deontological ethics, natural law ethics, or utilitarianism.

17

Sanitizing the Apocalypse: Moral Extremes in *Fallout*'s Simulated Wasteland

Kenneth R. Pike

Today, the *Fallout* franchise boasts titles on a dozen gaming platforms, spanning multiple genres and inspiring one of the best-reviewed film/television adaptations in video game history. But for two weeks in 1997, its inaugural entry was conditionally canceled by Interplay Productions. The concern was substantially moral: Steve Jackson Games, whose tabletop role-playing game "Generic Universal Role Playing System" (GURPS) was the mechanical heart of the project, did not want its intellectual property associated with the level of violence portrayed in the wastes. Interplay gave Christopher Taylor and Timothy Cain two weeks to overhaul the mechanics; if they could not accomplish this, *Fallout* would be scrapped.[1] Desperation proved the mother of invention, the S.P.E.C.I.A.L. system was born, and the game went on to sell more than half a million copies—in those days, a blockbuster success for a computer role-playing game.

This was the first time *Fallout* endured moral scrutiny, but it would not be the last. In addition to its ubiquitous simulated violence, the game allowed players to use drugs, kill children, and engage in prostitution with characters as young as sixteen. Its direct sequel included the ability to sell companions as slaves and the chance to perpetrate genocide against a sentient race. Cain has suggested that *Fallout* was a "sandbox" game before that term was popularized; the goal was to simulate as many choices as possible while also simulating the consequences of those choices within a morally ambiguous setting. Simulated drug use led to simulated addiction. Killing virtual children made the player character a virtual pariah, attacked on sight by more civilized non-player characters. The content of the game's narrative epilogue was determined directly by player choices, whether valorous, ignominious, or indifferent. But even with unambiguous consequences attached, many in the real world regarded the simulation of (some) evil as abhorrent in its own right. Some countries banned the game entirely; others censored it. In the European release, for example, child non-player characters were rendered invisible, leading to an amusing problem where players could inexplicably lose inventory items to *nearly* undetectable underage pickpockets.[2]

Since Bethesda Softworks' acquisition of the *Fallout* franchise, player freedom has taken a back seat to public mores. In the sanitized wastes, slavery and drug addiction have received muted treatment. *Fallout 3* included child non-player characters, but made them unkillable. *Fallout 4* excluded prostitution entirely. It is not difficult to imagine prudential reasons for the tonal shift. Within months of *Fallout's* initial launch, the deaths of several teenagers were blamed on the video game industry: a 13-year-old who died while imitating *Mortal Kombat*[3] and three high school students killed by a classmate with a penchant for first-person shooters.[4]

A few months after the release of *Fallout 2*, a dozen teenagers were murdered at Columbine High School. Simmering public concern about video games soon boiled over into full-blown moral panic.[5] During the next decade, significant political and philosophical attention was drawn to the phenomenon of virtual vice and the possibility that it could have real-world consequences. Protecting sales by avoiding bad press is probably sufficient practical motivation for watering down the player freedom that characterized the *Fallout* franchise's origins. But the possibility of bad press is itself the result of certain widespread (though by no means universal) moral intuitions concerning the appropriateness of simulated evil, namely, that it is (at least sometimes) wrong to *depict* wrongdoing. Foundational to the *Fallout* franchise, however, is the idea that it may be wrong to *not* depict wrongdoing.

Where Your Shadow Lies

One way to do philosophy is to craft stories ("thought experiments") that inspire a certain intuition in the audience. Daniel C. Dennett (1942–2024) called these "intuition pumps."[6] In the world of video game ethics, there is an intuition pump known as "the gamer's dilemma," after the shortened title of a paper by contemporary philosopher Morgan Luck.[7] Luck asks: Can anyone who thinks it is morally permissible to simulate (some) serious moral wrongs, like murder, consistently believe that it is morally *impermissible* to simulate other serious moral wrongs, like the sexual abuse of a child? He says:

> Whilst I am not suggesting that virtual [child abuse] should be deemed morally permissible, I do wish to make it clear that if it is not, then a significant portion of popular entertainment (those which feature representations of murder) may also be brought into question. Consequently, the questions raised concern not only players of computer games, but most members of popular culture.[8]

By highlighting congruence between murder and child abuse, Luck "pumps" the intuition that maybe there is something morally wrong with virtual murder. This is a conclusion—call it the "media impacts morals" theory—that the video game community has vocally decried for decades, often through outright mockery. Video games aren't real, after all. It seems a safe bet that *literally no one* has become a (charismatic!) drug addict in real life as a result of popping grape Mentats in *Fallout 3*. No one has committed actual genocide after terminating Gruthar's band of Deathclaws in Vault 13. And there are surely no cannibals in the world today who got their start as *Fallout: New Vegas* players, stealthily consuming the virtual flesh of digital human corpses. Video games and other media might play a causal role in genuine vice for individuals who struggle to distinguish fantasy from reality, but that's a question for mental health professionals—not the entertainment industry. Call the idea that games do not influence real-world morality the "it's just a game" theory.

If "it's just a game," why draw the line at putting a slug or two into some of the more annoying residents of Little Lamplight? The prudential response—to protect sales by avoiding a harsh content rating or bad press—is downstream from an apparently widespread moral intuition that it is nevertheless wrong to even *depict* certain kinds of wrong, because "media impacts morals." Gamers are not the first consumers to grapple with such concerns. In many countries, content advisories appear on movies, music, comic books, and other entertainment media as a direct result of moral concern that entertainment corrupts (at minimum) the youth. Arguments over such intervention stretch back millennia; the ancient Greek philosopher Plato (428–348 BCE) wrote extensively on why he believed the construction of an ideal community depended on careful regulation of entertainment. He believed that uncensored music and poetry threatened the education of wise community leaders, corrupting their moral development through the perpetuation of falsehood and vice. His famous "Allegory of the Cave" will sound familiar to *Fallout* fans:

> Compare the effect of education … on our nature to an experience like this: Imagine human beings living in an underground, cavelike dwelling, with an entrance a long way up.… They've been there since childhood … able to see only in front of them, because their bonds prevent them from turning their heads around. Light is provided by a fire burning far above and behind them. Also behind them … a low wall has been built, like the screen in front of puppeteers above which show their puppets.… There are people along the wall, carrying all kinds of artifacts that project above it.… Do you suppose … that these prisoners see anything … besides the shadows that the fire casts on the wall in front of them? … The prisoners would in every way believe that the truth is nothing other than the shadows of those artifacts.[9]

The Allegory *can* be read as a story about politics—powerful people putting on a show that keeps their prisoners not only powerless and oppressed but ignorant of their oppression—and the *Fallout* franchise draws deeply from that well. But Plato wasn't just writing about politics, he was writing about *epistemology*—about how it is that we come to know anything at all. For Plato, the shadows represent the world our physical bodies inhabit, sometimes called the "material" world. Outside the cave is what Plato regarded as the "real" world, the world of permanence and perfection, the world of thought and ideas—the world of the Forms. As shadows, material things are distorted imitations of a higher reality, so Plato is suspicious of anything that tends to increase our enjoyment of, or attachment to, the material world.

Even worse, for Plato, are mere *representations*—paintings and plays, for example—which are an *additional step removed* from the real, the good, and the true. Your cardboard T-51 cosplay armor is a far cry from real power armor, and further still from the one true, ideal Power Armor, the Platonic Form of which all power armor is but a metaphysical shadow—but at least your cosplay can be worn *like* armor. A *photograph* of your T-51 cosplay *looks* like power armor, but as a photograph, it is even *less* truly power armor than your costume; the photograph is a shadow of a shadow (of a shadow). Plato thinks it evident that if we wish to be truly good, and not just *seem* good, we must understand things as they truly are, not as they merely seem. That means turning away from shadows, toward the light.

If it were possible to introduce Plato to the *Fallout* franchise (perhaps by catching a ride in a randomly encountered blue police box), he would likely find it all a little disgusting. Video games, like paintings and poems, are shadows of shadows. For Plato, their only possible redemption might be in a capacity to inculcate virtue by teaching us something true. Plato would seize the gamer's dilemma by the horns: it is wrong to do wrong, even virtually, because pretending to do wrong things corrupts us. "Media impacts morals." A video game that teaches us truth and goodness *might* be morally permissible, but a video game simulating vice would not. It's not that *Fallout* fans are training to become murderers or cannibals or child abusers *specifically*. Rather, by playing such games, we "will be brought up on images of evil, as if in a meadow of bad grass, where [we] crop and graze in many different places every day until, little by little, [we] unwittingly accumulate a large evil in [our] souls."[10]

In the Name of Progress and Healing

Not everyone in ancient Athens accepted Plato's demanding view on morality in the arts. His most famous acolyte, Aristotle (384–322 BCE), argued that humans naturally delight in imitation and storytelling, and can benefit even from the depiction of evil deeds and their tragic consequences. In *Poetics*, he suggests that a major function of dramatic art is to arouse certain emotions in the audience, "wherewith to accomplish [the] catharsis of such emotions."[11] *Poetics* is a challenging text—to this day, scholars debate its meaning—but gamers often speak of the emotional benefits of gaming. This can be in the context of real-world emotions; spending an evening lobbing mini nukes at Super Mutant behemoths is surely a healthier purgation of stress than yelling at one's roommates or co-workers. But the idea also applies to fully simulated experiences. The dazzling wonderment of emerging from Vault 101 for the first time, or the anger at discovering Anna Holt's betrayal of Project Purity, presents opportunities for players to *practice their emotions*. This is done in much the way (and for substantially the same reasons as) one might practice for a musical performance or an athletic competition: to become better.

Emotions are not the only thing Aristotle encourages us to practice. Contemporary philosopher Marcus Schulzke argues that the *Fallout* franchise, and *Fallout 3* in particular, cultivates

> what Aristotle called "*phronesis*"—the practical wisdom of knowing how to act morally in particular situations. According to Aristotelian virtue ethics, morality is not a matter of learning universal laws. It is learning how to be good by strengthening one's practical wisdom to the point that it is capable of resolving moral dilemmas as they arise. Practical wisdom is essential even for those who believe in a moral code as it is the skill that allows one to recognize when to apply a particular rule. By situating players in a virtual world in which they can test their *phronesis* and improve it without suffering from the adverse consequences actions real world [sic], video games serve as an invaluable educational tool.[12]

Interestingly, Schulzke's praise embraces the "media impacts morals" conclusion. Because "media impacts morals" is often deployed as a criticism of video games, gamers have often responded that "it's just a game." But even Plato was open to the idea that, with appropriate curation, art could *elevate* our souls as surely as it could corrupt them. "Media impacts morals" may actually be a *better* defense of gaming than "it's just a game," provided we can articulate the relevant moral content. Schulzke suggests that, for the *Fallout* franchise, the relevant moral content is the opportunity to practice moral reasoning. There are many "sandbox" video games, and many games where player choices influence outcomes, but the *Fallout* franchise's combination of significant player freedom with detailed and lasting narrative consequences is rare, and rarely done well. Indeed, entries in the franchise tend to draw criticism from fans, specifically when they fall short on this measure—the dramatically simplified "dialogue wheel" implemented in *Fallout 4*, for example, often left players guessing as to what their avatar was actually going to say, impairing the choice-and-consequence experience *Fallout* players have come to expect from the franchise.

Of course, not every choice can be simulated! Even if practical concerns like publicity and sales were not an issue, game developers would still be constrained by finite budgets and processing power. Why not devote *all* those resources to the simulation of morally praiseworthy—or at least overtly pro-social—activities? The Aristotelian insight is that the Platonic approach of limiting artistic narratives to the strictly praiseworthy would deprive us of valuable opportunities for catharsis and moral reflection. Much of the satire in the *Fallout* franchise revolves around this very insight. It is especially evident in the many manifestations of "Vault Boy," the in-universe mascot of Vault-Tec Corporation, but also in the forced optimism (or "toxic positivity") of many Vault Dwellers—perhaps most memorably, Lucy "Okey-Dokey" MacLean in Amazon's TV adaptation. Lucy is in many ways the exception who proves the rule; her Platonic upbringing was basically successful, gifting her with both remarkable competence and genuinely unfeigned optimism. As her story unfolds, however, she is repeatedly confronted with evidence that she has been underprepared for a wide range of emotions and experiences.

Suppose this is right—that it is both morally permissible and frequently beneficial to simulate disturbing events and blameworthy choices. It remains the case that not every choice can be simulated. Not every story can be told. Which stories, then, should we tell? Here, the gamer's dilemma reasserts itself. If it is morally permissible to simulate at least some serious wrongs, then game developers (along with other artists) face a puzzling question: Which are the *right* wrongs to depict?

The Best of the Many Simulations I've Run

When *Fallout* was first released, it was the industry standard for computer role-playing games to include printed manuals. *Fallout*'s manual, the *Vault Dweller's Survival Guide*, was written as if to an actual resident of Vault 13. Within the manual, the game is presented as a simulation intended to prepare Vault Dwellers for life in the wastes:

> The Vault-Tec Research Group has determined that after a long period of security, many Vault-Dwellers will feel "uncomfortable" with the idea of returning to the outside world. The SimTek 5000 will provide a safe and reassuring return to life on the outside world.[13]

One suggestion made to the putative Vault Dweller operating the SimTek 5000 explicitly concerns the permissibility of simulated choices: "Obviously, we don't condone some of the actions performed in the game world as appropriate, or even legal, actions in the real world. Don't confuse the two."[14] This establishes, somewhat recursively, the proper function of *Fallout*: its fictional authors wanted to craft a simulation that could prepare Vault Dwellers for the shock of life in the wastes, while its actual authors aimed to craft an entertaining simulation of such a simulation.

Fidelity is the accuracy with which a simulation imitates the genuine article. As a prototypical sandbox title, *Fallout* aimed to maximize player freedom within the boundaries of the game's narrative framing and technical limitations. In many ways, *Fallout* is inescapably low fidelity; simple graphics and scripted conversations are a far cry from a robustly simulated reality. But by offering choices and consequences where most video games offer only linear progression, *Fallout* offers a surprisingly high-fidelity simulation of *choice*. One of the most common events simulated in the *Fallout* universe is death, and players can choose to kill essentially every non-player character in *Fallout*, including children. Perhaps more importantly, however, it is possible to complete the central *Fallout* storyline without directly killing any non-player characters at all—though some still die as a result of player actions. Not all *Fallout* games can be completed without simulated bloodshed, and pacifism is almost never the easiest path available to players, but in the world of video games, the possibility of non-violent resolution is an unusually high-fidelity simulation of choice, encompassing unusually diverse opportunities for catharsis. Outside of combat (or non-combat), most *Fallout* plotlines can also be pursued in a non-linear way. Performance-enhancing drug use is optional. Most non-player characters are both potential allies *and* potential enemies. The wastes are hostile and unforgiving, but player characters need not be either.

Fallout 3 increased simulation fidelity through visual improvement and the introduction of rudimentary physics for in-game objects, but reduced player choice in other ways. Interestingly, a quest line in Vault 112 alludes (perhaps unintentionally) to the change; the player finds Stanislaus Braun, creator of the Garden of Eden Creation Kit, living as a child ("Betty") in the simulated prewar neighborhood of Tranquility Lane.[15] The other inhabitants of Vault 112 also occupy the simulation, but the choices available to them are governed by Braun's preferences. For the most part, the simulation is a domestic monochrome paradise,[16] but this is only to heighten the distress experienced by the residents when something surprising occurs, either by accident or in accordance with Braun's sadistic whims. While Tranquility Lane presents as a high-fidelity simulation of a prewar suburb, it does not meaningfully simulate *freedom* for its residents (even, if the player executes the system failsafe, for Braun himself). Should future entries in the *Fallout* franchise lean more toward the expansive, Aristotelian, SimTek 5000 approach to simulated choice and the depiction of wrong? Or should the series continue to move more toward Braun's vision of ideal simulation—carefully controlled, high fidelity in presentation, punctuated by negativity only when sufficiently entertaining?

Concerning the nature of choice, there is a joke, possibly originating in the movie *Ninotchka*[17] but today commonly told with reference to the

French existentialist philosopher Jean-Paul Sartre (1905–1980). The joke is that Sartre arrives at his favorite café and orders a coffee with no cream. A few minutes later, the waiter comes back and says, "I'm sorry, Monsieur Sartre, we are all out of cream. Would you prefer no milk?" Even Plato might agree that actual choice is preferable to its mere appearance.

A post-apocalyptic simulation that does not allow players to choose to abuse drugs, does not give players practice choosing *not* to abuse drugs. A video game that does not simulate the choice to become a prostitute does not invite players to exercise the emotions relevant to *not* becoming a prostitute. Rather than excusing the horror and violence of the *Fallout* franchise under the rubric of "it's just a game," gamers should embrace the idea that "media impacts morals" as an affirmative defense of the franchise. The right wrongs to depict are whichever wrongs *can* be depicted, within the constraints of the development process, to maximize the simulation of choice and the practice of relevant moral judgments and emotions.

Because *Fallout*, at its finest, *isn't* just a game. It's a *morality simulator*.

Notes

1. Timothy Cain, "Fallout: A Postmortem," PowerPoint presentation, Game Developers Conference, San Francisco, California, March 8, 2012, at https://youtu.be/T2OxO-4YLRk.
2. I-Know-All, "Why No Kids?," Fallout 2 forum, Neoseeker, April 5, 2004, at https://www.neoseeker.com/forums/3073/t362751-no-kids.
3. Wilson v. Midway Games, Inc., 198 F. Supp. 2d 167 (D. Conn. 2002).
4. James v. Meow Media, Inc., 90 F. Supp. 2d 798 (W.D. Ky. 2000).
5. Sanders v. Acclaim Entertainment, Inc., 188 F. Supp. 2d 1264 (D. Colo. 2002).
6. Daniel C. Dennett, *Intuition Pumps and Other Tools for Thinking*, (New York: W.W. Norton, 2013).
7. Morgan Luck, "The Gamer's Dilemma: An Analysis of the Arguments for the Moral Distinction Between Virtual Murder and Virtual Paedophilia," *Ethics and Information Technology* 11 (2009), 31–36.
8. Luck, "The Gamer's Dilemma," 36.
9. Plato in John M. Cooper ed., *Plato: Complete Works*, (Indianapolis: Hackett, 1997), 514a–515c. *Republic*, trans. G.M.A. Grube, rev. C.D.C. Reeve.
10. Plato, *Republic*, 401c.
11. Aristotle in Jonathan Barnes ed., *The Complete Works of Aristotle: The Revised Oxford Translation*, Vol. 2., (Princeton: Princeton University Press, 1984), 1449b. *Poetics*, trans. I. Bywater.
12. Marcus Schulzke, "Moral Decision Making in Fallout," *Game Studies* 9.2 (2009), https://gamestudies.org/0902/articles/schulzke.
13. Interplay Productions, *Vault Dweller's Survival Guide*, (1997), 2–1, https://archive.org/details/FALLOUT_SURVIVAL_GUIDE.
14. Interplay Productions, *Vault Dweller's Survival Guide*, 3–3.

15. At some point in the development process, the virtual reality and life support pods in Vault 112 were labeled "Simtek 6000." This language was removed from the game some time before release but was discovered in unused texture art assets that shipped with the game. It is not clear whether the removal was inspired by the fact that the SimTek 5000, despite its prominence in the original game manual, was also never mentioned during gameplay (aside from its apparent appearance on a loading screen). Recursive simulation is a surprisingly frequent topic in philosophical thought experiments!
16. Tranquility Lane is highly reminiscent of the movie *Pleasantville*, which was released the same month as *Fallout 2*.
17. *Ninotchka*, dir. Ernst Lubitsch (Metro-Goldwyn-Mayer, 1939), 47:43.

18

Vault-Tec and the Moral Fallout of Human Experimentation

Bobbie L. Eicher

The *Fallout* series gives players the chance to inhabit the kind of future that people in the 1950s might have easily imagined. The styles, clothing, and advertising shown from the periods before the nuclear disaster are all very deliberately crafted to look like a mixture of the real world of that period with a dash of the science fiction of the era (for example, Codsworth the robot butler in *Fallout 4*). Even the bombs themselves, though they're dropped in 2077, have a design that closely resembles the bombs that were dropped at the end of World War II.

This gives us a prewar game world that closely resembles the real United States of the 1950s, in which Americans are deeply concerned about the threat of communism (though with China as the major threat in place of the USSR) and the potential for a civilization-ending war between the nuclear superpowers. In response to this situation, the US government hired Vault-Tec to build a series of underground facilities across the country with the intention of providing a safe hiding place for a portion of the nation's population if a nuclear war broke out. Vault-Tec created these structures but also quietly modified many of them to include experiments on the inhabitants without warning any of the potential "Vault Dwellers" of what they had planned. Given the dire state of the world, is it possible that Vault-Tec's experiments were justified, or is this just proof that Pip-Boys should have come with a properly calibrated moral compass?

A Better Future, Underground?

Vault-Tec's work to create a system of underground vaults at the behest of the US government has made them a major commercial and corporate power in the prewar *Fallout* setting. Though we never get the full details of the company's size or scope, it's clear that massive resources were required to carry out their task. Vault-Tec not only built a series of sophisticated underground facilities spread over a large geographic area, but they also stocked them with necessary supplies and the staff members to run the vaults and keep the necessary equipment operating. At the same time, they were able to run a public advertising campaign for the service and develop organized systems for determining and tracking exactly who would be allowed to enter a vault before it was sealed.

We know exactly how these vaults were presented to the public because *Fallout 4* shows a commercial that Vault-Tec used to advertise their service. The ad shows people a place to "wait out the horrors of nuclear devastation" with "all the amenities of your modern-day home," where teenagers can find someone to fall in love with and build their own families, and children can spend their time playing. Overall, the sales pitch promises an experience very similar to normal life, though lived entirely underground for as long as it takes the surface to become safe and habitable again. Everyone was promised that they would be allowed out of the vaults to go and repopulate the world as soon as it became safe.

This, however, is not what most of the people who signed up experienced. While Vault-Tec did run a small number of vaults that behaved as promised (including Vault 76, which serves as the starting location for *Fallout 76*), they operated for completely different purposes than people had been told. These were "control" vaults, intended to be used to help with the analysis of the medical, social, and psychological experiments that drove the majority of Vault-Tec's project.

Ethics and Experimentation

The *Fallout* games don't portray the vault experiments as something anyone should condone. Some of the experiments could plausibly have scientific value, such as the plan for Vault 13 (from *Fallout* and *Fallout 2*) to remain locked for 200 years to collect data on how the people would behave in isolation. Others are more sadistic in their design, such as Vault 11 from the same game, where inhabitants were told that they would have to sacrifice someone each year, or everyone in the vault would be killed. (Even this was a lie, with the program set to say the inhabitants' "commitment to human life is a shining example to us all," in the event they refused. In actuality, an election system emerged with factions vying to determine who would die each year.)

Is it unthinkable that scientists could do something like this? Unfortunately, it's not. In the early twentieth century, a lot of science focused on creating a better future for society collectively, even if it meant hurting some individuals. It was socially acceptable to believe that people should be thought of much like livestock, with consideration about which physical and mental traits are worth keeping as part of the species and who should be eliminated from the gene pool.[1] This attitude about sacrificing some people (especially those society thought to be less valuable) to benefit the larger community in the future led to experiments that were forced on participants and behavior among scientists and doctors that eventually horrified the public so much that a new set of standards was imposed to prevent it from happening again.[2]

Vault-Tec's experiments fit in very well with the world the *Fallout* series depicts because they fit the culture of the 1950s in the same way that the clothing and the advertising do. Our current attitudes about research and medical ethics didn't become widespread until the following decades, with pushes like the *Declaration of Helsinki* and the *Belmont Report*.[3]

Kant and Deontology

Going back a couple of centuries, the German philosopher Immanuel Kant (1724–1804) advocated deontology, an approach to ethics that focuses on actions being inherently right or wrong without consideration for the consequences of the action. Kant argued that all moral duties derive from a supreme principle of morality that he termed the "Categorical Imperative." He presented this principle in different ways that he calls *formulations*.

The first is often called the Universal Law Formulation (ULF): "Act only in accordance with that maxim through which you at the same time can will that it become a universal law."[4] A maxim here is a general rule for conduct, so he's telling us to adopt rules for behavior that could be followed by everyone everywhere without creating a contradiction. An example Kant offers for this is a man who wishes to borrow money, knowing that he will not be able to pay it back, but also knowing that no one is likely to lend to him without promise of repayment. Kant suggests a possible maxim that a person in deep distress should be permitted to lie to improve his situation. He goes on to argue that this fails the ULF test because if people in distress can lie to improve their situation, everyone will quickly know that such lying is happening and act accordingly. This makes the lying pointless, which creates a contradiction.[5]

The second is the Humanity Formulation: "Act in such a way that you treat humanity, whether in your own person or in the person of another, always at the same time as an end, never merely as a means."[6] The essential idea here is that humans should be respected as rational agents who can make their own decisions, have their own desires, and exercise autonomy over their own lives. Treating a person merely as a means is to act as if they are only a tool to be used to achieve something while ignoring their inherent value as a human. If you were to hire someone to clean your home, they would be serving as a means to achieve a goal. This is fine under the Humanity Formulation, so long as you also treat that person with respect as a person who has a right to make their own choices, such as when they're willing to work for you or what kind of payment they require. Exploiting or enslaving workers, on the other hand, treats them purely as a means of achieving your goals and not as humans deserving of respect and autonomy.

Utilitarianism

To some people, the only sensible way to know whether an action is good or bad is to look at the results. This focus on the consequences over the intention is known as *consequentialism.* Utilitarians are a subset of consequentialists who think the best way to judge an action is by the amount of happiness or pleasure the action produces. As Jeremy Bentham (1748–1832) put it, "It is the greatest happiness of the greatest number that is the measure of right and wrong."[7]

The goal of utilitarianism is the maximum good, and for a philosopher like Bentham, everyone's happiness is equally valuable. Making one person slightly unhappy to make another person very happy would be a net good. Making one person extremely unhappy to make a group of people somewhat happier could be good if the number of people is large enough that the overall amount of happiness increases.

That said, utilitarians recognize that actions also have indirect effects on bystanders. They wouldn't necessarily agree with something as extreme as killing one innocent person so that their organs can be used to save the lives of several other people, just because the number of lives saved works out well. Valuing the consequences of an action means that *all* the consequences matter. If you save a few people while causing everyone else to lose faith that their doctor would never harm them to help someone else, the impact goes far beyond the people who are directly involved. Other people could lose trust in doctors and the medical system entirely, leaving them to live in fear or die of treatable illnesses because they refused to seek treatment.

Utilitarianism comes in two broad types. *Act utilitarianism* calls for every action to be judged individually based on whether it will maximize happiness or not, whereas *rule utilitarianism* aims to identify rules that people can follow to maximize the overall happiness in the world over time. This latter approach means that there may be some actions that have a negative impact, but the action should still be taken because following the rule behind the actions has the overall effect of increasing happiness.

Rule utilitarian thinking resembles Kant in the sense of wanting to identify a clear system of rules that everyone should follow as opposed to trying to consider every action separately. Sometimes, a rule utilitarian and a Kantian will arrive at similar rules, but the thinking behind the rules is very different. A rule utilitarian arguing for a rule against lying is focused on the ways that mistrust and betrayal reduce overall happiness, and therefore, a world without lies would be happier. Kant opposes lying because the lie itself violates the autonomy of the person being deceived. Even when discussing a hypothetical question of whether it would be permissible to lie to a murderer about the location of his intended victim, Kant argued that lying is still not acceptable because it would violate the autonomy of the murderer (though other choices like refusing to answer at all, locking the door, calling for help, and that kind of thing are all acceptable).[8]

Do the Ends Justify the Vaults?

To weigh the vault experiments against these ethical frameworks, we need to start by considering what Vault-Tec actually did. We know that they deceived many of the vault residents, because we get the chance to see the advertisement in *Fallout 4*, along with the exact pitch the Vault-Tec salesman makes when he comes to the door to persuade the player to reserve a place in the vault. Even when the bomb has dropped and you reach the vault itself, the Vault-Tec workers lie when they claim that the pods are just preparing you to go deeper into the vault rather than admitting that you are about to be frozen for an experiment in long-term human storage. This deception alone would be reason enough for Kant and many rule utilitarians to say that Vault-Tec was acting unethically.

If the residents were better off in the vaults, would that make it acceptable to lie to them about what to expect? A lot of people survived the nuclear war, but it's possible that Vault-Tec genuinely believed before the war that everyone who was not in a vault would die in a way far more horrible than anything they could experience in the vaults. In some cases, it even seems as if the vault experience was more terrible than Vault-Tec intended. Vault 11 was set up to congratulate its inhabitants for refusing to offer up a sacrifice, so Vault-Tec may never have anticipated how far the experiment would go before the final few remaining Vault Dwellers refused to cooperate.

Society managed to survive and move on to some degree, even for those who weren't in the vaults. Some characters became exceptionally long-lived, such as the Vault-Tec rep we meet at the beginning of *Fallout 4*, who survives to appear later in the game after becoming a ghoul. Still, we can generously assume that Vault-Tec didn't know something like this might be possible at all, and perhaps they believed that anything they might do to people in the vaults was still better than the certain death outside. After all, if you happen to be a utilitarian trying to maximize happiness in the world, you need to put a high value on making sure that you still have some living people available to experience it.

Another thing we need to consider, if we're going to weigh whether Vault-Tec's ends could have justified their means, is exactly what their ends were. The project clearly wasn't purely sadistic; they went to the trouble of having control vaults so that there would be a valid comparison to whatever data they gathered. If someone wanted to maximize the opportunities for tormenting helpless subjects, the control vaults would be wasted opportunities. This tells us there was actual information that they were trying to gather, and that Vault-Tec may have at least had reason to believe that they were taking actions that would lead to the greatest happiness for the greatest number, even though we can only judge them based on the outcomes from a utilitarian perspective.

The lore of the games does not give us much indication of what motivated Vault-Tec's leadership. There are hints and clues that have led to a lot of fan theories and suggested conspiracies with other powers like the United States government and the Enclave, but no firm proof about the details of the plan. Since we're trying to figure out whether it's possible Vault-Tec could have been justified, we'll focus on the theory that Vault-Tec believed that human life on Earth was eventually going to be doomed by a nuclear conflict (a common belief during the Cold War era), and they aimed to collect data that might allow them to create a long-term space mission to send some humans away from Earth to safeguard the survival of the species. This is consistent with some of the experiments we've seen in the vaults (both the study of long-term isolation and the attempts to freeze vault residents for centuries could plausibly serve that goal). Timothy Cain, one of the original main designers of *Fallout*, has said that he personally favors this explanation.[9]

A prospective space mission isn't officially included as canon in any of the *Fallout* games so far, but it generally fits well with the lore, and it provides a potential motivation for Vault-Tec powerful enough that it might justify their actions. So, if we pretend that we could be sure that this was their motivation and that they sincerely made their best effort to come up with experiments that provided data necessary to the project, could Vault-Tec have been making the right choice?

Kant would clearly denounce the project. He would focus on the way the Vault Dwellers were deceived and denied the opportunity to make their own choices about whether to sign up for the vaults based on an accurate understanding of the project. Even though Vault-Tec may have had the intention of saving humanity and perhaps did legitimately save the lives of some individual Vault Dwellers, they still lied to the public and kept people from making informed choices. Neither good intentions nor any positive consequences can do anything to make Vault-Tec's actions fit with the Categorical Imperative. This scenario is a clear example of treating people merely as means rather than as ends in themselves. Anyone that Vault-Tec experimented on was being reduced to a mere means of gaining important data, and not being engaged with as a valued human deserving of respect for their autonomy.

The utilitarian perspective is less clear. Utilitarians are more open to the idea that you can have goals so important that they can justify extreme actions that would be considered vile if done for another purpose, but that's not the entire story. A rule utilitarian might argue that Vault-Tec's decision to use deception and forced experimentation would hopelessly undermine their credibility and doom any later space program because no one would ever cooperate with the company again after knowledge of the experiments came out. Still, it's also possible that someone would argue that the highest rule should be that we must safeguard humanity as a whole, and so extreme measures can be justified if the circumstances are extraordinary enough.

It is easier to imagine justifying it from the act utilitarian approach, where the focus would be more narrowly on the outcomes of the specific project. The game doesn't give us a lot of information about exactly what proportion of people survived the vaults and what proportion would have likely survived outside the vaults, let alone other factors like the importance of the vaults to the survival of *Fallout*'s main characters and what long-term consequences that has for the world (which can vary depending on what ending you choose). It may be that a perfect calculation of the happiness in *Fallout*'s world would show that humanity is better off because of Vault-Tec's actions.

It's unlikely that many people play any of the *Fallout* games and reach the end feeling sympathy for Vault-Tec's goals. By the time the *Fallout* series began to be released, it was established practice in most of the world that an experiment should never be done on anyone who hasn't knowingly agreed to it, especially when the experiment includes a risk of harming the subjects. Still, we shouldn't completely dismiss the idea of a world where an actual Vault-Tec could exist that feels justified in these pursuits; real-world history proves that it isn't so far-fetched. People can be good at finding ways to justify the things they want to do, but the writings of people like Kant and Bentham give us a more thoughtful way of approaching the question of what kinds of actions are justified.

The *Fallout* series plays with some of the realities of culture in the early-to-mid twentieth century, including attitudes about nationalism and government, and the way that scientists should engage with research subjects and value their autonomy. Society went through an era where the focus was on maximizing progress and trying to build the best possible future for the collective. In the process, we saw exactly how far things can go if scientists, doctors, and government officials are allowed to act on the belief that individual autonomy and respect can be compromised for the sake of larger goals. The residents of *Fallout*'s vaults have learned the same hard lesson, and perhaps someday the game world will have its own declarations outlining proper research practices and ensuring that the horrors of Vault-Tec never happen again.

Notes

1. Megan Kalomiris, "Unfit to Breed: America's Dark Tale of Eugenics," The NIH Catalyst, last updated February 3, 2022, at https://irp.nih.gov/catalyst/29/4/unfit-to-breed-americas-dark-tale-of-eugenics.
2. Karen Norrgard, "Human Testing, the Eugenics Movement, and IRBs," *Nature Education* 1 (2008), 170.
3. The Declaration of Helsinki (1964) and the Belmont Report (1979) are two examples of foundational documents outlining ethical principles for doing research on humans. The former was created following the Nuremberg Trials in response to the Nazi crimes against humanity, while the latter was commissioned in the United States following public outcry over incidents like the Tuskegee Syphilis Study, where treatment for syphilis was withheld from Black men so that doctors could study the progression of the disease.
4. Immanuel Kant, *Grounding for the Metaphysics of Morals*, trans. Allen W. Wood, Vol. 4., (New Haven: Yale University Press, 2018), Ak.), 421.
5. Kant, *Grounding for the Metaphysics of Morals*, Ak. 4:422.
6. Immanuel Kant, *Grounding for the Metaphysics of Morals: With On a Supposed Right to Lie Because of Philanthropic Concerns*, trans. James W. Ellington, Vol. 8., (Indianapolis: Hackett, 1993), Ak.), 425–430.
7. Jeremy Bentham, *Bentham: A Fragment on Government*, trans. Ross Harrison, (Cambridge: Cambridge University Press, 1988).
8. Immanuel Kant, "On a Supposed Right to Lie from Philanthropy," in *Practical Philosophy*, trans. Mary J. Gregor (Cambridge: Cambridge University Press, 1996), 605–616.
9. Timothy Cain, "The True Purpose of Vaults in Fallout," YouTube, May 4, 2023, at https://www.youtube.com/watch?v=oWd4RBdeoaM.

Part 5

A BEAUTIFUL DISASTER: THE AESTHETICS OF *FALLOUT*

19

Genre Fusion and Its Fallout

Nathan Sheff

Suppose someone asks you to describe *Fallout*, either the games or the show. You could start with the setting, which is post-apocalyptic, taking place long after a worldwide nuclear war, and retro-futuristic, due to the World of Tomorrow 1950s cultural trappings of its prewar world. Concerning the games specifically, you might describe them in terms of their style of play; they're roleplaying games (RPGs) and, starting with *Fallout 3*, you might point out that they're first-person shooters (FPSs) with RPG elements.

But then you might start to wonder whether you can stop there. After all, *Fallout: New Vegas* has a special "Hardcore" mode, which imposes more demands on the player than regular play. For instance, player characters have to stay hydrated, fed, and well-rested, or else become encumbered and weakened. Does that make *New Vegas* a survival simulator, in addition to being an RPG/FPS?

Then there are the other thematic elements sprinkled liberally throughout the franchise: the Old West themes in the Mojave setting of the TV show and games, the sci-fi horror of *New Vegas*'s Vault 22, and the Lovecraftian horror of *Fallout 3* and *4*'s ghoul-infested "Dunwich" locations. At the same time, what ties it all together is giddy violence and an irreverent tone. Critical hits in the game can blow enemies to bits of flesh and bone (even more so if the player takes the Bloody Mess perk), and one of the opening scenes in the show features a pregnant woman mowing down raiders while a fork is stuck in her eye.

On paper, this sounds like a tonal mess, as if the developers threw a bunch of ideas at the wall to see what would stick, but as any *Fallout* fan will tell you, it all comes together to form a unique, cohesive, singular gaming experience. Somehow, it just works, and in its best moments the *Fallout* world manages to keep everything balanced. Entries in the *Fallout* universe often belong to multiple genres and categories of art at once, and this turns out to pose an interesting aesthetic challenge to creators and audiences alike. To understand this challenge, we'll have to get clear on what "categories of art" amount to. This will help us ask and answer two questions. First, why does it matter to us as an audience that *Fallout* belongs to any particular category rather than another? Second, what difference does it make to a work of art if it belongs to more than one category at a time, if it straddles multiple genres and styles at once? These questions belong to *aesthetics*, the area of philosophy that studies things like the nature of art, art criticism, and engagement with art.

Answering these questions will show us what makes *Fallout* unique (one might even say "S.P.E.C.I.A.L."). It manages to finesse the expectations it sets up in its audience and the inherent risk in taking on more and more expectations with every genre convention it adopts.

Categories of Art and Their Perks

Imagine you've recommended *Fallout* to a friend—maybe you lend them one of the games or tell them how much you liked the show. Next time you see your friend, you're eager to hear what they think. But much to your surprise (and chagrin), they tell you, "I didn't like it. I didn't learn anything about atom bombs or how they work. It was a total waste of time." This would probably give you pause. Did they play the wrong game? Watch the wrong show? But no, you confirm that the very thing you're now discussing is indeed *Fallout*. What is your friend's deal?

If this happened to me, I would say that my friend missed something really crucial. They've committed an unusual blunder in how they engaged with the work in question, how they "looked" at it. It's as if my friend had gone to a performance of *Swan Lake* and left unfulfilled because there weren't enough jokes, or rated a local food truck poorly because of its lackluster decor. *Swan Lake* isn't a comedy, so it's not supposed to be funny; and a food truck has plenty of features or qualities—what philosophers call "properties"—which seem to matter more when judging a food truck, things like the sort of food they serve, how fast the service is, or whether the food is any good. Decor just doesn't matter with food trucks; it's an irrelevant property because patrons aren't meant to spend time there. My friend would be judging the food truck by completely inappropriate standards, so their disappointment shouldn't surprise me. They'd be expecting the wrong sort of experience.

If your friend complained that the dearth of educational material about atomic physics in *Fallout* makes it a bad game or show, you'd probably draw the same conclusion. In a way, the game of aesthetic engagement was rigged from the start by their own misunderstanding. *Fallout* isn't "about" thermonuclear war in that way, so if they're expecting an experience similar to watching Christopher Nolan's *Oppenheimer* from playing a game where you can reprogram a casino's robot into being the town sheriff, that's their fault, not the game's. Your friend missed the point.

If this all sounds more or less correct, then you might agree with the contemporary philosopher of art Kendall Walton. In "Categories of Art," Walton addresses the following question: out of all the *properties* of a given work of art, which properties are the ones that matter from the aesthetic point of view? Which properties make a difference to how the audience engages with the work, and which ones don't? By "properties," philosophers typically mean something like "quality" or "feature." The whiteness of a marble bust is a property of the statue, for example, and being-a-first-person-shooter is a property of Bethesda's *Fallout* games (and *not* a property of the first two games from Interplay, which were turn-based RPGs with an isometric perspective).

Now consider the following claims:

1. The first episode of *Fallout* has a slow-motion sequence featuring gun violence.
2. The *Fallout* TV show is an adaptation of a video game series.
3. The first episode of *Fallout* has a slow-motion sequence that is over the top and funny.

All three claims attribute different properties to the show, but notice: Aren't there some intuitive, deeper differences between the properties? Don't these properties seem to belong to different kinds? The first and second claims describe the show from a neutral perspective—they attribute properties that seem objective. The third claim, on the other hand, seems less neutral. To say that something is "over the top" or "funny" isn't just describing it. Instead, it's the kind of thing you might read in a critical (positive!) review of the show. You might attribute these sorts of properties to something as a way to recommend it to your friend, or to draw attention to something you like. So, the third claim involves *aesthetic* properties, whereas the first two do not.[1]

Now, a question: What relationship is there between aesthetic properties (like being funny or over the top) and the other, non-aesthetic properties in the first two claims? Some philosophers have thought that not only are aesthetic properties significantly different from non-aesthetic ones, but also that the non-aesthetic properties in the first two claims differ from one another in a deep, important sense. To begin, notice that there seems to be a distinction between the kind of non-aesthetic properties in that first pair of claims.

Take the first property: having a slow-motion sequence. This is a straightforward, surface-level feature of how the show uses filming and editing to depict a sequence of events. It's a perceptible property right there on the screen, which the most casual viewer can recognize as easily as they might see the blueness of the vault jumpsuits or hear the pace of a part of the soundtrack. These are *formal* properties of the show. But the second kind of property is a little more subtle. Notice, for example, that some audience members might have no idea that the *Fallout* show continues a story told in a video game. That's because the property of being an adaptation isn't obvious to viewers in the way that colors, sounds, or even editing choices are. The *Fallout* show doesn't wear its status as an adaptation on its sleeve. So, being an adaptation is a *non-formal* property.

More specifically, we might say that it is a (merely) *historical* property, a property of the show's origins, but not something a viewer can see in the show. For you to watch the show *as an adaptation* is to bring outside knowledge to bear on your viewing experience.

So, restating the question above: Where do aesthetic properties come from? Do they emerge out of formal properties alone, or do they sometimes depend on non-formal properties as well? If you think the gratuitous violence of *Fallout* is part of its charm, is that just because of "how it looks," or could it also matter that, say, the creators meant it to be funny and made their editing choices accordingly?

Luckily for us, we don't have to settle this debate here, but Walton's point in "Categories of Art" is that, sometimes, which aesthetic properties we "see" in a work when we engage with it depends on non-formal features of the work, like what *kind* of artwork it is, what genre it belongs to, what the creator(s) wanted their audience to get out of it, and so on. Sometimes, the aesthetic properties of a work depend on what *categories* that work belongs to.

Now, some categories are pretty clear-cut, like medium. The *Mona Lisa* is a painting on canvas; Michelangelo's *David* is a marble statue; *Fallout: New Vegas* is a video game; the *Fallout* series is a TV show. But even though the question "What is the medium of *Fallout*?" seems simple, it's instructive to consider how we answer a question like that. Video games are a pretty diverse lot, so what makes something count as a video game?

Here's one thought: not only are video games played on electronic devices, they are *played* because they're games. Yes, they often have very important visual elements, like graphics, but video games aren't just meant to be looked at. According to contemporary philosopher C. Thi Nguyen, games in general (not just video games, but card games, board games, and so on) are partly defined, as a category, by how the audience is supposed to engage with them. Games prescribe a certain form of engagement. To put the point in Walton's terms, these prescriptions ("the game is meant to be played like *this*") are among the standard properties for the "game" category of art. This clues us in to some very general features of video games as a category. It tells us something about what constitutes the *standard* properties relative to the category of "game," those features that make something count as a game, rather than some other kind of art form.

To put the point the other way around: when a property is standard for a category, its *absence* from a particular work tends to disqualify it as a member of that category. For Nguyen, games typically present the player with obstacles that have to be overcome, according to the game's rules; games standardly afford a kind of striving. If a piece of software *doesn't* give its user a problem to solve, obstacles to overcome, or even an open-ended goal to strive for, then we might wonder whether it's really a game or merely a setting in which a "player" can mess around. If Nguyen is right about this, then striving would be one of the standard properties of games as a category.[2] This clues us in to some very general features of video games as a category. It tells us something about what constitutes the *standard* properties relative to the category of "game," those features that make something count as a game, rather than some other kind of art form. And with the concept of standard properties in hand, we can generalize from here, and pose questions like: According to what standard is *Fallout* a TV show, and not just a very long movie?

"Everyone Disliked That": Contra-standard Properties

Standard properties are those that make something count as a member of a category when they're *present*, and tend to count it out when *absent*. What about properties whose *presence* tends to rule it out? In addition to a category's standard properties, Walton also thinks each category has *variable* and *contra-standard* properties. Think of *Fallout 3* and *Fallout 4*. Both are games, of course, because they're meant to be played, but within the category of video game, there's a lot of leeway for game developers to make choices about, say, what the rules are, what sorts of gameplay loops are encouraged, or how the game looks and sounds. Just think of the difference in "look" between *Fallout 3* and *4*—a lot of players consider *Fallout 3*'s Capital Wasteland pretty drab in comparison with the bright palette of *Fallout 4*'s Commonwealth. The look and feel of a game are among the variable properties within a category, those things that distinguish one work from another, one game from another.

Contra-standard properties, meanwhile, tend to count against a work belonging to a category. They're not merely a rarity within the category, but something that (as Walton puts it) "does violence" to the category. Imagine if a *Fallout* game included an unavoidable quest in a vault classroom where the player has to write an entire book report on *Moby-Dick*, so that if you never read the book before, you'd have to go and read the whole thing before continuing. At this point, we'd start to wonder if this was really a video game or whether it was more like educational software. At the very least, we'd wonder if this "quest line" made the game an especially bad and baffling one.

So, for Walton, each category of art has its standard, variable, and contra-standard properties. This doesn't mean that these categories have strict, unambiguous boundaries, and it doesn't mean that every work of art has to belong to some category or other unambiguously. A lot of artistic innovation involves bucking convention and trying something new. Clearly. But categories of art don't have to be as sharp as scientific concepts in order to do their job. What these categories *do* for us is set expectations. They give us a baseline of familiarity so we can better appreciate and attend to those things that are unique to the work in question. If I know that *Fallout* games are RPGs, and I've played RPGs before, then I can better appreciate the perks and S.P.E.C.I.A.L. system for character creation. The standards built into categories help us get a grip on the work as we engage with it.

The boundaries between concepts and categories can often be difficult to pin down precisely. For example, while it's easy enough to say what's contained in the concept of a triangle, defining a category like "sandwich" is much trickier. Even so, unlike notions in logic or geometry, categories of art are allowed to have boundaries that are a little stretchy and blurry, as long as the audience can make use of them in aesthetic engagement, in getting the general feel for a work's aesthetic properties. Even so, as contra-standard properties show us, these categories have breaking points. When the general categories that a work belongs to are unclear to the audience, we literally don't know what to make of it, and that's a serious aesthetic liability for the artist. If we don't know what to make of their work, even in the broadest strokes, what has the artist accomplished?

Genre Fusion and Aesthetic Risk: Critical Hit or Critical Failure?

Clearly, *Fallout* belongs to a lot of different categories. Let's take one example from the game series, *Fallout: New Vegas*. Obviously, *New Vegas* is a game, but also, and more specifically, it's a video game in the roleplaying genre. "Video game" and "game" aren't categories that conflict, since video games are a type of game. Other categories are more obviously mutually exclusive, like "painting" and "video game." Walton's framework helps us see straight away that *New Vegas* doesn't have enough of the standard properties of paintings to belong to that category, and too many of the contra-standard properties of paintings. *New Vegas* has hardly any of the qualifying features to count as a painting, and a *lot* of disqualifying features.

Applying Walton's view in this way helps us make a more general point about the possible relationships between categories and how artworks fit (or fail to fit) into them. Since most of the standard properties for video games are contra-standard properties for paintings, and most of the standard properties of paintings are contra-standard properties for video games, it's no surprise that nothing is both a painting and a video game. It's hard to see how such a thing could possibly exist. We can also see why it's no surprise that all video games are ... well, games. All of the standard properties of games are *also* standard for video games.

Other types of categories don't obviously exclude one another in this way. "Post-apocalyptic" is arguably a category in its own right, with its own peculiar conventions and standard properties, and the same can be said for "comedy" as a category. RPGs have their standard, variable, and contra-standard properties, and likewise for shooters. And clearly, in some sense, these categories can all play nicely together. They're compatible in a way that "painting" and "video game" are not. But even though a work can be both post-apocalyptic *and* a comedy, these categories tend to narrow each other's scope. While it's possible to make a comedy in a post-apocalyptic setting, you couldn't make *just any* comedy in such a setting; any post-apocalyptic comedy will have to have *some* underlying darkness to it. The same goes for RPG and shooter. The first two *Fallout* games were turn-based RPGs. Once Bethesda introduced the shooter aspects, some of the roleplaying aspects from *Fallout 1* and *2* had to be changed accordingly.

These observations point to a broader lesson: for every category a work belongs to, that work has another set of standard properties to meet—it has more targets to hit. It doesn't have to meet *all* of them, but it has to meet enough to count. Likewise, it doesn't have to avoid *every* contra-standard property, but for every contra-standard property it has, the artwork better make it count by compensating in other ways. So, by making a video game with shooter elements, *and* roleplaying elements, with a setting for quests, levels, and stories that can be funny, *and* tragic, *and* suspenseful, *and* scary, game designers give themselves a narrower and narrower tightrope to walk. More categories mean more standards, and more standards mean more needles to thread. In other words, the more categories a game (or show, or any work) tries to belong to, the more opportunities the game designer has to screw it up.

When a game designer engages in genre fusion like this, they're taking an *aesthetic risk*. They're making a gamble: when players sit down with their game, the players will recognize all of the standard properties from all the different categories. If someone plays the game, and the game has that recognizable *feel* of a RPG, and at the same time, the recognizable feel of a shooter, then the designer has threaded that needle. They've successfully fused the categories. They've given the gamer something that they can make sense of; the gameplay loop is familiar as an RPG and as a shooter.

Notice, too, that this kind of fusion doesn't just put pressure on a designer to meet the standards of different genres. They also have to either *avoid* including contra-standard properties or, if the inclusion of contra-standard properties is unavoidable, the developer has to *finesse* their inclusion. This is no mean feat. Making games takes a lot of time, and massive open-world epics like the recent *Fallout*s are team efforts. So, it's all too easy to leave the final product unbalanced in some way.

To appreciate this point, think of all the options offered by *Fallout*'s character-building system—the S.P.E.C.I.A.L. stats and perks—and the possible playing styles they afford. One player might want to play as a fighter who shoots first and asks questions later; another might want to play as a smooth-talking diplomatic type; yet another might want to do a bit of both, but with a special focus on melee weapons instead of guns. (And still more players, this author included, will play the game several times just to try every character build under the sun.) To give gamers an RPG as such is to make an implicit promise: "Play how you want, build whatever character you like, and you will have a rewarding experience unique to your style."

But what if the melee weapons just aren't as fun as the guns? What if there aren't that many opportunities to use your speech skills? What if one type of character build is so overpowered that it's hard *not* to use it when playing? These are genuine liabilities that a designer has to keep in mind if they want to make good on the promises implicit in the game's genres. It is in this sense that developers take an aesthetic risk: the possibility of flubbing the execution is very close at hand.[3] The standard property that makes your game a shooter might be a *contra*-standard property relative to RPGs. And indeed, a lot of criticism—positive or negative—of entries in the *Fallout* franchise centers on whether certain compromises in design really panned out as intended. Some design choices can inadvertently unbalance the gameplay.

Aesthetic Appreciation as a Category-assisted Targeting System

Let's return to those questions we posed earlier. What is it to you, the viewer or gamer, if *Fallout* belongs to one category rather than another? And what difference does it make if it belongs to *more than one* at a time? Sometimes it can be hard to see the relevance of an abstract question about the nature of art to everyday, uncomplicated enjoyment of a show or video game. If Walton is right, though, *whenever* we sit down to play a game or watch a show, we are (consciously or not) bringing certain expectations to the table. So, when the next season of the show comes out, or *Fallout 5* drops, remember to bring the right mindset to the couch (or gaming chair) and set your expectations accordingly. The only way to engage with a work of art authentically is to appreciate it for what it is, and that means engaging with it *as* art of a particular kind.

Notes

1. To see how Walton himself makes the relevant distinctions, see Kendall Walton, "Categories of Art," *Philosophical Review* 79 (1970), 334–367.
2. For details, see C. Thi Nguyen, *Games: Agency as Art*, (New York: Oxford University Press, 2020). See especially chap. 6 for Nguyen's account of game rules as prescriptive frames; for his account of striving play, see chaps. 1 and 2.
3. For more on this notion of aesthetic risk, see Duncan Pritchard, "Aesthetic Risk," *Think* 17. Spring 2018, 11–24.

20

Putting Broken Glass Back Together: Freedom Through Modding in Bethesda-era *Fallout*

Chris Lay

Here's a contentious claim: Bethesda, owner of the *Fallout* franchise since 2007, fundamentally doesn't understand *Fallout*. I won't be trying to settle whether or not this claim is true, but it's hard to deny that a swath of the fandom feels this way—especially those players weaned on the original *Fallout* developer Interplay/Black Isle's role-playing titles from the 1990s. *Fallout 76*'s bungled launch may have puzzled and frustrated fans,[1] but Bethesda's original sin might be the substantial retcons made to precious *Fallout* lore, like casting Elder Lyons and his Brotherhood as heroic saviors in *Fallout 3* rather than the morally ambiguous (possible) technofascists of earlier games. Older fans often maintain that Bethesda *Fallout* just "feels" different. There's a quirky, irreverent bleakness characteristic of the Interplay/Black Isle titles that seems absent from most of Bethesda's output (the Obsidian-developed but Bethesda-published *New Vegas*, with such oddities as the Elvis-impersonating Kings gang, often gets a pass from fans).

Yet, *Fallout* wouldn't be the mainstream juggernaut that it is without Bethesda. While the PC originals quickly attracted a cult of devoted stalwarts, Bethesda's first bite at the apple obliterated those numbers and made *Fallout* a household name; *Fallout 3* generated more than $300 million and sold nearly five million copies *in its first week* alone.[2] Indisputably, many newcomers to the franchise snagged *Fallout 3* on the promise that it was the evolution of The Bethesda RPG™, a formula for a highly customizable experience with an unparalleled degree of freedom and exploration that saw breakout success in 2006's *The Elder Scrolls IV: Oblivion*. Most of these new players couldn't tell an Enclave Mk II suit from Brotherhood T-45 power armor and didn't care that maybe Super Mutants shouldn't have been in the Capital Wasteland because the Forced Evolutionary Virus that created them was stuck on the West Coast with the original *Fallout*'s antagonist, the Master. Bethesda's reimagining of a series that had been dormant for seven years just seemed like a bizarre, novel world to get lost in.

There's a real tension here. *Fallout* is undoubtedly the gaming behemoth it is *because* of Bethesda, in spite of the fact that Bethesda's *Fallout* titles are both a departure from what some original-series fans loved and are lousy with bugs. That last point is something everyone can agree on: Bethesda games are really buggy. This isn't unique to their *Fallout* titles; the studio's development history is a trail of ambitious games shot through with glitches both big and small. Players even have a name for these (by now expected) technical problems: "Bethesda jank." So, why do so many unsatisfied players continue to buy Bethesda-developed *Fallout* games just to (apparently) grouch about them online?

One possibility is that their excitement comes from dreaming about how players will modify the games to make them their own. "Mods" in *Fallout 4* range from simple quality-of-life enhancements, like making roads visible on the Pip-Boy map, to creating bespoke weapons, equipment, environments, and characters whole cloth.[3] Some players think that modding is mandatory to enjoy *Fallout*—mods fix something broken or incomplete. To their credit, Bethesda encourages, supports, and outright enables the *Fallout* modding community. *Fallout 4* launched alongside a suite of modding tools; Bethesda hosts and promotes official mods on its website; and many of these same mods can be browsed and installed from fully integrated in-game menus on both PCs and consoles. Writers often emphasize the freedom that players of Bethesda's *Fallout* games have in navigating sprawling open worlds and choice-based narratives, but what about the even greater freedom that Bethesda gives players to just make a better *Fallout*? That's what we're going to investigate in the rest of this chapter. How is *Fallout* modding an expression of philosophical freedom for players and modders, and what is Bethesda's part in it?

"And at the End of the Day, You'll Need to Make a Choice. Make It the Right One"

With a robust enough set of modding tools, no amount of dissatisfaction over Bethesda's changes to *Fallout* or disappointment with "Bethesda jank" can keep fans away from the series. With the keys in hand to reshape titles like *Fallout 4* as they please, players can simply make the game they want to play, like the staggering and widely acclaimed *Fallout: London*, a "DLC-sized" mod that transplants *Fallout 4* into the eponymous British city, bringing completely new enemies, quests, and fully-voiced dialogue along for the ride.[4] As much as some modders may grumble that they're stuck "fixing" Bethesda's busted games—obnoxiously running from bug to bug like Preston Garvey rushing between Minutemen settlements—they also seem to derive immense satisfaction from the creative freedom modding allows. And modding is just as much a win for gamers who have no particular love for Interplay/Black Isle *Fallout*, as they get a boatload of user-created *Fallout* content to play. It might be that what makes Bethesda *Fallout* special is just how much the studio weaves modding into its titles and even empowers modders.

I previously mentioned "creative freedom," so we need to narrow down what that could mean. One option is the freedom to create meaning or choose what's meaningful, and that definition is at the center of much of existentialist philosopher Jean-Paul Sartre's (1905–1980) work.[5] Sartre asserted that we—human people—are "absolutely free." This might give the reader pause, since there are plenty of things we're unable to do, like leaping 20 feet in the air without *Fallout 76*'s Marsupial mutation. But Sartre wasn't talking about the freedom, options, or ability to do whatever you imagine.

Obviously, there are serious constraints on what we're biologically, socially, and practically capable of doing: for one, you don't have the Aquaboy perk, so you can't breathe underwater. Outside of physical impossibilities, there are also sometimes public consequences so severe that my apparent "choice" might not seem like a live option at all. *Fallout 4* permits players to both side with the Railroad in the quest "The Battle of Bunker Hill" and tell Father what they did, but players can't then stop Father from banishing them from the Institute. Likewise, you're "free" to faff around in the original *Fallout* all you like, ignoring the time limit on getting Vault 15's water filter—but this isn't a real possibility if you'd like to finish the game. Sartre and his long-term romantic and philosophical partner, Simone de Beauvoir (1908–1986), called these concrete conditions that both situate and limit us in a social world "facticity."[6]

Even if we can't *act* with absolute freedom because of the reality of our individual facticity, what we can do—and this is Sartre's point—is determine what sorts of things are valuable to us. As Beauvoir stressed, whether certain actions or beliefs are important or not is ambiguous; we have to sift through these competing values and *give* them meaning through our choices. When Deacon tells the player they'll eventually have to choose a faction to support in *Fallout* 4, he gets close to Sartre and Beauvoir's notion of freedom. He's spot-on that meaning comes from the choices we make. What he misses is that the rightness of the choice comes from the meaning we invest in it—there isn't a "right choice" that preexists our ability to assign meaning.

If the game design of Bethesda's *Fallout* titles affords freedom in choosing how to play, modding is probably the ultimate expression of meaning-making. Someone playing unmodded, vanilla *Fallout 4* can elect to ignore the main questline and commit to dozens of hours of base building or even something seemingly pointless, like vowing to collect every wayward teddy bear in the Commonwealth. However, the vanilla player arguably isn't "making" meaning; they're just picking priorities among the game's existing features. Someone using mods injects *new* meaning into the game, reframing the structure of the experience to better suit their desires.

Unhappy with *Fallout 4*'s selection of hairstyles for women? There's a mod for that. Aggravated by bullet-spongey foes that shrug off your skillful headshots? Install a mod that dramatically increases headshot damage for all enemies cursed with a skull and brain. Some mods offer minor, unintrusive fixes, like removing the door-opening animation before load screens. Some improve textures (and come recommended over Bethesda's official high-resolution graphics patch, which is both poorly optimized and a bloated, dizzying 58GB).[7] Others make substantive and sweeping changes to gameplay, like expanding the settlement system to something closer to a city-building simulation. Whatever way of engaging with the game that a player chooses as meaningful, there's likely a mod for it, three updates deep, that's ready to be installed—and, if not, the tools are there to make it.

"The Game Was Rigged from the Start"

Don't get the wrong idea: even modders are limited by a certain facticity. Mods aren't converting *Fallout* to entirely new game engines (the software used to build games, like Unity or Unreal), and most don't completely overhaul the underlying mechanics either. Boundaries for modders are largely set by the developmental and technological choices made by the game's original design team. Bethesda's Creation Engine is built for making open-world RPGs that specifically play like *The Elder Scrolls*, not go-kart racers or a dating sim about romancing ghosts. Even if modders *did* radically rework *Fallout 4* into something like *Fallout Kart*, all of the characteristic gameplay features of *Fallout* would have been removed. So, it wouldn't be a case of a player choosing meaning for a *Fallout* game.

Because modding choices are at least somewhat defined by the structure of the game, we can start to see how another classical philosophical dimension of freedom is involved—namely, the clash between whether actions are freely chosen or determined by something else before we "choose." Here's how it works: some might argue that synths in *Fallout 4* can't make free choices because everything they do is a result of some programming instruction or another. Their actions are caused by something like a complicated conditional statement—"If the Sole Survivor draws on me, then I'll fire my weapon"—that tells them how they have to act. In this case, philosophers might say that the synth's actions are *determined by prior causes* rather than free choices. There aren't actually choices to be made: "The game was rigged from the start," as Benny admits before shooting the Courier in the head to open *Fallout: New Vegas*.

Baruch Spinoza (1632–1677) provides us with a relevant (and complicated) theory of causal determinism that I'll cut down to the bare essentials.[8] To Spinoza, the whole universe (Nature) is a constellation of interrelated causes; every event, action, and even thought has a preceding event, action, or thought that brought it about. This sounds like the strictest determinism possible, as it robs both physical and mental activity of any kind of "free choice." (Dogmeat is lying on the mat because his legs carried him there, and his desire for a soft place to curl up simultaneously produced a parallel mental "decision" to lie on the mat.) But Spinoza thought that humans have a peculiar way of finding genuine freedom within Nature's causal web: because we have the capacity to understand how all of Nature's causes are interconnected, we're uniquely equipped to also recognize our own place within its vast architecture. Once we do, we see that no causes act on us *from the outside*, as we and all other things are united *in* Nature together; we might call this recognition of internal causes "immanent freedom."

Unexpectedly, Spinoza's image of ourselves as part of a web of causes is a little bit like how a modder relates to their modding toolkit. See, what hasn't been said so far is that modding is a complex and sometimes daunting process. It makes changes to a game's base code, and, if done carelessly, can disrupt ordinary game functions or even make something unplayable. Just *installing* mods is sometimes downright arcane, as adjusting plugin files, getting the load order right for stacking multiple mods, and finding the correct directories can feel like consulting the *Krivbeknih* (*Fallout 3*'s *Necronomicon* stand-in). Successful modding demands an understanding of how the player and the game's structure are linked—how to effectively work within those structures and, most importantly, how to keep from burning everything down in the process. The modder isn't some divine maestro floating outside the tools and choosing where everything goes by executive fiat. It's actually a lot more like Spinoza's model. Knowing how you, as the modder, fit into the comprehensive system of tools that forms, say, the *Fallout* Creation Kit is really a way of exercising immanent freedom.

The *Fallout* Creation Kit is Bethesda's (free) editor for simplified modding and sharing completed mods in *Fallout 4* (it's a version of the same toolset that Bethesda's own developers use). It's not the *only* way that players can mod *Fallout 4*, but it certainly streamlines things. Bethesda's support doesn't stop with the Creation Kit either. *Fallout 4* includes dedicated menus for both normal mod browsing and the Creation Club, a built-in store where players can purchase curated mods—like new dog breed models for Dogmeat or self-contained quests—that have been officially developed by Bethesda and community modders hired to create new content. Moreover, *Fallout 4* became the first game to offer these sorts of traditionally PC-only, in-depth modding options to the notoriously prohibitive console space.[9] There's even a Bethesda mod manager to make installing mods a breeze for less mod-savvy players who might be intimidated.

I'm not gushing over Good Guy Bethesda for these decisions—the company has lots to gain financially from, say, a monetized Creation Club storefront that's also available to PlayStation and Xbox gamers. The point is that the studio has worked mod support into the digital infrastructure of *Fallout 4* (and *Starfield*, rereleases of *Skyrim*, and probably whatever its next non-multiplayer-focused *Fallout* turns out to be). Modding accessibility is just part of what it is to be a Bethesda RPG like *Fallout*, and it's this accessibility that opens players to the absolute freedom to choose meaning (through modding) and the immanent freedom of acknowledging how you fit into a larger system (of modding tools).

"The Kings Are About an Idea, You See? Where Every Man Is a King in His Own Right"

Though they seem applicable to both *Fallout* modding and Bethesda's approach to it, the kinds of freedom we've reviewed so far don't quite capture what you probably thought about when reading the words "creative freedom" earlier in the chapter. The most commonsense definition is likely "making something" (like an artifact), but that still doesn't entirely do justice to a more philosophical reading of "creative freedom." For Simone Weil (1909–1943), the idea is more that we're most free when we engage in creative labor *for ourselves*.

Weil understood freedom as the convergence of thought and action, where what we do perfectly follows what we think, and she believed that self-directed manual labor brings the greatest harmony between the two.[10] As her philosophy matured, she would explicitly call this kind of hard work a spiritual foundation for everything else we do.[11] For Weil, a Far Harbor fisherman just scraping by is freer than a merchant at *Fallout 76*'s plush Whitespring Resort, even if the merchant has an "easier" or "better" life by most measures. The fisherman has direct contact with his work and its products that the merchant—several steps removed from the production of her wares—lacks. Admittedly, the work that Weil has in mind isn't creative in the way that art is usually considered creative—instead, it's *productive* and solves problems. But this isn't all that different from *Fallout* modding as a process that fixes perceived shortcomings in Bethesda's games.

As the paradigmatic example, let's take a longer look at *Fallout: London*. A true "total conversion" mod replaces all of a game's assets while still using the original game's framework under the hood. *London* doesn't replace *all* of *Fallout 4*'s assets, but it does include enough new environments, character models, enemy types, weapons, and quests that calling it a total conversion isn't that far off. There's professional voice acting, a multi-act plot, and a clever adaptation of *Fallout*'s Americana staples to suit a distinctly British taste. For instance, the Pip-Boy has been replaced by the handheld Atta-Boy (with new perk animations to boot), Dogmeat is now Churchill (an adorable English bulldog, naturally), and there's a score of custom factions for the

Wayfarer to buddy up to or betray, like the Pistols (a group of communal anarchists clearly inspired by their punk-rock namesake in more ways than one). All told, the mod was a formidable undertaking that took nearly five years to develop, and it looks like brand new *Fallout*.

In fact, that's exactly what it is to many fans who've been starving for a new single-player *Fallout* in the decade since *Fallout 4*'s launch. That's the first problem that the mod is solving, but it isn't the only one. Beyond the desire for more single-player *Fallout*, fans have been clamoring to see how the rest of the world was affected by the nuclear, well, fallout of the series' Great War. Yet, Bethesda has emphatically resisted, maintaining that the American setting is crucial to *Fallout*'s identity.[12] Now, *Fallout: London* offers players the chance to experience the *Fallout* world beyond the United States.

Fitting with Weil's account of labor, *Fallout: London* took a monumental amount of work to produce, but the effort is very much *for themselves*. *London* is a free mod: the team earns no profit from their work. Of course, the developers clearly also made *London* for a prospective throng of fans who they hoped would be enthusiastic to play it. But this hardly challenges Weil's point, because the *London* team certainly wasn't forced or commissioned by others to complete the work. Choosing to make the mod ultimately fulfilled a need the members had, namely to see their creative desires expressed concretely—lining up thought with action in the way that Weil thinks only labor can.

According to Weil, the freedom in making something from your own effort but without being compelled by others is the most essentially human thing that you can do—it's how we can live well. This is the life of a king, just like *New Vegas*' The King observes in the quote that headlines this section. But the life of someone "free to follow his own path, do his own thing" might sound like too much for some of us. Creative freedom could be a burden if creativity always requires novelty. Modding shows us that creative freedom doesn't have to generate something entirely new, though. Moira Brown, *Fallout 3*'s enthusiastic shopkeeper/tinkerer, puts it aptly, asking players how to put broken glass back together and explaining, "Even if the pieces fit, you can't make it whole again the way it was. But if you're clever, you can still use the pieces to make other useful things. Maybe even something wonderful . . ." Putting an arguably broken *Fallout* game back together still makes a useful thing, too. In the case of mods like *Fallout: London*, it also makes something wonderful.

Notes

1. I should note that *Fallout 76* has since been patched with improvements that have led much of the community to not just warm on the title but celebrate it, like expansive, character-rich questlines, playable ghouls, and even radioactive fishing.

2. Brendan Sinclair, "*Fallout 3* Ships 4.7 Million in First Week," GameSpot, November 10, 2008, at https://www.gamespot.com/articles/fallout-3-ships-47-million-in-first-week/1100-6200678.
3. Because *Fallout 4* is the title that's gotten the most modding attention from both Bethesda and the fandom, that's also the game I'll be focusing on in terms of modding. *Fallout 3* has an impressive modding community, too, and there's even a modding scene for *Fallout 76*, though the options are drastically reduced because of shared-space, online requirements.
4. Joshua Wolens, "One of the Biggest *Fallout* Modding Projects in Years Is About to Release, and If It Goes Wrong It Could 'Kill the *Fallout* Modding Scene,'" *PC Gamer*, March 12, 2024, at https://www.pcgamer.com/games/rpg/one-of-the-biggest-fallout-modding-projects-in-years-is-about-to-release-and-if-it-goes-wrong-it-could-kill-the-fallout-modding-scene.
5. See Jean-Paul Sartre, *Being and Nothingness: An Essay on Phenomenological Ontology*, trans. Hazel E. Barnes, (London: Methuen, 1957). and "Existentialism Is a Humanism," in Walter Kaufmann ed., *Existentialism from Dostoyevsky to Sartre* (New York: New American Library, 1975).
6. Simone de Beauvoir, *The Ethics of Ambiguity*, trans. Bernard Frechtman, (New York: Citadel Press, 1948).
7. Brendan Lowry, "Warning for *Fallout 4* Players: Avoid the High Resolution Texture Pack, Use These Mods Instead," Windows Central, April 15, 2024, at https://www.windowscentral.com/gaming/warning-for-fallout-4-players-avoid-the-high-resolution-texture-pack-use-these-mods-instead.
8. Baruch Spinoza in Seymour Feldman ed., *Ethics*, trans. Samuel Shirley, (Indianapolis: Hackett, 1992).
9. Jeff Grubb, "*Fallout 4*'s First Console Mods Now Live on Xbox One," VentureBeat, May 31, 2016, at https://venturebeat.com/games/fallout-4s-first-console-mods-now-live-on-xbox-one.
10. Simone Weil, "Reflections Concerning the Causes of Liberty and Social Oppression," in *Oppression and Liberty*, trans. Arthur Wills and John Petrie, (New York: Routledge, 2001).
11. Simone Weil, *The Need for Roots*, trans. Arthur Wills, (New York: Routledge, 2002).
12. Wesley Yin-Poole, "Todd Howard Explains Why Bethesda Plans to Keep Fallout Set in the US," IGN, April 30, 2024, at https://www.ign.com/articles/todd-howard-explains-why-bethesda-plans-to-keep-fallout-set-in-the-us.

21

Some Video Games Are S.P.E.C.I.A.L.

Katia S. Franco

There are literally millions of video games, so it takes something truly remarkable to stand out.[1] Many games offer mere escape from our troubles,[2] but some invite us to get invested in a richly detailed world where we discover fascinating characters and their intricate interrelationships, while resolving spectacular moral dilemmas that stick with us long after we've stopped playing. Such games are special, and playing one of them can be a meaningful and highly memorable experience, reminding us about the power of our moral decision-making, and in doing so, helping us experience the joy of doing philosophy. *Fallout 4* is special.

The Allure of Escape

On the surface, *Fallout 4* doesn't have anything to do with our everyday life. Its post-apocalyptic wasteland is full of raiders, ghouls, Super Mutants, Deathclaws, robots, and synths, all of which you are free to avoid or engage with, and some of which you have the option to save or befriend. The synth storyline, one of several woven together in *Fallout 4*, is of particular interest here. (The details that follow reveal the broad strokes of this storyline but, in my view, don't ruin its particularly surprising and moving aspects that you experience when playing the game.)

In the world of *Fallout*, various resources are scarce, including technology, but one cryptic place that seems to avoid this problem is the Institute, short for the Commonwealth Institute of Technology, which grows out of the remains of MIT after the nuclear apocalypse. As the name suggests, it is a place of advanced research, but its exact purpose is somewhat of a mystery, since those belonging to the Institute are secretive about what goes on there. If you play *Fallout 4*, you discover that part of what the Institute does is create synthetic humanoids or artificial humans, better known as synths.

Generation 1 and 2 synths are entirely mechanical and easily identifiable as such, but Gen 3 synths are biological constructs that are incredibly hard to distinguish from humans, and even they themselves usually don't know they are synths. (There are similarities between synths and terminators from the *Terminator* franchise in that there are increasingly more complex and human-like terminators, as well as replicants from *Blade Runner*, who may not know they are what they are, like Gen 3 synths.) There is a question of whether Gen 3 synths are sentient, self-aware beings, a question that the player of *Fallout 4* is invited to ponder. Depending on how you answer that question, you can either support the synths who want to escape the Institute to lead their life as they choose, hunt them down as a danger to humanity, or support the Institute in one of its nefarious projects of replacing specific people in towns around the Commonwealth with identical-looking synths who don't know they are synths, implanted with those people's memories, in order to spy on the people of those towns unbeknownst even to themselves.

All this sounds far removed from our reality, which is precisely why games like *Fallout 4* are appealing to some players looking for escape. The signals that we are not in our actual world but in a different one are numerous, inviting us to set aside whatever troubles we might be escaping.

But under the futuristic wasteland skin of *Fallout 4*, there are realistic and immersive mechanisms of decision-making. Decision-making is at the core of our agency, and *Fallout 4* (and some other role-playing games) offers us numerous opportunities to make difficult and impactful decisions, particularly the moral kind. This allows us to get immersed and emotionally invested in the fate of the game world and its characters. It is this immersion and emotional investment in a world, facilitated by closer approximation of our reality rather than a further departure from it, that grants us so much more than the escape we might be expecting.

Immersion Through Agency

When gamers describe something as immersive or realistic—words often used interchangeably—we're usually referring to the quality of the graphics and the visual similarity to our reality.[3] The more detailed a video game is, and the more visually similar it is to our own reality, the more immersive we tend to think it is. For example, if we compare the graphics of the older *Fallout 3* game (released in 2008) with those of the newer *Fallout 4* (released in 2015), the newer game has better graphics, which might lead us to describe *Fallout 4* as more immersive. Likewise, even though the world of *Fallout* has gone through a series of nuclear explosions, it is nonetheless clearly a world that is meant to be visually very similar to ours in the 1950s, had the transistor not been invented, and had it experienced a nuclear apocalypse.

The visual medium is naturally suited to generating immersion through representation: the more accurate the visual representation of, say, a person, the more immersive that visual experience is.[4] So part of the explanation why *Fallout 4* is an immersive game is the accuracy of its visual representation, achieved through improved graphics and the visual similarity of the *Fallout* world to our actual one, among other things. But these visual virtues of *Fallout 4* and other video games like it aren't enough to explain or support the sort of immersion that leads to hours of gameplay and deep emotional investment that the players experience. What explains that is tapping into our agency: specifically, the intricate, thoughtful, and difficult moral decision-making that games like *Fallout 4* offer us.

When we first encounter Gen 1 or 2 synths, we might marvel at the technological advancements of the *Fallout* world, but it is not until we encounter Gen 3 synths, who we first think are humans (in part because they think they are humans), that we are swept away by the emotional consequences of deciding whether something is a self-aware entity and how it should be treated. On the one hand, Gen 3 synths are created by humans, likely with malicious intent, but on the other, those synths are neither aware of being created nor do they demonstrate any malicious intent. These facts lead to a complex cluster of decisions, all of which have mixed consequences for the world of *Fallout* and a deep emotional impact on the player.

Making life-and-death decisions ourselves, rather than passively observing them being made, is part of what is so impactful about games like *Fallout 4*.[5] But more than that, it is the moral nature of such decisions, rather than their complexity or high stakes alone, that has such a deep emotional influence on us.[6] We don't just observe synths being saved or killed as in a movie; we decide the fate of specific, named synths with whom we establish a relationship. We go through the moral calculus of what it would mean for the world of *Fallout* and what it would mean for us as the decision-makers, and then we observe the game's feedback to us, sometimes with elation, sometimes with sorrow, sometimes with relief. This is what gives *Fallout 4* and games like it their impressive immersive character—the realism of just how emotionally impactful moral decision-making can be. We have to weigh the unweighable, choose between the incomparable, and then be forced to observe the consequences, which we already imagined. The heartbreak of going through this process is mitigated only by the sense that we made the right decision.[7]

The magnitude of moral decision-making in *Fallout 4* far exceeds the magnitude of our everyday moral decisions, but this isn't a drawback. Rather, we are drawn to it as part of the immersive gaming experience. When we experience such moral decision-making in a video game for the first time, we know that we're in for an entirely different kind of adventure, a much more epic one than anything we had hoped for.[8] It is not the expected departure from reality but rather the unexpected realism of moral decision-making, along with its emotional consequences, that makes playing *Fallout 4* such a special experience. We usually think of immersion as visually generated, so when it is generated through the involvement of our moral decision-making, which is central to our agency and is particularly emotionally charged, the result is remarkable.[9] It gives us a rare opportunity to tap into the immense power of our mental capacities (often underutilized in our everyday life), which is precisely what doing philosophy involves.

The S.P.E.C.I.A.L. Experience

In playing *Fallout 4*, you will be confronted with the discovery that a person you've come to know is actually a synth, hated and hunted by a powerful group, and used for espionage unbeknownst to themselves by their creators. The fact that they look just like any other person is striking. A thought comes to mind: it could've been me in their shoes.

To someone else, I'd be indistinguishable from a synth, and until that occurs to someone, whether I'm a person and all that goes with it doesn't even come up as something to think about, let alone something to prove in order to survive. How would I prove to someone else that I'm self-aware, that I think, that I'm a person? A version of this question weighed on Alan Turing (1912–1954) as he was developing the first digital computer, foreseeing the path it would unfold for humanity, heading toward AI—a question we are trying to answer to this day.[10]

Since *Fallout 4* is fiction after all, and playing it is something we do voluntarily, we get to set such agonizing questions aside when they become too much. But pondering them, especially when there is no obvious answer, and especially from the first-person perspective, gives us much more than an escape from our everyday problems. It provides us with a special experience that can stick in our memory and have a significant, long-term effect on us.

Part of that experience is having our imagination reawakened. We get to walk the post-apocalyptic wasteland, imagining how best to resolve its problems and, among other things, what it's like to be a synth, realizing that it's just a stepping stone to an endless universe of other perspectives. For example, we might not be able to imagine what it's like to be a bat right away,[11] but perhaps we can do so if we start by imagining being a synth and then trying out perspectives that are further and further removed from our own.[12]

Regardless of whether we can successfully imagine occupying radically different perspectives as a result of playing *Fallout 4*, becoming more acutely aware of there being such perspectives can be enough to rejuvenate the mind. Sometimes, all it takes to invigorate mental skills like imagination and decision-making[13] is reshuffling our space of possibilities: what wouldn't occur to us becomes a possibility, and what seemed far-fetched becomes a likely scenario. This happens naturally when we are kids, playing pretend, but as adults, we sometimes need help with that.[14] Playing *Fallout 4* can be that help, granting us innovative ideas and refreshing the patterns of our thinking, allowing us to alter the habits of our minds, if we so choose.

Dusting off our imagination and reshuffling the space of possibilities can also help us gain clarity with respect to our own problems, which we wanted to escape in the first place. But rather than merely escaping them, we are gifted with an opportunity to tackle them afresh and reassess them in our minds.

In a way, then, making life-and-death moral decisions in *Fallout 4* and experiencing their consequences in a controlled environment reminds us about the untapped strength of our mental capacities, the immense satisfaction of challenging them more than we normally do, and the rewarding feelings of making the right decisions in difficult circumstances.

This is the joy of doing philosophy, rather than passively consuming it—pushing our mental capacities further and further, exercising them in a morally significant setting while managing the emotions that come with it, and rationally responding to the feedback we get about our decision-making. Video games like *Fallout 4* are playgrounds for the mind, where it can be active in a way it doesn't get to be with other media. Getting to make difficult moral decisions and getting to witness their consequences from the first-person perspective, contextualized in a detail-rich but still fictional world, is a unique way of thinking through philosophical issues. It's not just a different way of conducting thought experiments that help us figure out what our philosophical views should be (though it can be that, too),[15] nor is it just a different way of exercising our agency (though it can be that as well).[16] It's the closest we get to living out and refining our philosophical views in a controlled environment because, in an important way, how we make moral decisions in video games like *Fallout 4* is exactly like in our reality: it is emotionally significant to the point of agonizing over which course of action to take.

For those of us who already love this active aspect of doing philosophy, *Fallout 4* is quickly recognizable as a bounty of riches compared with the austerity of traditional philosophical training, in which *The Matrix* is often considered a high-water mark for engaging stimulation. For those of us unfamiliar with philosophy as a discipline, *Fallout 4* is an equally, if not more, enjoyable experience, especially if one comes into it only looking for escape. Whether the moral dilemmas throughout *Fallout 4* are recognized for what they are, agonizing over them reminds us of the power of moral decision-making, whether in a video game or in reality—the power to affect other people's lives and to shape our own private world, in the moment and in our life's story. They remind us that, to borrow from Tolkien, what is for us to decide is not the times in which we live but what to do with the time that is given us.

Most video games don't stick in your mind like that. They come and go, having served their temporary purpose. But some stick around, affecting us not only while we play them but long afterwards. Some video games are special.[17]

Notes

1. Binh Tran, "How Many Video Games Are There in the World? (2025 updated)," Gamespublisher.com, February 26, 2024, at https://gamespublisher.com/how-many-video-games-are-there-in-the-world-2025.
2. Escapism as one of the motivations for gaming is well documented, though there is disagreement over how to define it and which consequences it has, for example, in Zsolt Demetrovics, Róbert Urbán, Katalin Nagygyörgy, Judit Farkas, Dalma Zilahy, Barbara Mervó, Antónia Reindl, Csilla Ágoston, Andrea Kertész, and Eszter Harmath, "Why Do You Play? The Development of the Motives for Online Gaming Questionnaire (MOGQ)," *Behavior Research Methods* 43 (2011), 814–825; Lucas M. Marques, Pedro M. Uchida, Felipe O. Aguiar, Gabriel Kadri, Raphael I. Santos, and Sara P. Barbosa, "Escaping Through Virtual Gaming—What Is the Association with Emotional, Social, and Mental Health? A Systematic Review," *Frontiers in Psychiatry* 14 (2023), 1257685; Rosalynd Fraser, Jan Slattery, and Igor Yakovenko, "Escaping Through Video Games: Using Your Avatar to Find Meaning in Life," *Computers in Human Behavior* 144 (2023), 107756.
3. Those who work on the nature of immersion introduce fine-grained distinctions between immersion, presence, realism, involvement, emotional content, and other related terms that become precise and technical, and lead to disagreements over their definitions. Those details don't play a role here, but for those interested in them, some good places to start include Bob G. Witmer and Michael J. Singer, "Measuring Presence in Virtual Environments: A Presence Questionnaire," *Presence* 7 (1998), 225–240; Mel Slater, "Measuring Presence: A Response to the Witmer and Singer Presence Questionnaire," *Presence: Teleoperators and Virtual Environments* 8 (1999), 560–565; Mel Slater, "A Note on Presence Terminology," *Presence Connect* 3 (2003), 1–5; Mel Slater, "Immersion and the Illusion of Presence in Virtual Reality," *British Journal of Psychology* 109 (2018), 431–433.
4. Some think that representationalism has the resources to explain key features of consciousness as well, including Fred Dretske, *Naturalizing the Mind*, (Cambridge, MA: MIT Press, 1995). Michael Tye, *Ten Problems of Consciousness* (Cambridge, MA: MIT Press, 1995), and William Lycan, *Consciousness and Experience* (Cambridge, MA: MIT Press, 1996), but its success is questioned by, for example, Ned Block, "Mental Paint and Mental Latex," in Enrique Villanueva ed., *Philosophical Issues, 7: Perception* (Atascadero, CA: Ridgeview, 1996) and David Chalmers, *Conscious Mind* (Oxford: Oxford University Press, 1996).
5. There is evidence that going through moral decisions for oneself, rather than passively observing or even evaluating the moral decisions of others, involves more of and different brain processes, as reported by Beverley Garrigan, Anna L.R. Adlam, and Peter E. Langdon, "The Neural Correlates of Moral Decision-making: A Systematic Review and Meta-analysis of Moral Evaluations and Response Decision Judgements," *Brain and Cognition* 108 (2016), 88–97.

6. It is evident that moral decision-making has a significant emotional component, as reported by Joshua D. Greene, R. Brian Sommerville, Leigh E. Nystrom, John M. Darley, and Jonathan D. Cohen, "An fMRI Investigation of Emotional Engagement in Moral Judgment," *Science* 293.5537 (2001), 2105–2108, and discussed by Jesse Prinz, "The Emotional Basis of Moral Judgments," *Philosophical Explorations* 9 (2006), 29–43, as well as Ellen Fridland, "Motor Skill and Moral Virtue," *Royal Institute of Philosophy Supplements* 80 (2017), 139–170
7. For a different look at how the *Fallout* games, particularly *Fallout 3*, involve moral decision-making, check out Marcus Schulzke, "Moral Decision Making in Fallout," *Game Studies* 9 (2009), 1.
8. In fact, Bethesda (the studio that made *Fallout 4*) is known for jarring lapses in visual immersion, and even beloved for some of the "jankiness" of their games, precisely because of the freedom in decision-making and action they grant the player, demonstrating their understanding of what makes their games so special, as noted by Jordan Gerblick, "Skyrim Lead Admits 'Bethesda Games Could Have a Higher Degree of Polish', but Some Jank 'Could Be Forgiven' Because of How Much You Can Do in the RPGs," Gamesradar+, October 15, 2024, at https://www.gamesradar.com/games/the-elder-scrolls/skyrim-lead-admits-bethesda-games-could-have-a-higher-degree-of-polish-but-some-jank-could-be-forgiven-because-of-how-much-you-can-do-in-the-rpgs.
9. Some see the way games in general (and not only video games in particular) involve our agency as making agency an art medium and those games artworks in that medium, for example, C. Thi Nguyen, *Games: Agency as Art*, (Oxford: Oxford University Press, 2020).
10. For some very candid and insightful thoughts on advanced machines and AI, check out Alan Turing, "Computing Machinery and Intelligence," *Mind* n.s. 59.236 (1950), 433–460.
11. That we cannot imagine what it's like to be a bat is one of the claims argued for by Thomas Nagel, "What Is It Like to Be a Bat?," *The Philosophical Review* 83 (1974), 435–450.
12. That we can scaffold our imagination to help us imagine significantly different experiences is a claim defended by Amy Kind, "What Imagination Teaches," in Enoch Lambert and John Schwenkler eds., *Becoming Someone New: Essays on Transformative Experience, Choice, and Change*, (Oxford: Oxford University Press, 2020), 133–146.
13. To see why imagination is a skill and how it factors into our decision-making, check out Amy Kind, "The Skill of Imagination," in Ellen Fridland and Carlotta Pavese eds., *The Routledge Handbook of Philosophy of Skill and Expertise*, (Abingdon: Routledge, 2020), 335–346.
14. For a fascinating account of how children's pretense play is the beginning of a "lifelong mental capacity to consider alternatives to reality" at the core of rational thinking (p. 28), which playing video games like *Fallout 4* harnesses, check out Paul Harris, *The Work of the Imagination*, (Oxford: Blackwell, 2000).
15. Some think that video games can indeed present us with philosophical thought-experiments, for instance, Marcus Schulzke, "Simulating Philosophy:

Interpreting Video Games as Executable Thought Experiments," *Philosophy & Technology* 27 (2014), 251–265.

16. Some think that games make an unusual use of our agency, or ability to act, for example, Nguyen, *Games*.
17. Special thanks to my husband, Ian Franco, for help with many details in this chapter, including the title, and to my father, Nick Samoylov, for introducing me to video games.

22

Aesthetics in the Age of the Atom

S. Evan Kreider

Bethesda Softworks released *Fallout 3* in 2008, a decade after original *Fallout* developers Black Isle Studies released *Fallout 2*. In that time, video game technology had come a long way, making the sequel a significantly different experience than its predecessor. It was well received by gamers and critics, but some noticed strong similarities to Bethesda's other recent titles in the *Elder Scrolls* series, *Morrowind* (2002) and *Oblivion* (2006). This raises some interesting philosophical questions. Is *Fallout 3* simply another fantasy role-playing game (RPG) with a thin veneer of post-apocalyptic aesthetic? If so, is the change of aesthetic itself trivial, or does it add something of substance to the gaming experience? These questions can be addressed by viewing *Fallout 3* through the aesthetics of philosophers like Aristotle, Francis Hutcheson, and Clive Bell.

Aristotle and Aesthetic Didacticism

Aristotle (384–322 BCE) endorses a kind of aesthetic *didacticism* (from the Greek *didaktikos*, meaning "able to teach"), where art serves the function of teaching the audience. In Aristotle's *Poetics*, he especially analyzes tragedies in terms of their moral content, seeing them as a means of communicating important philosophical truths about moral obligations and providing an opportunity to practice our moral responses to difficult scenarios, ahead of encountering analogous situations in real life.[1]

The main way that tragedies accomplish this is through *mimesis*, typically translated as "imitation." In this respect, Aristotle falls within the modern aesthetic classification of *representational* theories of art, where art is meant to represent a specific subject matter. In dramatic plays, this happens in obvious ways: actors imitate people (real or mythical), their words, and their actions. The sets and costumes also contribute to the imitation, but for Aristotle, the most important elements of tragedy are the plot (which imitates actions and events), the moral character of the protagonist and others on stage (revealed through their actions and words), and the dialogue (which allows the characters to explicate moral issues and lessons thereof). Aristotle pays special attention to the plot as the most important element, arguing that plots should have a unity, length, and internal logic that allows the audience to focus on the main sequence of actions and events in a single sitting, presented in such a way that the consequences of the characters' actions make sense and impart the correct moral lessons.

The point of this is twofold. First, the plot is meant to arouse certain emotions in the audience. According to Aristotle, tragedies are written to arouse feelings of fear and pity, primarily toward the tragic hero and by way of the tragic consequences that follow as the logical result of his or her own flawed behavior.[2] Second, this arousal should provide the opportunity for the audience to undergo a catharsis of these emotions. Aristotle is unclear about what this catharsis entails, but some modern philosophers have interpreted it as a purging of the relevant emotions, a way of "letting off steam" and ridding oneself of such negative feelings.[3] Other philosophers see catharsis as a perfecting of the relevant emotional responses, primarily for the purpose of ethical improvement, so that the audience will better respond to real-life tragic responses. Either way, the result should be for the better, ethically speaking, complementing the moral lessons explicitly taught by the tragedy through the plot and dialogue.

Fallout 3 offers clear applications of Aristotle's analysis. As a work of post-apocalyptic science fiction, it lends itself to exploring a variety of themes, makes points about ethics and politics, and offers opportunities for catharsis. For instance, *Fallout 3* is clear about the tragic consequences of war, as the opening lines indicate: "War. War never changes ... blood has been spilled in the name of everything: from God to justice to simple, psychotic rage." We learn that the war and resulting fallout are the result of conflicts between the United States and China over resources. The United States is led by a president whose election is suspect from the beginning and turns out to be an advanced AI who simply assumed control and created a persona along with a backstory that included a vague account of his election. Factions fight for influence in the Capital Wasteland, and the game's protagonist must navigate all the challenges of this setting, ultimately deciding the fate of the Capital Wasteland's people.

However, it's not clear that the science fiction setting of Bethesda's *Fallout* offers anything truly different from the themes, lessons, and catharsis available from fantasy role-playing games such as Bethesda's very own *Morrowind* and *Oblivion*. *Morrowind* deals with conflicts among the godlike beings Dagoth Ur and the Tribunal (particularly Vivec) and their cults and factions. Similarly, *Oblivion* deals with supernatural threats while also focusing on political conflict and intrigue related to the Empire and the protagonist's role as the "Hero of Kvatch" who ultimately saves the province of Cyrodiil and becomes its champion. Though the games themselves do not explicitly present themselves as such, they could be viewed as analogs to real-world political and religious struggles, thus allowing all the same reactions as one might have to a post-apocalyptic setting.

One might argue that it's psychologically more natural to apply these themes in a science fiction context, because it's easier to think of the characters and settings as representations of our own future. Even when science fiction is set in the distant past (as in *Star Wars* with "a long, long time ago"), we tend to envision it as in the future (the technology of *Star Wars* is sometimes referred to as "futuristic"). However, that's not a very strong philosophical connection, just a common psychological one. Considering that, we might find stronger distinctions between *Fallout* and the *Elder Scrolls* series by taking a different philosophical approach.

Hutcheson and Aesthetic Pleasure

Francis Hutcheson (1694–1746) was one of the first philosophers to develop a fully modern theory of aesthetics that treats aesthetic objects (such as nature and art) and our reactions to them as distinct subjects. His empiricist epistemology, a view that all knowledge is fundamentally grounded in observation and sense data, provides a foundation for his aesthetics. Early empiricists made a distinction between the primary and secondary qualities of objects. Primary qualities are, from the point of view of physics, the actual qualities of the object, and consist in mathematically quantifiable properties such as size, shape, and number. Secondary qualities are not, strictly speaking, properties of the objects themselves, but properties that the primary qualities give rise to in our psychological perception and experience of them, including qualitative properties such as color and sound. For example, a plucked string and its effects can be explained fully in physical terms of its primary qualities such as the movements of the materials of which it is made and the vibrations it causes in the air molecules nearby, but the sound of the music note it produces is a secondary quality that occurs in our minds as our brain's interpretation of the vibrations as they strike our eardrum, stimulate auditory nerves, and so on.[4]

Hutcheson agrees with Aristotle about the mimetic nature of art, seeing most forms (other than music) as mimetic. For example, a portrait literally imitates the visual appearance of its subject, and some of our enjoyment comes from seeing the resemblance between the two. However, art also has what Hutcheson calls "absolute beauty" independent of any mimetic features it may have. According to Hutcheson, our external senses (e.g., vision) are complemented by internal senses, mental capacities to generate additional ideas from those we receive from our external senses. Humans have an aesthetic sense that responds to a feature of our empirical experiences that Hutcheson calls "uniformity amidst variety." In the case of absolute beauty, "uniformity" means the order, and "variety" means the complexity of the perceptual experiences.[5] For example, a song has an orderly structure (perhaps an AABA form, which is a section repeated twice, a contrasting section, then the initial section again) and a harmonic complexity (perhaps specific chords, scales, and variations). An internal sense responds to this order and complexity, resulting in aesthetic pleasure, something distinct from non-aesthetic pleasures (which often fulfill practical needs, such as quenching one's thirst with water). Hutcheson refers to this pleasure in order and complexity (and sometimes the internal sense which gives rise to the pleasure) as beauty.[6]

The distinction between external and internal senses also explains variations in personal taste. Just as variations in the workings of an external sense (e.g., color blindness) result in different experiences, so too variations in the workings of the internal sense of beauty explain why two individuals may have the same perceptual experience but different responses in terms of the pleasure they experience from it. For example, two people with the same sense of hearing might listen to the same song and yet only one person enjoys it. Hutcheson suggests that the internal senses can be more or less accurate in the same way that external senses can be, and so he might want to claim that some people are "wrong" not to enjoy an objectively good song (they have "poor taste," just as one might have poor hearing). However, there's nothing that rules out some legitimate variation of taste as well (just as people might legitimately enjoy different food and drink).

There's a lot to be said for the pleasurable aspects of *Fallout*—gamers usually just call it "fun"—in terms of its orderly elements. As an RPG, its order is largely presented through its gameplay rules. These rules provide an orderly structure for character creation with the S.P.E.C.I.A.L. attributes (Strength, Perception, Endurance, Charisma, Intelligence, Agility, and Luck), the skill system (for example, Barter, Persuade, Sneak), and perk abilities (for example, Gunslinger, Lady Killer, Night Person) that distinguish a player character among different players or different playthroughs. There are also rules for skill use and combat, though those largely take place "under the hood" and are handled by the computer or console. *Fallout* also shows orderly gameplay in terms of its quest structure. Each game has a main quest, which, in the case of *Fallout 3*, begins with the player character trying to find their father. The main quest is further supplemented by various side-quests, some of which facilitate the completion of the main quest, others of which simply allow more gameplay and opportunities to improve one's character. In these respects, *Fallout* offers a highly orderly gaming experience.

Fallout also offers plenty in terms of enjoyable complexity, what gamers sometimes refer to as "crunch." The aforementioned character generation offers detailed options that are more complex than many other RPGs. For example, an RPG could reduce the number of attributes of the S.P.E.C.I.A.L. system (perhaps just three attributes, such as Physical, Mental, and Social), which would handle the same things but with a simpler list. So too, many games offer far fewer than the thirteen skills found in *Fallout 3* (for example, by combining multiple ranged weapons skills such as Big Guns, Energy Weapons, and Small Guns into a single Ranged Weapons skill). *Fallout 3* also offers plenty of crunchy gear and equipment, giving items various statistics themselves, such as weight (which determines whether the character is over-encumbered) and condition (which can affect the item's ability to work properly). There is also the crunchy gameplay of repairing and creating items such as weapons, ammo, and medical aid, which requires appropriate player character skill levels, materials, and workspaces. For players who enjoy complex gameplay, this level of crunch is precisely one of the things that draws them to the *Fallout* series.

Once again, we're left with the concern that there's nothing substantially different between *Fallout* and the *Elder Scrolls* series. *Morrowind* and *Oblivion* likewise have order and complexity, both in terms of character creation and gameplay, and similar kinds as well: detailed character stats, crunchy gear and equipment, the ability to create and repair items, and so on. As before, we could simply explain this in terms of psychological rather than philosophical differences. However, in this case, Hutcheson offers us a philosophical explanation of the psychological difference: personal taste reflects variations in internal senses of beauty. Since some gamers' senses will be different than others, they will find the order and complexity of the post-apocalyptic setting and gameplay more or less fun than that of classic fantasy. Though this is somewhat more philosophically satisfying, it would be nice if we could still find a more substantial difference between the games, and one that references the games themselves rather than the gamers' subjective reactions to them.

Bell and Aesthetic Formalism

The art critic Clive Bell (1881–1964) was a proponent of an approach to aesthetics known as formalism. Bell was a fan of post-impressionist painting and argued against critics who disparaged such art on the grounds that it was not realistic enough. Against mimetically realistic art that closely resembles the appearance of its subject, Bell argued that it was no more than a slavish copying of things and that it contributed nothing aesthetically distinctive. Instead, art should help us capture the true nature of things by drawing attention to what is important about them, reflecting reality better than the mundane appearances of things themselves do. According to Bell, good art does this by means of its "significant form." By this phrase, Bell seems to mean the formal features of the work of art. These features are the abstract elements that make up the work, independent of any mimetic resemblance to which they might contribute (e.g., lines, colors, and shapes), that capture important aspects of reality in a way that evokes what he calls our "aesthetic emotions."[7]

As with "significant form," Bell could have been clearer about his notion of "aesthetic emotions." At times, he seems to collapse into an expressive theory of art, wherein an artist is simply communicating an emotion to the audience through the art. However, he does clarify in other contexts that aesthetic emotions have no particular relation to everyday emotions such as happiness, sadness, anger, and so on. Instead, aesthetic emotions are distinct emotions only experienced in response to works of art, and their content "brings us closer to true reality." In other words, he suggests that an artist sees the true form of reality (whatever that is) and shows it to us through art.

One might be forgiven for thinking that Bell's theory sounds a lot like Hutcheson's, but there are important differences. Although Hutcheson refers to a formal property of art ("uniformity amidst variety"), this property is secondary to and simply arises from the fundamental nature of art, which, according to Hutcheson, is representational. As a result, Hutcheson would have been critical of post-impressionist art for not being realistic enough, whereas Bell rejects direct resemblance and simplistic mimesis as mere slavish copying. For another matter, Hutcheson's characterization of aesthetic feeling is simply another form of pleasure, in some ways no different than any other pleasure, but one that arises solely from the experience of aesthetic properties. Bell avoids reducing the aesthetic emotion to pleasure, even allowing for the possibility that it causes no pleasure at all and that it could involve a completely different kind of feeling, one that relates us to "true reality" in some way.

Fallout 3 clearly involves very different formalistic aesthetics than does an *Elder Scrolls* game, which one can think of in terms of their respective styles and genres. An obvious example is the Vault-Tec company's advertising mascot, Vault Boy. He is rendered in a distinct two-dimensional cartoon style that evokes an atomic age aesthetic, and his optimistic attitude (expressed by his broad smile and thumbs-up gesture) provides a clear formal counterpart to the death and destruction of the post-atomic apocalyptic setting. The in-game computer technology, such as computer terminals that provide information or require hacking and the player character's personal wrist computer "Pip-Boy" have a distinct style reminiscent of 1970s computer technology, rendered in all its 8-bit green or yellow glory. The appearance of the towns and their inhabitants has the veneer of old westerns, complete with the occasional cowboy hat.

On the other hand, *Elder Scrolls* games such as *Morrowind* and *Oblivion* involve a completely different set of aesthetic formalisms. Rather than drawing from the look and feel of more recent centuries, they are rendered in the style of ancient and medieval world qualities, such as lush green forests and large pure bodies of water, in addition to towns and cities with art and architecture one might see in a college course on the art of the ancient world. Instead of using in-game writing that looks like simple computer fonts, the *Elder Scrolls* games use old-fashioned scripts on signs, for example, suggesting pen-and-ink handwriting, chiseled carvings, and so on. This is not just limited to visual formalisms either but includes game music, both diegetic and non-diegetic. For example, while in *Fallout*, the player character might listen to twentieth-century country music on the radio on one's Pip-Boy, in *Morrowind* the player often hears the "walking from town-to-town theme" (accompanied by rather amusingly heavy-handed Foley-effect footsteps) which has the distinct sound of a pseudo-medieval Ren Fest.

Fallout and *Elder Scrolls* games are formally distinct games. Despite the similarities in gameplay structure (and legitimate criticisms thereof), they provide the player with aesthetically distinct experiences. The games deliver these experiences through very different formal qualities, which could not be confused by gamers who take more than a passing glance at the games. No gamer has ever spent more than a minute playing and come away unsure whether they had just played *Fallout* or the *Elder Scrolls*, thanks to their aesthetic formalisms.

Fallout for Its Own Sake

Fallout 3 was very well received and still has a reputation as a fantastic game almost two decades later. However, even its fans had some concerns that it was not much more than *Morrowind* or *Oblivion* with a coat of paint, as it were. On closer look through the lenses of philosophical aesthetics, we can see there is nothing much to be concerned about. As a game with a very different style, *Fallout 3* had some practical and psychological advantages to presenting certain political and moral themes, as well as just offering different kinds of fun for different gamers' tastes. More importantly, *Fallout 3* is a formally distinct work of art from any *Elder Scrolls* game, and as such, deserves our appreciation as a work of art, existing for its own sake.

Notes

1. Aristotle, *Poetics*, trans. Richard Janko, (Indianapolis: Hackett, 1987).
2. Aristotle, *Poetics*.
3. This was a standard view in the field of dramaturgy and has roots in Freudian psychoanalysis.
4. Francis Hutcheson, *An Inquiry into the Original of Our Ideas of Beauty and Virtue*, rev. ed., (Indianapolis: Liberty Fund, 2008).
5. Hutcheson, *An Inquiry into the Original of Our Ideas of Beauty and Virtue.*
6. Hutcheson, *An Inquiry into the Original of Our Ideas of Beauty and Virtue.*
7. Clive Bell, *Art (1913)* (Whitefish, MT: Kessinger, 2008).

23

Player Narrative and Dying Well: Re-examining the Ending of *Fallout 3*

Daniel Guy Baldwin

It's the year 2277. In the heart of the Jefferson Memorial sits Project Purity, a feat of engineering designed to provide fresh water on a mass scale, something not easily found in the irradiated wastes of the Capital Wasteland. A young man stands outside, forced to make a choice. To activate the machine, he must enter the control chamber, which is filled with lethal radiation. Project Purity was the lifework of his father, whose dead body already lies within the heart of the chamber. Mustering up the courage, he enters the chamber and punches in the activation code—2-1-6—a reference to the Bible quote his father recited to him when he was young. Revelation 21:6: "I am Alpha and Omega, the beginning and end. I shall give unto him who is athirst the fountain of the waters of life freely."[1] The purifier turns on. The young man dies. Roll credits.

This is the original pre-*Broken Steel* ending of *Fallout 3*, which has generated much ire since its release in 2008. It is the ultimate sacrifice of the one for the many. But why did this generate so much frustration for the playerbase? Why was the ending ridiculed as nonsensical? As being "dumb as hell"?[2] Poor writing may be to blame, but I believe it goes beyond this. It goes to the heart of character identity and player motivation.

In role-playing games (RPGs), as in life, we create narratives to ground the identity we inhabit. This forms one basis of narrative ethics, which is loosely defined as an approach to ethics that involves utilizing stories rather than any strict reliance upon rules or principles. It is not a definitive methodology or moral theory, but an approach in which stories aid ethical understanding. Following this approach, I would argue that my identity is informed by the story I create from my life events. The interpretation of these past events becomes part of the life story I am crafting, and this story informs my future actions. Thus, I should act in a certain manner because it fits the story I have created for myself. In the real world, this narrative informs my personal identity and action; in RPGs, it is usually the player character's. One difference is that in RPGs, the player can create a desired narrative for their character prior to any in-game events occurring (especially on repeated playthroughs). Knowledge of the plot and game mechanics can be used to create a foundational character background that provides both in-game motivation for the player character's actions and external motivation for the player to actually play the game. Why should I blow this man's head off? Well, because my character is an evil bastard, naturally.

In real life, our narrative culminates in our death and the end of experience. As such, in video games, death tends to be the default fail state. But need it be? Admittedly, death can come at the wrong time within any story. It can disrupt and destroy the narratives we build for ourselves. People often die unexpectedly before their time, their story cut short. An early death is most often a bad death. Indeed, death is an evil for most people, who want to go on living. Thus, wanting to stave off death is not irrational.[3] Of course, in RPGs we can always reload the last save, but I've yet to experience this in real life.

None of this is to say that *Fallout 3*'s ending was bad simply because it was a death. Actually, a good death is something we should aspire to in both RPGs and real life. Death can be a redemption for a life poorly lived or a fitting ending to the story of heroism, but it must always be contextualized within the narrative of an individual's life. The same must be done for *Fallout 3*'s ending. It is not an inherently bad ending. The issue is that it often does not fit the player-created narrative that provides the reason to act.

Beyond Good and Evil (There's Neutral Too)

One of the main systems that can be used to define character identity in *Fallout 3* is the Karma system, which was introduced in *Fallout 2*. This system of moral judgment borrows its name from a concept referring to the law of cause and effect found in various Eastern religions, such as Hinduism and Buddhism. Good actions lead to good karma, with better karma leading to better rebirths in the cycle of reincarnation. Ignoring the metaphysical and ethical implications of whether this is a genuine feature of the in-game world or merely a means to inform the player of the general perception of their character, the Karma system influences the premade narrative and gameplay as well as personal player narrative.

Actions in-game often have karmic weight; they provide good or bad Karma, eventually resulting in a character being classified as good, neutral, or evil. Karma both restricts and expands what a character is able to do in both a mechanical and narrative sense. Narratively, I may decide to blow up the town of Megaton because it is an evil thing to do, and as an evil character, it's fitting for my identity. A good character may be narratively limited from doing so, though they are not strictly limited from it in regard to gameplay. The player could still do it if they wished. It is always a possibility. But the narrative constructed by the player may restrict them from this action, as it would be unfitting to the character's story. Other actions may be narratively encouraged. If I wish for my character to experience redemption, then it makes sense for the evil character to begin doing good actions. These narrative limitations are, in a sense, self-imposed. I, as a player, am in control of this story, and I can shape it how I wish.

There is a parallel to be drawn here to life. If I view myself as a good person informed by my interpretation of my past life events, then I may refrain from committing a harmful action on that basis. It's not what a good person would do; therefore, I shouldn't do it. My action is narratively limited by my story-driven identity. And, like in *Fallout*, certain actions may be narratively encouraged. I am a good person (or at least I want to be), so I should commit to this action.

In terms of gameplay mechanics, some actions are only available to a character with a specific level of Karma. In *Fallout 3*, having a sufficiently high or low Karma will cause the player to be pursued and attacked by Talon Company mercs or the Regulators, respectively. Certain followers also have certain karmic requirements of the player. The Super Mutant Fawkes will only join the party of good characters, whereas Sergeant RL-3—the Mister Gutsy–style military robot—will only follow neutral characters. Other possible followers have no such requirements. The ghoul bodyguard Charon will happily follow anyone so long as they have purchased his contract.

These mechanical restrictions can help or hinder player narrative. Karma can prevent me from choosing options that I, as a player, desire and perhaps even those I genuinely believe my character would do. Alternatively, it can provide a reason to adapt the story of my character so that I can achieve those desired options. If my character is good but I want Sergeant RL-3 to join the party, then perhaps this shift from good to neutral can be narrativized into a story of an overly trusting, naive Lone Wanderer becoming a more pragmatic, stoic individual after their exposure to the harsh realities of the Capital Wasteland.

Translation of mechanics into narrative requires a level of flexibility and creativity on the player's part. This is not to say that all players do this. Some may simply enjoy the game mechanics without the need for narrativization. I may revel in the sight of a Deathclaw being atomized or take joy in the sight of a mini-nuke being launched into an unsuspecting group of bystanders. The motivation to play the game and for in-game action comes from elsewhere. Indeed, there is debate as to whether narrative is required for identity at all. Contemporary philosopher Galen Strawson denies that he and others understand their lives as a story or that narrative understanding is even required for a good life. Strawson has little concern for his far past or far future and constructs no narrative to link them to the present.[4] Comparably, it could be said of video games that certain players have a mechanical understanding of character identity—the character identity exists so that they may experience the game mechanics, and any narrative required is merely a means of delivering that experience.

But it seems to me that the narrative aspects form a large part of the appeal of RPGs and do provide motivation to play in this context. RPGs, by their nature as role-playing games, want a player to inhabit a role. There is a character that wants to be played, an identity that needs to be formed, and events that require an interpretation. There is a story waiting to be told. But, of course, the player is not the only one crafting a story here.

Narrative Paradox

Narrative paradox results from the conflict between the premade story and the freedom of player agency. I may be limited in my action because of the story the game wants to tell. This is especially prevalent in RPGs, which encourage player-created narratives whilst also trying to deliver a pre-authored story. Thus, although my character may be inclined to behave in a certain manner, this can be undermined by the story forcing certain actions upon me that do not align with my character's narrative.

This is not to say that restrictions on the player always result in narrative paradox. Nearing the end of the game, the player is captured by the Enclave and taken to their hidden base in Raven Rock. Thus, a narrative restriction has been placed upon the player. They cannot leave the base until the desired pre-authored story has been told. But the player still has the ability to act in a manner that aligns with their character narrative. Do they shoot their way out? Do they use their silver tongue to buy themselves some time? Do they simply sneak past the enemies without raising the alarm? The player still has agency to act in accordance with their character's story.

Even reaching the end of this sequence, the player is made to take the modified Forced Evolutionary Virus from Enclave president and supercomputer John Henry Eden. Within the premade story, Eden's intent is for the player character to insert the virus into the water purification system of Project Purity. This modified Forced Evolutionary Virus would be lethal to all humans with even slight mutations. The only survivors would be those who had avoided the effects of the radiation-filled world (Enclave members and Vault Dwellers). Simply being forced to take this virus does not cause any major narrative paradox because the player can still choose what exactly to do with it. They do not have to use it; they are simply given the option. Overarching pre-authored stories only become problematic for player-created narrative when no options present themselves that can be aligned with the character story. Now, let's go back to the ending of *Fallout 3*, which I believe contains the greatest example of narrative paradox within the entire game.

A Super Mutant, a Robot, and a Ghoul Refuse to Walk into a Control Chamber

To return to the scene described at the beginning of this chapter, let's imagine it is my character standing in the rotunda, which contains the control chamber of Project Purity. To briefly summarize his narrative, after exiting the vault, he soon adapted to the wastes by becoming entirely egoistic and self-serving. Initially, his selfish actions were justified by a need to survive. A couple of caps stolen here, some Dandy Boy Apples there. A man's gotta eat. But a couple of caps were never enough. He always wanted more. Eventually, this would lead him to murdering innocent Wastelanders, enslaving children, detonating an atomic bomb at the heart of a town, and generally not being a very nice person, all for financial gain. It is a story of a survivalist quickly becoming corrupted by greed. Karmically, he is an evil man. He feels little remorse for his actions since they have been rationalized as being done in the name of survival.

So why should this evil character, who has no need for redemption, enter the water purifier, knowing it will kill him, when that is completely at odds with the narrative that I, as the player, have constructed? Consider that when I am presented with the evil option of tainting the water supply with the modified Forced Evolutionary Virus, this does not seem something that *my* evil character would do. If everyone dies, then who is left to be exploited for his gain? In terms of player-created narrative and character identity, this death would be a bad one. It would disrupt my motivations for playing the game as this character. It would make the previous experience less meaningful overall.

However, it would be in the character's interest for Project Purity to begin pumping out clean water. Perhaps there are caps to be made there. I can generate a reason based on the previously constructed narrative for my evil character to want to do this good action. But that reason requires him to live. Entering the control chamber means certain death, and so this must be accounted for within the narrative. How can he, as the character, and I, as the player, get around this? Considering our options, we remember his follower Charon, who coincidentally is immune to radiation.

Earlier, I mentioned the followers Fawkes, Sergeant RL-3, and Charon, who can each accompany the player. All are immune from radiation and can be asked to enter the chamber of Project Purity to activate the purifier instead of the player. All of them refuse for their own reasons: Fawkes claims that it's the character's destiny and he would not rob us of that; Sergeant RL-3 says something similar about having to finish what your daddy started; Charon simply claims he has saved the player's ass enough times already.

Does this mean that the player character has to die? Are there no other options? Attempting to exit the rotunda presents the player with the message that the doors have locked behind them, so simply shirking the decision is not an option. This is narrative paradox. Player action has been limited by the pre-authored story, and the player may be forced to take action not necessarily in line with their character's identity. There is a disconnect between player motivation and character narrative. If the player wants to activate Project Purity, someone has to enter the control chamber. If my evil character must sacrifice himself, then my motivation to play and to act in-game, which stems from the narrative identity I have created for the character, has been undermined. It no longer matters. For this character, this ending is a bad one. This death is a bad one.

Fortunately, another option presents itself. Also accompanying the player during the final sequence is Brotherhood of Steel paladin Sarah Lyons. She will happily sacrifice herself in place of the player so long as the player informs her of the activation code. This is how the player can be freed from the narrative paradox and the character freed from a bad death.[5] But this raises the question of why the developers would not allow radiation-immune followers to act in Lyons's place, especially when it was considered that the player might ask them to do so. Perhaps that simply boils down to bad writing. Furthermore, whether the player is willing to sacrifice Paladin Lyons may also come down to the narrative of their character. Perhaps Paladin Lyons has been integrated into the player-created story in a way in which the character would not wish to sacrifice either her or themselves. For some characters, it is still an impossible situation.

A Story of Death or the Death of a Story

The main issue with the ending of *Fallout 3* is that it often does not fit the player-created narrative, which provides the character, and indeed the player, with their motivations. Whether it is altruistic or egoistic, good or evil, benevolent or malevolent, self-sacrifice cannot always be easily incorporated into our narratives. There needs to be some narrative reason that makes sense. This is especially true when there are options denied to the player, such as sending in a character immune to radiation, which would not cost the character their life.[6] Allowing the player to send in Sarah Lyons certainly reduces the level of narrative paradox, as more options mean a higher chance of one fitting within the character narrative. But if, in my character's final moments, I am forced into actions that undermine who they are, then it leads me to question why I played the game that way in the first place. It lessens the meaning of the entire experience. A good death is one that allows the meaning of the whole to remain intact. Dying well requires us to be able to incorporate death into the narrative we have authored. For many characters, *Fallout 3*'s ending would not be a good death. It is too sudden and unexpected. It is too hard for the player to make sense of it in relation to the story they were trying to tell.

This might lead us to say then that it is a failing of the player, not the game, that they allow their character narrative to become so disrupted as to damage the overall meaning of playing the game. Narrative is flexible. It is an interpretation of events (fictional or real) told to an audience. In this case, the player is both the author of their character narrative and its audience. In life, we can't control exactly what happens to us, but we are afforded a level of control of the interpretation and integration of those events into our story. This is a fictional instance of a similar occurrence. An event is forced upon me. I must make sense of it narratively. Sometimes this is simple. The entirely good utilitarian has no qualms about sacrificing themselves for the greater good. The absurdly evil misanthrope has no issue poisoning the watering hole and sending Sarah Lyons to her death. There are no narrative paradoxes or disruptions here because the character narratives are relatively simple and straightforward.

Flexibility is required when narrative disruptions occur, and disruptions are more likely to occur when a player-created character narrative is more complex. To return to my evil character, perhaps another solution to undo the narrative paradox is to rationalize the self-sacrifice by presenting it as him having a sudden epiphany. He realizes all the harm he has done to the world and sees this as his final opportunity to redeem himself. The story of the character is mine to control. But it is not always that simple. The player has invested hours into a certain narrative, and to change the story at the last moment does not necessarily feel satisfying. Whether my character's death is good or bad depends both on the specific narrative I have constructed for the character and my own personal traits, which influence how easily I am able to adapt to disruption of that narrative.

The original sacrificial ending of *Fallout 3* can be a good ending, it can be a good death, as long as the player is aware of it and can build their character narrative around it or can quickly adapt the narrative to the pre-authored structures. On most initial playthroughs, however, the player would be unaware of the ending and not necessarily able to rationalize it within their narrative. That would be a death which comes too soon. That would be a bad death. That would be a death which throws the narrative-based identity that motivates the player into confusion. That would be a death which a large number of *Fallout 3* players would, and indeed did, find disappointing.

Notes

1. The Holy Bible, Revelation 21:6 (King James Version, 1769).
2. Tiago Svn, "Revisiting 'Fallout 3's Ridiculous Ending," Cracked, September 11, 2022, at https://www.cracked.com/article_35271_revisiting-fallout-3s-ridiculous-ending.html. "Dumb as hell" is one of the kinder phrases to be found online regarding Bethesda's writing and *Fallout 3*'s ending.
3. Christine Overall, *Aging, Death, and Human Longevity: A Philosophical Inquiry*, (Berkeley: University of California Press, 2003), 104–106.
4. Galen Strawson, "Against Narrativity," *Ratio* 17 (2004), 428–452.
5. There is also a somewhat hidden option of doing nothing. If the player waits long enough, Project Purity explodes and kills the player regardless. For some characters, this may be a better death for their narrative. I say this ending is

somewhat hidden as, until writing this chapter, I had no idea it existed at all. This may be one way out of the narrative paradox presented but it does not necessarily make itself obvious within the game as the player is both encouraged and naturally inclined to act.

6. Admittedly, Bethesda did eventually add the option of sending in a follower in the DLC *Broken Steel* (which also retconned the death of the main character if the player chose to sacrifice themselves), but seemingly begrudgingly, as the end narration still highlights that the player has failed to follow the example of their father.

Part 6

APOCALYPTIC PSYCHOLOGY

24

Loss, Care, and Morality in *Fallout*: An Ethics of Care Approach

Karen "Kat" Schrier

Even though *Fallout 3* and *Fallout: New Vegas* are two of my favorite games, I almost turned off *Fallout 4* during its opening scenes. In it, I discovered that I was a Sole Survivor who had escaped a Great War and was cryogenically frozen in Vault 111. I also saw my in-game spouse get murdered and my baby son get kidnapped. This hurt deeply. It had only been a few months since losing my real-life baby son, and I wasn't emotionally prepared for even a digital version of that grief.

But I should have expected this. Games in the *Fallout* series feature themes like grief and loss, as their narratives revolve around the destruction of society as we know it. The basic story is this: you are a survivor amid post-apocalyptic nuclear destruction. There's a sudden and prolonged societal collapse. There's also a need to rebuild humanity in a world with limited potable water and safe food, ruined homes, and few non-radioactive spaces. Individuals need to reimagine what humanity is now, given these new constraints.

Grief, loss, and care are integral to *Fallout 3* and *4*. As we'll see, care is a response to, or even resistance to, loss and moral despair in the barren wasteland, and, by playing the games, we can learn about ourselves and society.

The Ethics of Care

The ethics of care is a philosophical approach that integrates care, connectedness, compassion, responsiveness, relationships, and our caretaking responsibilities into moral decision-making.[1] According to contemporary theorists and researchers like Nel Noddings (1929–2022), Carol Gilligan, and Joan Tronto, ethical decision-making is not just about objective or universal rules or outcomes, but also about context, connection, and caring. Recognizing this, care ethics emphasizes the importance of nurturing relationships, depending on others, and being responsible for the needs of those in your care. Moral decision-making involves a moral agent having a "desire or inclination toward" someone else's feelings, possibilities, or needs.[2] Our care for someone (along with the reasoning behind it) guides our ethical attention. It shows us that if we are taking care of a child, a parent, a pet, a spouse, or even our fellow community members, we are in a "caring-for" relationship with them. Accordingly, we should calibrate our ethical decision-making by integrating our understanding of their needs, any relationship information, and our obligation and responsibility to take care of them.

Traditional philosophical approaches, such as some interpretations of Kantian ethics, posit that moral decision-making should be devoid of any emotion or consideration of one's relations to others. The ethics of care approach, however, rejects dichotomies between reason and emotion. Relational data, emotions, needs, caretaking, and societal expectations of care, all become salient evidence to use alongside other information when making ethical decisions.

But how are we defining care? Though "care" is often an unclear term, we can define it as "an attitude of appropriate concern," as well as a practice or a skill.[3] Contemporary philosopher Shannon Vallor explains that it takes practice and time to develop caring, and we may not always care appropriately or meet the needs of those we care for, even those that are not human.[4] Tronto and her co-author, contemporary philosopher Berenice Fisher, define care as an activity "that includes everything that we do to maintain, continue, and repair our 'world' so that we can live in it as well as possible."[5]

Thus, care can be toward a specific person, or it could even be toward a group, like the caregiving that players of *Fallout* might do toward virtual creatures, a potential romantic interest in the game, or an in-game collective like the Brotherhood of Steel. This affects how we might interpret or reinterpret games. It means that we can see games as emotional, care-filled, and ethical experiences.[6] Care can extend to virtual characters because they serve as mirrors and mediators for human values, relationships, and emotions. We can't help but care for characters in books, movies, television, and games, because they bring us into their story, and we spend time interacting with their needs and perspectives. Likewise, they help us to explore how we care and which values matter to us, even though they aren't real.

Ethics of Care Applied to Gaming

Researchers like John Murphy and José Zagal have suggested that it is useful to incorporate alternative moral perspectives into games. Games have often been considered a male domain, and philosophy has traditionally emphasized impersonal, objective perspectives amid a male-dominated public sphere. So, unsurprisingly, analyses of games have also focused on masculine frames of morality.[7] My own research suggests that this is a false dichotomy, in that all players may have emotions, care relationships, and myriad perspectives to use when playing a game, regardless of their gender identity.[8] In *Fallout*, we can use an ethics of care approach to understand how care and emotions emerge from the "bleeds" or blurs between in-game and out-of-game, particularly those that support ethical engagement.[9] For instance, despite experiencing both real-life grief about a son and (in *Fallout 4*) "fictional" grief about a son, I continued playing the game. I was highly motivated to not just complete the game, but to find my in-game son as quickly as possible. I felt a responsibility to take care of this virtual character, and an obligation to fulfill caretaking and relationship-building to ensure his safety.

How might we apply the ethics of care approach to digital people and creatures in virtual worlds, stories, and games? How can we more deeply reflect on and understand our play and our relationship with loss and care? What are some of the caring relationships we are able to foster or imagine in *Fallout*? In what ways are we able to care about its virtual characters and communities? To address these questions let's focus on three different specific care relationships: the father in *Fallout 3*, the son in *Fallout 4*, and Dogmeat in both games.

Care and Fallout: Ethical Acts in a Broken World

Fallout 3's Father: "It's a Big World Out There. … What Kind of Person Are You Going to Be?"

At the start of *Fallout 3*, you are immediately thrust into vault life. You begin as a baby who is being cared for by your parents in Vault 101. This serves as a tutorial and a way of customizing your character, so that you can learn about the game and grow alongside your avatar. It also serves as your first moment of loss, as you immediately hear your father shout as your mother dies in childbirth. As you grow into adulthood within the vault, you complete a number of tasks under the watchful eye of your father. You walk to him (and learn how to move), move a ball, open a gate to a playpen, and choose your skills or abilities. You also learn about the Pip-Boy system, which plays the role of a surrogate parent that takes care of you on your journey through the wasteland. Once you turn 19, you learn that your father has escaped the vault. Despite his leaving a note asking you not to follow, your first goal is to escape and try to find him in a town called Megaton. This loss is a microcosm of the larger societal loss, where vaults have become tombs, cities are in ruins, creatures have mutated, and trust is scarce.

Your relationship with your father is an important relationship in *Fallout 3*, though one that you have only a limited opportunity to build. You may not feel the loss of this character viscerally because you never had much time to spend with your virtual father. As an idea, goal, or memory, however, it propels the narrative, with you leaving the vault and exploring the wasteland. In using your parental loss as a game goal, *Fallout 3* evokes care as an act of world-building. You learn about the Capital Wasteland as you wander through decaying urban infrastructure, meet survivors, give water to beggars, aid settlements, and heal companions. This shows an ethic of care as a moral responsibility not just to one's father but to one's status as a restorer of humanity.

Dogmeat as Companion: "Want to Come with Me? It's Dangerous Out Here all Alone"

While there are many different opportunities for building relationships with citizens of the wasteland in the *Fallout* franchise, none stay in my mind as long as Dogmeat, the canine creature that remains by your side as you slay ghouls, beat Super Mutants, and face off against Deathclaws. After wandering the wasteland as a solo player in *Fallout 3*, you can recruit Dogmeat as your companion (follower) as part of your journey. In the "Man's Best Friend" side-quest, Dogmeat can either be found in the scrap-yard or near the (old) National Mall. Meeting Dogmeat offers a reflective and profound opportunity to shift from lone wanderer to caregiver. Caring for Dogmeat is both practical in terms of gameplay and also emotional, in that you are mutually attuned to each other. Dogmeat/Dog also appears in *Fallout 4* and is similarly loyal and caring. For instance, he is unwavering no matter what your moral actions are, unlike other companions who might disapprove of your decisions (and will make that known).

In terms of the ethics of care, this relates to responsiveness. You anticipate Dogmeat's barks or listen for his growls, which alert you to nearby enemies. You can send him on mini-quests to fetch supplies like ammunition or weapons, and he may not return for days, increasing your worry and desire to find him. Dogmeat's loyalty—running into battle at your side or foraging for mole-rat meat or stimpaks—is an example of relational reciprocity: care met with commitment.

Caring for and about Dogmeat also raises the stakes of the game, such that we don't just feel that we are playing, but that we are emotionally embedded in a world that matters. It reminds us that even amid loss and catastrophe, it's not just about bleak survival, but also about building relationships so that our time (however long) is meaningful.

There are other possible followers, too, who, over time, you can form connections with, like the powerful Star Paladin Cross, a ghoul named

Charon, and a guilt-ridden human named Preston Garvey, who worries about lost colonists. Dogmeat, though, is a memorable in-game pet who not only supports your gameplay but also connects with you and helps establish your emotional place in the world. I even bought a Dogmeat stuffed animal so I could build a more concrete connection to the digital creature.

The Son in *Fallout 4*: "They Had no Right to Take You! You Were My Son.... Our Son ..."

The loss of one's kidnapped son in *Fallout 4* serves as a counterpart to the loss of one's father in *Fallout* 3. From the very beginning of *Fallout 4*, you find out that you are a "sole survivor" of an apocalyptic nuclear war, living in Vault 111. You discover that you have lost your spouse, and that your young child has been taken. This time, your wandering through the wasteland is motivated by a desire to find your son, Shaun. These losses also reflect other breakdowns: of family structures, of social norms, and systems of care. Loss and grief color all of your interactions, and emotionally underscore the broader societal loss of what life had once been like in Boston. Every quest is imbued with the urgency of parental responsibility and care.

Looking for your son, and discovering his transformation from young child to the (possibly problematic) Institute's leader and scientist, you experience the moral tension between wanting to support a safe, cared-for community and wanting to care for your child. Can you still care for someone who is complicit in morally dubious experiments? You might ask, should you kill him? Reconcile with him? Find out more?

These dilemmas reflect ethics-of-care concerns: conflicting loyalties, moral ambiguity, and the pain of care that isn't or shouldn't be reciprocated. What do you do when your care relationships are in contradiction with each other—caring for your son versus caring for the larger Commonwealth?

When I played *Fallout 4* and finally found my son in the Institute, I stopped playing the game. I knew what would happen next, and I considered my own unique goal to be complete. I had taken care of my virtual son by finding him, and I had taken care of myself by putting down the controller until a day that I could handle losing even a virtual son again.

By focusing on your relationship with your son and your journey toward him, *Fallout 4* embodies the ethics of care. It helps us to explore the difficulty of making moral decisions and how emotional responsibility and obligations toward care relationships affect our morality. Moreover, it shows how care can be complex: it can be painful, uncertain, joyous, and even unreciprocated. Care is not just one and done. Rather, it is an ongoing struggle that can be peppered with grief, ambiguity, tension, and love.

Civic Responsibility and Communities of Care

Players confront remnants of lost, mutated humanity everywhere: Nuka-Colas in almost-empty vending machines, lone teddy bears in deserted homes, vault memorials, makeshift churches, and companions like Preston Garvey who are struggling with memories of the past. Traditional care institutions (like schools, hospitals, playgrounds, and government buildings) are covered in debris, showing quite literally the decay of society.

Fallout encourages you to grapple morally with how to rebuild. It also enables you to view how emergent communities decide how to care for their members (or treat their enemies). In *Fallout 3* and *4*, you can bear witness to (and join in some cases) factions that each have differing value systems and ideas about how humanity should be restored. For instance, in *Fallout 3*, you can experience the Family, a cannibalistic society that has its own five key laws, such as "Kill not our kindred; slay only the enemy. This is our justice."

You can also talk to and potentially join the Brotherhood of Steel, an authoritarian, military-focused, jingoistic group that cares for its citizens through advanced technology, but which limits your ability to be individualistic and unique in restructuring society. Factions and organizations like the Brotherhood of Steel, Minutemen, the Institute, or the Railroad offer competing visions of restoration. Do we rebuild through military power? Through grassroots organizing? Through creating synths? Through the liberation of the oppressed (synths)? Each allegiance is a moral stance concerning the kind of care society should prioritize.

From the ethics of care approach, you might choose the Brotherhood of Steel because they focus on using technology to protect civilians and help those who are vulnerable (even if it seems they are sometimes idealistic and even foolhardy about it). The Elder Owyn Lyons, the leader of the East Brotherhood, cares about the protection and well-being of those in the Capital Wasteland region, and, for example, gives clean water to settlements. The Brotherhood prioritizes loyalty and their relationships to each other and the people they protect. Personally, I reluctantly joined the Brotherhood of Steel mostly because of what I felt was their powerful ability to help me "win" the game.

Throughout the series, you can also more directly engage in care-filled worldbuilding and meet your ethical responsibility to rebuild society. In *Fallout 4*, for instance, you can engage in settlement management. You're able to rebuild not through the conquest or subsumption of settlements, but by constructing homes, assigning jobs, and protecting the civilians who live in those areas. Such actions are not just about survival, winning the game, or even helping to acquire a companion, Preston Garvey. Rather, they are also about creating dignity and belongingness for the virtual denizens who live there, and a more caring moral lens through which those citizens in turn view you and your avatar. You can create spaces where others (and you, as a player) can live, thrive, and feel a sense of safety.

Play as an Act of Care

The player's choices regarding moral decisions, role upgrades, companions, faction allegiances, and settlement management can reflect an ethics of care that prioritizes cooperation, emotional connection, and mutual support. We have focused on care relationships in the game, but there are also mechanics that might enable us to explore care and grief more readily. The dialogue system and options give you (sometimes) the ability to express and make choices that show you want to participate in care or express grief. You build relationships with different virtual citizens and companions by listening to their stories, learning their perspectives, or reacting to their needs. For instance, in *Fallout 4*, you can decide to keep Dogmeat with you and say, "Stay with me, boy. I'm not leaving you behind," expressing your responsibility to care for your pet companion. (He whimpers when you leave.) You can tell Preston Garvey that you will "help however I can. People are counting on us," which shows your commitment to community care. You can affirm the needs of ghouls, synths, and other beings you encounter. And, you can decide to adopt a synth son and care for him, something that gives you the opportunity to be the parent you couldn't be before.

Other mechanics that support care stem from the S.P.E.C.I.A.L. effects you can choose, namely, Charisma and Luck. Charisma (among other things) allows certain dialogue (speech) options to be unlocked, which leads to possible moral choices, storylines, quests, and character connections. For instance, when you first meet Preston Garvey, you can more easily persuade him to help you and earn his trust during the quest "When Freedom Calls." He gives you access to useful armor and weaponry, and this sets you up for a better relationship with the Minuteman faction. Thus, higher charisma can help to influence other characters and enable ways that other characters might treat you. Luck enhances all skill levels, including charisma.

Certain levels of different S.P.E.C.I.A.L. effects can also unlock perks, like Black Widow and Animal Friend in *Fallout 3* and *Fallout 4*, or Inspirational and Local Leader in *Fallout 4*. Inspirational Leader allows your companion to do more damage in combat or help you carry more items (something I always needed since I was constantly dropping scavenged items in vacant houses). In *Fallout 4*, Dogmeat has a perk associated with him, Attack Dog, that unlocks at various levels of your avatar's Charisma level. This helps enhance his combat prowess and his ability to support you.

The Black Widow perk gives you certain dialogue options that can lead to unexpected and rare combinations. You can use the perk to seduce Mister Burke in Megaton and convince him not to go through with his plan to detonate a bomb. This keeps the Mayor, Lucas Simms, alive and also keeps Megaton from exploding. A real-life friend noticed that his game looked completely different from mine, and it was due to this storyline possibility that I had unlocked only because I was a female main character and had unlocked the Black Widow perk as my first perk before reaching Megaton.

The Karma system in *Fallout 3* itself reinforces a desire to play with intention and care. When you are engaging in the morality system, you can earn positive Karma when killing a bad character or doing a good deed (like caring for a citizen and giving water). Negative Karma is earned by killing good characters or making uncaring dialogue choices.

Likewise, Affinity is the system by which citizens and companions in *Fallout 4* either agree with or disagree with your moral decisions, and decide whether to align with you based on your values. Every time you choose whom to align with and what matters to you, you are performing care and deciding how to rebuild after loss.

Care as an Act of Protest

An ethics of care approach to *Fallout* shows us that moral life stems from the messy terrain of relationships, not just rights or rules. *Fallout* is not about clear-cut dichotomies like good versus evil or survival versus death. Instead, it's about the slow, complicated work of tending to others, building relationships, and imagining better worlds. Caring is not separate from but part and parcel of world-building and flourishing.

The games help us to uncover our own morality against the stark backdrop of loss and grief. Are we nurturing and building villages in *Fallout 4*? Are we embracing vulnerability by loving Dogmeat or fostering other companions? Are we helping communities take better care of their people, or are we purposefully causing chaos and instability?

Ultimately, the wasteland provides the experience of widespread loss as well as the potential for growth, restoration, and care. In a universe like *Fallout*, where survival is the main objective and society has collapsed, care relationships become a radical act of protest against the stark landscape and monstrous creatures. Whether we are caring for Dogmeat, protecting settlers, or confronting our lost son, our choices matter—to the game, to ourselves, and to the communities we inhabit both virtually and in real life.

By caring, we fight in a different way. It's not the aggressive type of violent combat that is typical of *Fallout*. Rather, each act of care reveals a new type of civic arrangement, one which isn't just about personal survival or the reinforcement of old hierarchies, but about rebuilding and reconnecting with each other. An ethics of care lens helps us see that moral life in *Fallout* (and beyond) can be about collective healing, growth, and repair, and not just societal and individual destruction.

Notes

1. Carol Gilligan, *In a Different Voice: Psychological Theory and Women's Development*, (Cambridge, MA: Harvard University Press, 1982); See also Carol Gilligan, "Women's Place in Man's Life Cycle," *Harvard Educational Review* 49 (1979), 440: "women not only define themselves in a context of human relationships but also judge themselves in terms of their ability to care. Women's place in man's life cycle has been that of nurturer, caretaker, and helpmate, the weaver of those networks of relationships on which she in turn relies"; and Nel Noddings, *Caring: A Feminine Approach to Ethics and Moral Education* (Berkeley: University of California Press, 1984), 96.
2. Noddings, *Caring*, 9.
3. Shannon Vallor, "Moral Deskilling and Upskilling a New Machine Age: Reflections on the Ambiguous Future of Character," *Philosophy & Technology* 28 (2015), 119.
4. Vallor, "Moral Deskilling and Upskilling a New Machine Age."
5. Joan Tronto, "Care as a Basis for Radical Political Judgments," *Hypatia* 10 (1995), 141–149, and Joan Tronto and Berenice Fisher, "Toward a Feminist Theory of Caring," in Emily K. Abel and Margaret K Nelson eds., *Circles of Care: Work and Identity in Women's Lives* (Albany: SUNY Press, 1990), 36–54.
6. Karen Schrier, *We the Gamers: How Games Teach Ethics and Civics*, (New York: Oxford University Press, 2021).
7. John Murphy and José Zagal, "Videogames and the Ethics of Care," *International Journal of Gaming and Computer-Mediated Simulations* 3 (2011), 69–81; Virginia Held, *The Ethics of Care: Personal, Political, and Global* (New York: Oxford University Press, 2006), and Virginia Held, "Caring Relations and Principles of Justice," in James Rachels and Stuart Rachels eds., *The Right Thing to Do: Basic Readings in Moral Philosophy*, 5th ed. (New York: Oxford University Press, 2010), 78–84.
8. For example, consider the experience of men playing *Fable III* and caring for their mentor Walter (a virtual character in the game) or the greater virtual society of Albion. Karen Schrier, "Avatar Gender and Ethical Thinking in *Fable III*," *Bulletin of Science, Technology, and Society* 32 (2012), 375–383.
9. Peter Rauch, "Playing with Good and Evil: Video Games and Moral Philosophy" (unpublished master's thesis, MIT, 2007); John Murphy and José Zagal, "Videogames and the Ethics of Care," *International Journal of Gaming and Computer-Mediated Simulations* 3 (2011), 69–81. See also Matthew Farber and Karen Schrier, "Beyond Winning: A Situational Analysis of Two Digital Autobiographical Games," *Game Studies Journal* 21 (2021), http://gamestudies.org/2104/articles/farber_schrier.

25

Obsessed with "The End" and What Comes After

Eric D. Wesselmann and J. Scott Jordan

Post-apocalyptic stories focus on the end of civilization as we know it and what comes afterwards.[1] The specific events that jumpstart the apocalypse vary. Sometimes it's a nuclear holocaust, a pandemic, or an environmental catastrophe. The event could be supernatural in nature, such as a zombie invasion or even Divine Judgment, like in the book of Revelation, or it could be a slow-burn threat like diminishing birth rates, abject poverty, hunger, drought, or a global lack of fuel.[2] In the *Fallout* franchise, the key event is a nuclear war between China and the United States, resulting in much of the United States being a barren, resource-deprived wasteland filled with various types of predators, both human and non-human.

Though the specific cataclysms in post-apocalyptic stories often reflect the anxieties of the cultures in which they were created, what these stories typically share is that the events transform their characters' physical and social environments from the familiar to the alien, both to them and to the audience.[3] The protagonists of these stories commonly find themselves in environments dominated by multiple physical and social threats, especially from those surviving humans who strive for power by exploiting others, such as the *Fallout* show's raiders, who abduct Hank MacLean, or the Vault-Tec executives who have been conducting experiments on citizens of the vaults since the war began. Thus, *Fallout*'s audience experiences a hypothetical world in which human life is characterized best by a phrase from philosopher Thomas Hobbes (1588–1679): "nasty, brutish, and short."[4] Further, post-apocalyptic stories often end ambiguously as to what comes next (if anything) for the characters and the world generally. Thus, scholars of post-apocalyptic stories argue that these narratives can serve both as simulations of what might happen in the future and allegories of the present for audience members.[5]

These stories are popular across diverse mediums and cultures throughout history, especially in Western Europe and the United States.[6] For example, the *Fallout* franchise has released several video games across multiple platforms since 1997, one television show, and several tabletop and card game adaptations. This popularity is paradoxical: Ernest Becker (1924–1974) argued that humans generally are terrified at the prospect of their demise and are motivated to avoid thinking about it as much as possible.[7] So why would people choose to consume narratives that remind them of their own mortality as well as the potential destruction of everything they know and hold dear? Why are these stories so popular across diverse mediums and cultures? Philosophers, psychologists, and other scholars have studied the reasons people report for consuming media that provoke negative emotions, generally assuming that people choose media purposefully to fulfill various psychological (e.g., cognitive, emotional, and motivational) functions.[8] So, what psychological functions do post-apocalyptic stories serve?

World-famous horror/sci-fi author Stephen King argues that some of the most effective horror and sci-fi stories provide audiences an opportunity to confront and control their fears in a safe way, sometimes providing the opportunity to imagine how they would respond in similar situations. Philosophers and psychologists studying these genres have made similar arguments.[9] Post-apocalyptic narratives, which typically have elements of both horror and sci-fi, likely provide similar benefits to audiences. Indeed, these stories focus on the lives of people who manage to survive the initial calamities and how they, and future generations, attempt to reforge communities and ultimately a new civilization. Post-apocalyptic stories like *Fallout* may have their greatest narrative attraction because of how the central characters respond to their extreme situations. For example, after the Ghoul takes Lucy to organ harvesters and trades her for two months' worth of the chemical vials he needs to survive, she ultimately escapes, and while doing so, finds him passed out on the ground. Of course, this is an extremely new type of experience for her. Yet despite the extremity of the situation, she resorts to the kindness and values with which she was raised ("The Golden Rule") and gives the Ghoul the life-sustaining vials. Such an action reveals to viewers the possibility of retaining our values and humanity in post-apocalyptic contexts that seem devoid of them.

In popular culture, people tend to associate the term *apocalypse* with catastrophic destruction and destabilization. But the original Greek form of the word *apokalypsis* often translates to "an uncovering" or "a revealing." As sci-fi actor/fan Wil Wheaton notes, many of these are "[stories] that tell us what we could be and warn us about where we're going."[10] Thus, one may ask what apocalyptic narratives *reveal* to audiences about ourselves, our cultures, and ultimately human nature. This chapter explores the various ways that stories like the *Fallout* franchise can provide audiences with both challenges and opportunities to explore general human concerns with potential threats to psychological needs that people must have fulfilled to be both psychologically and physically healthy. We'll also see how these stories can provide audiences with an opportunity to engender hope, an important emotion in helping people both navigate personal traumas and take action to reshape their environments in ways that they value.

Considering Media Narratives and Audience Needs

Humans have several needs that must be fulfilled to be both physically and psychologically healthy, such as a sense of personal security, control, and meaning.[11] Typically, people wish to avoid threats to these needs in real-life situations, and when they experience these situations, their attention and motivation are directed toward viable options to meet these needs. People also wish to avoid seeing others experience these threats. Generally, people are hardwired neurologically to experience the emotions of others vicariously when they see these emotions expressed in daily life, which many scholars describe as *empathy*.[12] Psychologists who study peoples' experiences with fictional narratives have argued that similar processes occur with characters in the stories people consume.[13] However, this presents a conundrum—why would people actively engage with stories that make them experience emotions they would normally avoid in "real" life? Philosophers have often described this situation as a *paradox* that has yet to be resolved fully.[14] Why would viewers of the *Fallout* show want to experience emotionally intense events, like when Snip Snip, the organ-harvesting robot, threatens to operate on and kill Lucy MacLean?

Many philosophers across centuries have addressed this paradox and have taken different approaches, each of which works well for some examples, less so for others.[15] As such, there likely is no one-size-fits-all explanation for why people consume stories that provoke negative emotions. Instead, the "truth" lies in the complex interaction between individual preferences of audience members and the specific situations that the story's characters find themselves in and how these situations are resolved. One common view that some philosophers and social scientists share is that people are more likely to enjoy stories that provoke negative emotions when they know these stories are fiction and they know they have some type of control over their consumption of the stories.[16] They can choose when to play a *Fallout* game or watch Maximus battle mutant animals and fiends, knowing that it is fiction, and they can choose when to stop if their vicarious experiences of negative emotions become too intense.

Other philosophers have argued that audience members choose these stories ultimately because there are other emotional or cognitive benefits that compensate for the immediate negative emotions (such as fear, disgust, or sadness) provoked by the experience.[17] But in what ways could watching Lucy and Norm MacLean learning the horrible truth about their father's role in the nuclear apocalypse (and their mother's tragic fate) provide audiences with compensatory benefits to make it an ultimately fulfilling media experience? It may be within the ways that the characters navigate the various threats to their fundamental needs, needs that the viewers also share and work to satisfy, albeit in a more mundane setting than a post-apocalyptic world. For example, though audiences are not members of the Brotherhood of Steel, they likely can understand the pain and anger that

Maximus feels when being mistreated by fellow members Titus and Thaddeus, as this type of mistreatment can be common in people's everyday experiences.

Finding Security After the Apocalypse

Perhaps a key pleasure comes from learning about how individuals such as Lucy, Maximus, and the Ghoul can survive in post-apocalyptic environments. Humanist psychologist Abraham Maslow (1908–1970) created a theoretical hierarchy of needs that people must satisfy to reach their full potential. The most basic needs of this hierarchy were focused on satisfying physiological needs (like food and water), and physical safety (protection from predators and shelter from the elements). Maslow argued that when these basic needs are not satisfied, other concerns, such as a sense of belonging or self-esteem, become less important.[18] When people feel their safety is threatened, they often seek ways to restore that security, sometimes at the expense of other needs like personal freedom, including other people's freedom.[19] For example, the Vault 33 Council rejects Lucy's pleas to organize a search party and leave the vault to find her father, suppressing her personal freedom by arguing it jeopardizes everyone's safety. Though the Council's rationale likely seems reasonable to most people, the sacrifice of personal freedoms for safety can be taken to violent and abusive extremes, like with Hank's justification for Vault-Tec's starting the war to "get rid of the factions" and to destroy Shady Sands in order to ensure peace and safety for his community and the future. It's important to note that psychologists have revised Maslow's theory, recognizing that the ranking of needs is more complicated in the sense that Maslow does not account for individual differences in one's priorities and values.[20] For example, Cooper Howard is not willing to sacrifice personal freedoms for the safety that Vault-Tec offers, and Lucy's need to be with her father supersedes the safety of the vault and the psychological and physical needs it satisfies. Audience members likely find themselves reflecting on their own needs and values while imagining what they would do in these circumstances.

Related to safety concerns, other psychologists have argued that humans (and related primates) evolved to attend to fear-relevant cues in their environment automatically in order to learn to avoid these threats in the future.[21] Recently, studies have found that people can experience *morbid curiosity*, a motivation to learn information about prospective survival-related threats, and this curiosity also increases their desire to consume fictional media that focuses on survival threats (like virus-related films during a pandemic).[22] It is possible that viewers of *Fallout* and other post-apocalyptic media experience a similar form of morbid curiosity that draws them to these stories. Some audience members may think that knowing what types of threats may exist in desolate places like the wasteland, and what people may need to do to survive (like drinking contaminated water), and what types of injuries may prove fatal when bereft of modern health care may give them insights to use if they are ever in similar (albeit less fantastical) survival situations.

Reestablishing Control Amidst Chaos

Wil Wheaton argues that stories depicting apocalyptic or dystopian warnings can "make people feel very small and very out of control."[23] Some of the events in *Fallout* would surely have a similar effect. Perhaps some viewers gain different benefits from watching *Fallout*'s protagonists overcome seemingly insurmountable odds. People generally have a psychological need to feel that they are in control of their destiny or at least can have a significant impact on their immediate environment.[24] For example, Maximus decides to take control of his destiny when Titus, the abusive knight he serves, is mortally wounded, and Maximus decides to let him bleed out, thus allowing him to take Titus's armor and live the life of a knight. Though audience members likely never have to make the type of decision Maximus was forced to make, they will have their own personal struggles that require mastery and control of their own destiny. In the context of horror, some fans report that watching these films provides them with inspiration to confront their own fears and problems, sometimes by directly identifying with the survivor characters.[25] It is possible that some fans of the *Fallout* series and other types of post-apocalyptic narratives derive a similar sense of strength from these stories.

Rebuilding Meaning from the Rubble

People respond negatively to the idea that their lives may simply be at the mercy of uncontrollable forces or randomness. Indeed, people have a general need to find meaning in their lives and in the world broadly, and this meaning can be derived either through sacred or secular worldviews.[26] Researchers have found that making people explicitly think of their death can heighten their need to fortify these meaning-related belief systems. These belief systems can offer a general sense of immortality, whether literally in the context of religious beliefs in an afterlife, or symbolically by contributing to a social system in which they can live on through their familial or cultural contributions.[27] We can see examples of this when Maximus says that the Brotherhood has given his life meaning, in Lucy's dedication to "The Golden Rule" and the vault's purpose for "Reclamation Day," and even the Vault 4 citizens' dedication to the Flame Mother.

Of course, beliefs about literal versus symbolic immorality would not offer equal protection in a true end-of-the-world scenario where there would be no remnants of human society and culture to continue beyond one's own earthly demise.[28] Perhaps that is why audiences become so invested in seeing how people continue to struggle, live, and perhaps even flourish after the Great War of 2077. If these characters' stories, and society broadly, ended with the Great War, then perhaps *our* stories would be at an end too. If these characters can still persevere despite the upheaval of society as audiences know it, then the story provides a sense of *hope*. Hope is an important emotion in helping people both navigate personal traumas and take action to reshape their environments in ways that they value.[29] Perhaps it is this spirit of hope, as embodied in Lucy's optimistic "all-American can-do spirit," community-oriented nature, and her moral values that she struggles desperately to preserve in a hostile environment, that endears her to audiences and helps them identify with her as a focal character of the series.

Navigating What Comes After Apocalypse

Popular post-apocalyptic narratives like the *Fallout* franchise have valuable functions psychologically and culturally. They provide us with a space for introspection, for collective dialogue, and for hope. They move us to ask ourselves, *what* do we value, *who* do we fear to become, and *how* do we work to become what we aspire to be personally and collectively? Media scholars Chase Pielak and Alexander H. Cohen argue that post-apocalyptic narratives can provide audiences with a way to think about what they value about being human and how they may use these values to make meaningful changes in their real-life environments to work toward a future they desire. As Maximus tells Lucy, "Everyone wants to save the world, they just disagree on how." Lucy, Maximus, the Ghoul, Lee Moldaver, the Brotherhood of Steel, and even Hank and Vault-Tec all have ideas about how they think the world should continue. The key questions for the audience are how they respond to these characters' differing views, who they side with, and what that inspires them to do as they think about the current state of our own world. As the *Fallout* series poster says, "The world deserves a better ending." If we assume this show is a distorted mirror, *our* ending ultimately is up to us.

Notes

1. Films that fit within an apocalyptic vs. post-apocalyptic cinema category may be debated based on whether the narrative focus is on the cataclysmic event itself or how humanity continues afterward. Charles P. Mitchell, *A Guide to Apocalyptic Cinema* (Westport, CT: Greenwood Press, 2001). We choose to

use "post-apocalyptic" as an umbrella term because both types of films fit within our broader arguments.

2. Claude Gaillard, *After the World Ends*, (Paris: Pulse Editions, 2021); Mitchell, *A Guide to Apocalyptic Cinema*; Chase Pielak and Alexander H. Cohen. *Living with Zombies: Society in Apocalypse in Film, Literature, and Other Media* (Jefferson, NC: McFarland, 2017); Annie Rehill, *The Apocalypse Is Everywhere: A Popular History of America's Favorite Nightmare* (Santa Barbara: ABC-CLIO, 2010).
3. Pielak and Cohen focus mostly on post-apocalyptic films that involve zombies. We posit that many of their arguments can apply to other types of post-apocalyptic narratives.
4. Thomas Hobbes, *Hobbes's Leviathan*, (Oxford: Oxford University Press, 1952), 97.
5. Gaillard, *After the World Ends*; Mitchell, *A Guide to Apocalyptic Cinema*; Pielak and Cohen, *Living with Zombies.*
6. Gaillard, *After the World Ends*; Rehill, *The Apocalypse Is Everywhere.*
7. Ernest Becker, *The Denial of Death*, (New York: Free Press, 1973).
8. See for example, Thomas Ruggiero, "Uses and Gratifications Theory in the 21st Century," *Mass Communication and Society* 3 (2000), 3–37. Ron Tamborini, Nicholas David Bowman, Allison Eden, Matthew Grizzard, and Ashley Organ, "Defining Media Enjoyment as the Satisfaction of Intrinsic Needs," *Journal of Communication* 60 (2010), 758–777.
9. Stuart Hanscomb, "Existentialism and Art-horror," *Sartre Studies International* 16 (2010), 1–23. https://doi.org/10.3167/ssi.2010.160101; Stephen King, *Danse Macabre* (New York: Berkley Books, 1981); Glen D. Walters, "Understanding the Popular Appeal of Horror Cinema: An Integrated-interactive Model," *Journal of Media Psychology* 9 (2004), 1–35.
10. David A. Weiner, dir., *In Search of Tomorrow* (CreatorVC, 2022), https://www.imdb.com/title/tt11341742.
11. Patrick J. Carroll, Aaron L. Wichman, Robert Agler, and Robert Arkin, "The Regulation of Personal Security," *Journal of Theoretical Social Psychology* 2023 (2023), art. #7593709, https://doi.org/10.1155/2023/7593709; Lauren A. Leotti, Sheena S. Iyengar, and Kevin N. Ochsner, "Born to Choose: The Origins and Value of the Need for Control," *Trends in Cognitive Sciences* 14 (2010), 457–463; Travis Proulx and Steven J. Heine, "Death and Black Diamonds: Meaning, Mortality, and the Meaning Maintenance Model," *Psychological Inquiry* 17 (2006), 309–318.
12. Mark H. Davis, "Measuring Individual Differences in Empathy: Evidence for a Multidimensional Approach," *Journal of Personality and Social Psychology* 44 (1983), 113–126; Abigail A. Marsh, "The Neuroscience of Empathy," *Current Opinion in Behavioral Sciences* 19 (2018), 110–115.
13. Raymond A. Mar and Keith Oatley, "The Function of Fiction Is the Abstraction and Simulation of Social Experience," *Perspectives on Psychological Science* 3 (2008), 173–192; Keith Oatley, "Fiction: Simulation of Social Worlds," *Trends in Cognitive Science* 20 (2016), 618–628.
14. Noël Carroll, *The Philosophy of Horror, or Paradoxes of the Heart*, (New York: Routledge, 1990).
15. Aaron Smuts, "Art and Negative Affect," *Philosophy Compass* 4 (2009), 39–55.

16. Hanscomb, "Existentialism and Art-horror"; John Morreall, "Enjoying Negative Emotions in Fictions," *Philosophy and Literature* 9 (1985), 95–103; Walters, "Understanding the Popular Appeal of Horror Cinema.
17. Smuts provides a summary of these arguments, as well as other perspectives for why someone would consume art that provokes negative emotions. Our motivational need-threat approach best fits with Smuts's discussion of the "ahedonic compensatory" theories, though there may be aspects of the other perspectives that align with our arguments. We remain agnostic and are excited to see how future media-focused philosophers and psychologists engage with our suggestions.
18. Abraham H. Maslow, *Toward a Psychology of Being*, (New York: Van Nostrand, 1968).
19. Nathan Cheek, Elena Reutskaja, and Barry Schwartz, "Balancing the Freedom–Security Trade-off During Crises and Disasters," *Perspectives on Psychological Science* 17 (2022), 1024–1049; Omri Gillath and Joshua Hart, "The Effects of Psychological Security and Insecurity on Political Attitudes and Leadership Preferences," *European Journal of Social Psychology* 40 (2010), 122–134.
20. Mahmoud A. Wahba and Lawrence G. Birdwell, "Maslow Reconsidered: A Review of Research on the Need Hierarchy Theory," *Organizational Behavior and Human Performance* 15 (1976), 212–240.
21. Arne Öhman and Susan Mineka, "Fears, Phobias, and Preparedness: Toward an Evolved Module of Fear and Fear Learning," *Psychological Review* 108 (2001), 483–522.
22. Marissa A. Harrison and Erika J. Frederick, "Interested in Serial Killers? Morbid Curiosity in College Students," *Current Psychology* 41 (2022), 3768–3777; Coltan Scrivner, "An Infectious Curiosity: Morbid Curiosity and Media Preferences During a Pandemic," *Evolutionary Studies in Imaginative Culture* 5 (2021), 1–12 https://doi.org/10.26613/esic.5.1.206.
23. Weiner, *In Search of Tomorrow*; Carroll, Wichman, Agler, and Arkin, "The Regulation of Personal Security."
24. Gilad Feldman, "Making Sense of Agency: Belief in Free Will as a Unique and Important Construct," *Social and Personality Psychology Compass* 11 (2017), e12293, https://doi.org/10.1111/spc3.12293; Leotti, Iyengar, and Ochsner, "Born to Choose."
25. Deirdre D. Johnston, "Adolescents' Motivations for Viewing Graphic Horror," *Human Communication Research* 21 (1995), 522–552; Eric D. Wesselmann, Jeffery H. Kahn, Jordan A. Arellanes, and Aubrey D. Thimesch, "Exploring the Motives for Watching Horror Movies: A Replication and Extension," *Psychology of Popular Media* 14 (2025), 502–506.
26. Roy F. Baumeister and Brenda Wilson, "Life Stories and the Four Needs for Meaning," *Psychological Inquiry* 7 (1996), 322–325; Proulx and Heine, "Death and Black Diamonds."
27. Mark Dechesne, Tom Pyszczynski, Jamie Arndt, Sean Ransom, Kennon M. Sheldon, Ad Van Knippenberg, and Jacques Janssen, "Literal and Symbolic Immortality: The Effect of Evidence of Literal Immortality on Self-esteem Striving in Response to Mortality Salience," *Journal of Personality and Social Psychology* 84 (2003), 722–732; Erez Yaakobi, Mario Mikulincer, and Phillip R. Shaver, "Parenthood as a Terror Management Mechanism: The Moderating

Role of Attachment Orientations," *Personality and Social Psychology Bulletin* 40 (2014), 762–774.

28. Uri Lifshin, Jeff Greenberg, David Weise, and Melissa Soenke, "It's the End of the World and I Feel Fine: Soul Belief and Perceptions of End-of-the-world Scenarios," *Personality and Social Psychology Bulletin* 42 (2016), 104–177; Clay Routledge, Andrew A. Abeyta, and Christina Roylance, "Death and End Times: The Effects of Religious Fundamentalism and Mortality Salience on Apocalyptic Beliefs," *Religion, Brain and Behavior* 8 (2016), 21–30.
29. Thomas C. Bailey, Winnie Eng, Michael B. Frisch, and C.R. Snyder, "Hope and Optimism as Related to Life Satisfaction," *The Journal of Positive Psychology* 2 (2007), 168–175; Laura J. Long and Matthew W. Gallagher, "Hope and Posttraumatic Stress Disorder," in Matthew S. Gallagher and Shane J. Lopez eds., *The Oxford Handbook of Hope* (Oxford: Oxford University Press, 2018), 233–242.

26

The Wasteland Is Hell. So, Why Go There?

Greg Littmann

> Look around you, Danse. Look at the scorched earth and the bones that litter the wasteland.
> —Arthur Maxon, Brotherhood of Steel East Coast Division Supreme Commander, *Fallout 4*

I was searching for scrap in the ruins of a store in Boston when it started to rain ghouls. The place had seemed empty when I crept in, but I hadn't noticed the gaping hole in the ceiling. Up there on the second floor, a crowd of them had been shuffling around, just waiting for some scavenger to wander underneath. I tried to put my back to the wall and take out as many as I could with headshots from my sniper rifle, but there were too many. Going into V.A.T.S. only made things worse. Now they were pouring over me in slow motion. There were so many of them that I couldn't have made much of a meal when they tore me to bits. They probably got a mouthful apiece.

That was just one memorable death among so many horrible demises; I've lost count of them. I've been impaled by radscorpions, riddled with bullets by Super Mutants with miniguns, filleted by Deathclaws, fried by the laser eyes of Assaultron robots, and evaporated in nuclear blasts, among other horrors. And if death in the wasteland is cruel, living can be worse. I've eaten dried radroach, washed down with filthy, irradiated water, as I looked out over the ruins of what had once been a bustling city. I've watched thousands of men and women slaughtered, hundreds at my own hands. And the ugliest thing of all has been some of the horrible people I've met. Bandits, slavers, religious nuts, and cannibals; I've faced them all. There have been callous mercenaries like Conrad Kellog, who shot my wife for refusing to give up my infant son, power-crazed leaders like Shaun, dictator of the Institute, who plans to conquer the Commonwealth with synths, and insane killers like Pickman of Pickman's gallery, who loves to create art with human blood. Behind everything is the mocking presence of Vault-Tec, the corporation that saved me from nuclear annihilation—only to make me part of its deranged and vicious experiments on Vault Dwellers.

The wastelands of *Fallout* is a hellish place. So why do you and I come here? We do it for fun! Enduring this hell is our idea of recreation! But why do we find it fun to experience the sorts of things in a game that we would *hate* to experience in real life? I don't want to be shot at by desperados, eat cockroach for lunch, and gaze out over the rubble where millions of people died. You probably don't either. So why is it fun to pretend to do these things in a *Fallout* game?

What we say about the attraction of the dark elements of *Fallout* games will have implications that go beyond this one game series. Franchises like *Deus Ex* (2000), *Bioshock* (2007), and *Borderlands* (2009) also explore dark, violent, anarchic futures, while other popular franchises like *Grand Theft Auto* (1997), *Diablo* (1997), and *The Witcher* (2007) are set in worlds just as grim. In fact, almost any computer role-playing game (RPG) is going to send you, at some point, to an area overrun by something awful, whether it be *Call of Duty* (2003) posting you somewhere that swarms with enemy soldiers, *Resident Evil* (1996) assigning you to fight viral zombie outbreaks, or *Final Fantasy* (1987) or *World of Warcraft* (2004) giving you quests to go slaughter herds of monsters.

Of course, the puzzle of the attraction of such dark entertainments is older than computer games. Computer RPGs stem from pen-and-paper RPGs, in which player characters face similarly horrible situations. *Dungeons and Dragons* (1974) sends you down to the dungeon, where the monsters and traps are, or out into the perilous wilderness. Other games are set in darker worlds yet, such as the horror game *Call of Cthulhu* (1981) and the dystopian *Cyberpunk 2013* (1988). Some games are similar to *Fallout*. *Gamma World* (1978) is set in an irradiated post-apocalyptic Earth filled with monstrous mutants, and was a direct inspiration for *Fallout*.[1] *Paranoia* (1984) also takes place after the apocalypse, but this time, the PCs are Vault Dwellers living in an insane, rigidly organized society.

In fact, the problem of the attraction of dark art is older and broader than *that*. Before there were dark role-playing games, there were dark films like *Citizen Kane* (1941), *Lawrence of Arabia* (1962), and *The Godfather* (1972); and dark novels like Herman Melville's *Moby-Dick* (1851), Leo Tolstoy's *War and Peace* (1867), and George Orwell's *1984* (1949). And before *that*, there were tragic plays, like William Shakespeare's *Hamlet* (1603), Christopher Marlowe's *Doctor Faustus* (1592), and Sophocles's *Oedipus the King* (429 BCE). With the puzzle dating back to ancient Greece, it should be no surprise that ancient Greek philosophers tried to solve it. Let's see if we can get some help from Aristotle.

Aristotle Puts on His Power Armor

One of the oldest and most persistent puzzles in the philosophy of art is why people are attracted to depictions of horrible things. The issue is first raised in writing by the ancient Athenian philosopher Aristotle (384–322 BCE). One of the most influential thinkers in history, Aristotle made seminal contributions to ethics, logic, metaphysics, politics, biology, psychology, and philosophy of art, among other subjects.

Aristotle never knew the pleasure of booting up his PC to go face the dangers and privations of a ruined world, armed only with a shotgun and an attitude. Still, he would likely approve of gaming. He states in his book *Politics* that music is legitimate even if it does nothing more than bring relief from stress. He writes, "For the end is not desirable for the sake of any future good, nor do the pleasures which we have described exist for the sake of any future good but of the past, that is to say, they are the alleviation of past toils and pains. And we may infer this to be the reason why men seek happiness from these pleasures."[2] If listening to music is good just because it helps you to unwind, then presumably the same goes for hitting the virtual ruins to waste some Wastelanders.

Aristotle should approve of gaming even if the game is bad art or if the way we play it involves little artistic appreciation. He says of the music enjoyed by common people, "[for] the vulgar crowd composed of artisans, laborers, and the like—there ought to be contests and exhibitions instituted for … [their] relaxation.… And the music will correspond to their minds; for as their minds are perverted from the natural state, so there are perverted modes and highly strung and unnaturally colored melodies. A man receives pleasure from what is natural to him, and therefore professional musicians may be allowed to practice this lower sort of music before an audience of the lower type."[3]

Playing computer games would be particularly worthwhile if you engage your intellect by designing the most deadly character build or strategically thinking your way through an assault. Aristotle writes, "It is clear … that there are branches of learning and education which we must study merely with a view to leisure spent in intellectual activity, and these are to be valued for their own sake."[4] As a Greek of good birth, Aristotle likely had training as a hoplite—a heavy infantryman armed with shield and spear. So if he played *Fallout*, I'm guessing he would want to use power armor and a two-handed melee weapon.

In fourth-century Athens, plays were either tragedies or comedies, and Aristotle was a big fan of tragic theater. Greek tragic theater, like parts of *Fallout*, was filled with scenes of suffering and loss. For instance, in Sophocles's play *Oedipus the King*, which Aristotle held in high regard, poor Oedipus learns that he unwittingly killed his father and married his mother, fathering several children with her. Taking it hard, he rips out his own eyes and goes off to be a wandering beggar. Aristotle could appreciate that it needed to be explained why we would want to see such things in tragedy, when the sort of events portrayed are precisely those we *don't* want to encounter in real life. We wouldn't want to see someone tear out their own eyeballs in reality, so why would we want to sit through a play in which it happens?

In his book *Poetics*, Aristotle explains the attraction. Through feeling pity and fear on behalf of the hero of a tragedy, we purge these feelings from our own souls. By feeling fear and pity for the likes of poor old Oedipus, we get these feelings out of our system. Aristotle calls the process *katharsis*, the source of our English word "catharsis." *Katharsis* refers to any kind of purging, including vomiting. So just as your body might benefit from spewing up some undercooked radroach that's just too hard to digest, so your soul might benefit from spewing up your feelings of pity and fear.

What goes for tragic theater might go for computer games like the *Fallout* games. If we can enjoy tragic theater because it purges us of our pity and fear, maybe we can enjoy the horrors of a *Fallout* game in exactly the same way. Perhaps through feeling pity and fear on behalf of our player character and the sympathetic survivors they meet, we can cleanse ourselves of these emotions. Is that why we like playing such dark games?

Aristotle Is Wounded in Battle, but Survives

Mystery solved? Not yet! Aristotle has some problems to face first. One is that it isn't straightforward to apply his explanation to games like the *Fallout* games. One important difference between tragic theater and RPGs is that RPGs blur the line between what we feel on behalf of a fictional protagonist and what we feel on behalf of *ourselves*, because they blur the line between things happening to the player character and things happening to the player.

Obviously, you, the player, do not taste the disgusting radroach meat or feel the pain of being struck by a bloatfly's venomous projectile stinger. Nor do you directly feel the emotional pain of separation from loved ones, such as the pain of the protagonist of *Fallout 4*, who sees their spouse shot and their infant son taken by strangers. On the other hand, the death of your player character does mess up the progress of your game, robbing you of treasure and experience, and does subject you to the experience of being killed. When your character dies in *Fallout*, something bad has happened to you, too. You might even swear and rage-quit! Given this, it seems that you might feel fear on your own behalf while playing, rather than just feeling fear on behalf of your player character.

An explanation of why we seek out dangerous situations in games has to take into account the fact that physical danger to our characters involves the danger of inconvenience to the player. Perhaps we can attain *katharsis* not just by feeling pity and fear for others, but by feeling small doses of pity and fear for ourselves. Or perhaps we put up with some bad things happening to us as players for the sake of something else we get from the game, maybe the *katharsis* we get through sympathy with the player character.

A more serious problem for Aristotle's purgation account is that throwing up is no fun. Sure, we all feel better after a good chunder, but the actual process of emptying the guts via the mouth is about as pleasurable as licking a mirelurk. But playing *Fallout* games *is* fun. I *enjoy* exploring the wastes and ruins, rummaging through trash and struggling to survive, fighting it out with raiders and mutated beasts. Like most players, I even get a kick from those high-danger situations where I have something to lose. A quest that sends me deep into unexplored territory or sets me some other daunting challenge is more enjoyable than a quest that gives me easy victories. If the point of playing *Fallout* were to purge myself through *katharsis*, it would make more sense if the game were unpleasant to play but I felt relieved afterwards. This is not just a problem for applying the Aristotelean account to games, but to any dark art, including tragic theater. People *enjoy* watching tragedies like *Oedipus the King,* which suggests that there's more to the appeal of dark art than purgation. I think Aristotle may have much to offer us as we hunt for the answer, but he hasn't given us the final answer yet.

David Hume Roams the Crumbling Highways

The next great contribution to the debate over the attraction of dark art was made by Scottish philosopher David Hume (1711–1776). Hume made important contributions to the philosophy of mind, metaphysics, ethics, and religion. Influential among scientists as well as philosophers, Hume's work was acknowledged by Charles Darwin as inspirational for the theory of evolution. A best-selling historian, Hume also served as a diplomat for the British government in France, Austria, and Italy. A gregarious man, he enjoyed experiencing new places and loved to socialize, often hosting social dinners. If Hume played a *Fallout* game, I'm guessing he'd play a character with high charisma and high endurance, who wanders the roadways making deals. He wouldn't be the deadliest hombre in the wastelands, but he'd get great prices on ammo.

Like Aristotle, Hume was fascinated by the puzzle of the appeal of tragic art. He wrote in *Of Tragedy* (1757), "It seems an unaccountable pleasure which the spectators of a well-written tragedy receive from sorrow, terror, anxiety, and other passions that are in themselves disagreeable and uneasy."[5] Hume's solution is that tragic subject matter allows the artist to arouse emotions in the audience, which can then be transformed into pleasure by skillfully mixing them with an experience of beauty. Our predominant emotion is appreciation of the artwork's beauty, but the power of that emotion is increased by harnessing and transforming the power of our subordinate negative emotions. Without the negative emotions the audience feels toward the tragic events they witness on stage, they wouldn't be so moved by the play's beauty as art, because there would be less emotion for the artist to work with. Hume notes that applying artistic skill to a boring subject fails to stir emotion, leaving the mind "in absolute calmness and indifference," so that it won't enjoy the beauty of the art. Think of the negative emotions roused by tragedy as the bits and pieces of junk you pick up in the shells of old buildings. In themselves, the rusty fans and broken alarm clocks and such are nothing but a burden, but with the right skills, you can scrap them and turn them into something you really want, like a shiny new rifle.

The transformation of negative emotions generated by watching tragedy can only occur if the negative emotions are already less powerful than the positive emotions generated by the beauty of the art. That's why adding massive amounts of suffering doesn't automatically make a tragic play more enjoyable: if the negative emotions we feel are too strong, they overwhelm our appreciation of beauty rather than being transformed by it.

David Hume never knew the joy of launching a *Fallout* game to go machine-gun some gangsters in a bunker or fire a mini-nuke into a crowded raider camp, but his solution might be applicable to *Fallout* games all the same. As we encounter the horrors of the post-apocalypse, our negative emotions are roused. We feel pity at the loss of millions when the bombs fell, and more pity yet for the victims of bandits and of Vault-Tec's insane experiments. We feel revulsion at the horrible damage that radiation has inflicted on the bodies of ghouls, yao guai, and other poor, mutated beasts. We feel the chill of fear as we try to creep our way through dark city streets, scanning the rooftops and alleys for snipers. These emotions are then transformed, by the skill of game designers and programmers, into enjoyment. As in the case of tragedy, the transformation can only work if our negative emotions are less powerful than our positive ones to begin with. In *Fallout 4*, when I found the little ghoul boy Billy, who had been trapped in a refrigerator for 200 years, this was too dark for me, and I didn't enjoy it.

However, the explanation for our enjoyment of the dark elements of *Fallout* games can't be quite the same as the explanation Hume uses for tragedy. Hume claims that when watching a tragedy, our negative emotions are mixed with an experience of beauty, with the subordinate negative emotions fueling the predominant positive ones. However, playing *Fallout* is not usually an experience of beauty, but just the opposite. We're given a damaged world, filled with gross monsters, ragged survivors, and the trash left behind by an America gone by. Perhaps our negative emotions mix with the thrill of success, whether that be victory in combat with slavering reptilian gulpers, or successful completion of a quest to retrieve some ancient technology. Still, even that wouldn't explain the pleasure of exploring a threatening new location, the thrill of fighting a battle that you're not sure you can win, or the excitement of fleeing for your life.

Another problem with Hume's explanation is that it doesn't explain *why* a weaker emotion should strengthen a stronger one when we are enjoying art. After all, it isn't generally true that when we have two conflicting emotions, the weaker emotion will increase the intensity of the stronger one. If my strongest emotion is delight that I made it through the robot factory, but I also have a weaker emotion of worrying that I should be working instead of playing *Fallout*, my worry about work needn't increase my enjoyment of my triumph over the sentry bots and Protectrons. Likewise, if my strongest emotion is frustration at my inability to make it through the old mines without being blasted to pieces by mole miners, and my weaker emotion is satisfaction at taking some of the scuttling bastards down with me, my satisfaction at killing mole miners need not make me feel more frustrated about not being able to make it past them. If anything, feelings of satisfaction would do the reverse, making the thwarting of my plans a little easier to bear.

Hume is silent about how exactly negative emotion is transformed into positive emotion by the artist. He tells us only that the displeasure is transformed into pleasure by their skill. Speaking about oratory, he writes, "This extraordinary effect proceeds from that very eloquence, with which the melancholy scene is represented. The genius required to paint objects in a lively manner, the art employed in collecting all the pathetic circumstances, the judgment displayed in disposing them: the exercise, I say, of these noble talents." If the noble game-design talents of *Fallout* developers allow them to summon negative feelings and then transform them into pleasure, Hume gives us no indication of why that should be possible or how it works, apart from suggesting that genius may be required to do it well.

Lost in the Wastelands

We still don't have a solution to the puzzle we began with: Why we should want to play a character who lives in the hellish wastelands of the *Fallout* games, a place that we would hate to experience in real life? It shouldn't be surprising that we didn't come to a solution. The mystery of the attraction of dark art is at least 2500 years old, and the appearance of interactive art like computer games adds new complications that only make the problem more difficult to solve. Just what *is* it that drives us to go sightseeing through a scarred and polluted world, filled with warped, dangerous animals and humans who are often malicious or insane? Why do we come back to hell to drink filthy water and sift through the ruins for scrap? Why put ourselves in situations where the ghouls will suddenly come pouring down on our heads and tear us to pieces with their fingernails? Just as all the most interesting quests are those you haven't managed to beat yet, so all the really interesting questions are the ones we haven't yet solved.

Notes

1. See this interview with *Fallout* designer Timothy Cain: "Classic Game Postmortem: Fallout," GCD Festival of Gaming, May 4, 2017, YouTube, https://www.youtube.com/watch?v=T2OxO-4YLRk.

2. Aristotle in J. Barnes ed., *The Complete Works of Aristotle*, (Princeton: Princeton University Press, 2025). *Politics*, book VIII.
3. Aristotle, *Politics*, book VIII, 2129.
4. Aristotle, *Politics*, book VIII, 2122.
5. David Hume, "Of Tragedy," in *Essential Works of David Hume*, (New York: Bantam Books, 1965), 441.

Index